MORE PRAISE FOR

MW00576125

As so many of us in the fields of ps professions seek to find a more holistic approach to ... g ... Norberg's *Consenting to Grace* offers up a rich banquet that is both quite novel and deeply grounded in Christian tradition. As each chapter unfolds we are invited to taste and see the wonders of God's grace freeing our hearts and souls, bodies and minds.

> *Rev. Penny Gadzini, Staff therapist, Creative Living Counseling Center,*
> *Allendale, PA; Pastor, Good Shepherd United Methodist Church, Queens, NY*

Sometimes our inner wounds are so loud that it is difficult to hear the whisper of the Spirit. Gestalt Pastoral Care has given me tools to help others move through noisy, stuck places to awareness of God's voice.

> *Rev. Betty Voigt, Spiritual Director, Sycamore, PA*

Often a set of symptoms cannot be diagnosed by usual medical tests, nor do they respond to usual medical treatment. Participation in a Gestalt Pastoral Care class has given me new tools to help my patients to identify sources of their anguish, to work through their internal conflicts, and to accept the healing available through the grace of God.

> *Dr. Margaret Y. Groff, M.D., Mechanicsburg, PA*

Our congregation has grown to embrace Gestalt Pastoral Care: four lay persons have taken the training described in *Consenting to Grace*, small groups have benefited from its healing methods and various individualized healing liturgies have been life-changing for some of our members. My pastoral identity and sense of how the Spirit is at work in congregational life have been transformed by the insights in this book.

> *Rev. Roy Hange, Charlottesville Mennonite Church;*
> *Overseer, Harrisonburg District, Virginia Mennonite Conference*

Tilda Norberg shares ways of saying "yes" to God's innate healing process; a "yes" which honors persons' boundaries, self-awareness and particular life experiences; a "yes" which has psychological, physical, spiritual, and relational integrity. This is a valuable resource for all of God's people, and for clergy and spiritual leaders in particular.

> *Rev. Wanda D. Craner, Gestalt Pastoral Care Minister; Minister of Spiritual*
> *Nurture, Pennsylvania Southeast Conference of the United Church of Christ*

CONSENTING TO GRACE

AN INTRODUCTION TO GESTALT PASTORAL CARE

TILDA NORBERG

PENN HOUSE PRESS

Consenting to Grace: An Introduction to Gestalt Pastoral Care
Copyright © 2006 Tilda Norberg

First revised edition, August 2006

Penn House Press
78 Clinton Avenue
Staten Island, NY 10301
(718) 273-4941
www.pennhousepress.com

Some material in this book has also appeared in slightly different form in *Stretch Out Your Hand* by Tilda Norberg and Robert D. Webber (Upper Room Books, 1998) and *Ashes Transformed* by Tilda Norberg (Upper Room Books, 2002). Used by permission.

The scripture quotations contained herein are from the New Revised Standard Version Bible, copyright © 1989 by the Division of Christian Education of the National Council of Churches of Christ in the U.S.A. Used by permission.

Cover picture: oil painting by Brother Eric of Taizé,
copyright © Ateliers et Presses de Taizé, 71250 Taizé, France.
Book and Cover Design: Daniel Bodah

Gestalt Pastoral Care website: www.gestaltpastoralcare.com

Publisher's Cataloging-in Publication Data

Norberg, Tilda.

      Consenting to grace: an introduction to gestalt pastoral care / Tilda Norberg. — 1st ed. — New York: Penn House Press, 2005.

        p. ; cm.

      ISBN-13: 978-0-9658707-1-9
      ISBN-10: 0-9658707-1-5
      Includes bibliographical references.

      1. Pastoral care. 2. Pastoral counseling. 3. Pastoral psychology.
    4. Gestalt psychology. 5. Holism. I. Title.

BV4012 .N67 2005   2005909048
253.5—dc22   0512
Printed in the United States of America

For George McClain, the "nice man" I met at Taizé,
for forty years my best friend, colleague in ministry, tender husband,
and the love of my life.

I give heartfelt thanks to my family who have been unfailingly supportive: George, always in my corner, who read and re-read the often-revised manuscript; Shana Norberg-McClain, soon to be a nurse-midwife, who midwifed the process of getting into print and offered cogent editorial suggestions; Noah Norberg-McClain, who was seldom too busy with his graduate studies to listen, encourage, challenge, offer computer help, and cook delicious meals; Dan Bodah, who took time from his job and law school to design the book, Dora McClain for her loving support and frequent phone calls from Indiana, and Silas Norberg Bodah for his energetic delight in exploring the world.

I am deeply grateful to my colleagues of Gestalt Pastoral Ecumenical Associates: Anne Cormier, Wanda Craner, Rhoda Glick, and Sara Goold, who supported, prayed, discussed, tested the manuscript in their classes, generously offered insights and stories, and helped me hone my ideas. You were an essential part of the process. Thanks also to Carolyn Davies who said, "When are you going to write the book you know you are called to write?" and, "Write a paragraph and say you're writing a book!"

I thank my students whose questions and comments helped me articulate and clarify, and who told me over and over, "We need this book!" The faithful support of The Prayer House Community was wonderful, especially Kim Baldwin, Peter Chepaitis, Cynthia Hollenbeck, Deborah Keller-Klimo, Gail Metzger, Rodney Miller, Ruth Ellen Ray, Lyn Reith, Patricia Roedema, Donna Joy Schmid, Janet Stanley, Pat Stiles, Anna Tantsits, and Joyce Thomas, who prayed, discerned and held my hand when I was discouraged. I'm profoundly grateful to the men and women who allowed me to tell their stories; you know who you are. Thanks to Bette Sohm for years of faithful assistance in the office, and to Maryalice Graham Fegeley for her careful proofreading.

TABLE OF CONTENTS

PART ONE

WHAT IS GESTALT PASTORAL CARE?

The Prologue introduces Gestalt Pastoral Care, a synthesis of Gestalt growth work, prayer for healing, and spiritual companioning. I share how this new way of doing ministry was born from the stop signs, dead ends, rutted roads, and magnificent boulevards in my own life's journey.

The first and second chapters present an overview of Gestalt theory, and describe how Gestalt integrates beautifully with Christian spirituality and good pastoral care.

Chapter Three focuses not only on what a Gestalt Pastoral Care minister actually does, but also on who she or he is. I offer some cautions and criteria to help decide if you are ready to explore using Gestalt Pastoral Care with others.

Keep in mind that there are two levels in assimilating and using the material in this book. The first and simplest is to adopt a Gestalt Pastoral Care *perspective* that can give new shape to already existing ministries of pastoral care, spiritual direction or healing. The second level involves becoming a Gestalt Pastoral Care *Minister* and calls for further training and certification. These two levels are explained in Chapter Three.

...the fullness of joy is to contemplate God in everything.
Julian of Norwich

PROLOGUE: BEGINNINGS

The birth of Gestalt Pastoral Care reflects both my own struggle with difficult events and circumstances, and God's faithful desire to make all things new. My particular journey has led through five formative experiences: a traumatic plane crash and subsequent vision of Christ, rejection as a woman pastor, the discovery of a new way to pray, a dream in which God spoke, and the astonishing healing of a severely ill man.

I share some of this movement of grace, not because this book is about me, but because my story is different only in the details from that of any person trying to follow God. If we stay awake, sooner or later we come face to face with God's redeeming, healing work, even in our not-so-special lives. Despite our human bent for sleep, God keeps teaching and prodding and baking delicious bread out of the most improbable ingredients imaginable.

A PLANE CRASH AND A VISION

In an instant my secure and loving world was shattered. On April 6th, 1958, when I was 16 years old, the course of my life changed forever. I still think of that day as a hinge between "before" and "after".

On that Easter Sunday, my parents were returning to our home in Saginaw, Michigan when their plane crashed in a fiery explosion just off the airport runway. Seconds after the initial impact, the plane exploded and burned, instantly killing all 47 aboard. I ran out on the airport tarmac and watched as more explosions and fierce heat made rescue impossible. Watching the huge conflagration, I knew with sickening, horrifying certainty that my parents were dead. Then terror, nausea, and merciful numbing shock.

As I stumbled back into the airport, the waiting room was besieged with utter pandemonium. People were shrieking, fainting, clutching each other. Alarms were screaming, sirens wailing. Panicked airport staff were running around helplessly, frantically.

As I stood frozen and terrified, suddenly the sights and sounds of the airport faded from my awareness. Instead, there was a sort of blank screen in front of me, except for something in my peripheral vision. I turned around several times, trying to see what was there. At last I saw that the elusive image was Jesus. I did not see him imaginatively in my mind's eye, as I have many times since. That night I saw him with physical eyes, standing there looking radiant and indescribably beautiful in his resurrected body. He was looking at me with great love and tenderness, and I recognized him at once.

As we gazed at each other, he spoke with an audible voice saying, "Don't be afraid; I'm always with you." He repeated these seven words many times, as if he were making sure that I understood.

During this encounter, a tumult of conflicting and intense feelings were mixing and swirling in me: terror and peace, horror and joy, dread and ecstasy, shock and certainty. I was a tree in a hurricane, shaken, buffeted, losing leaves and branches, nearly blown over. At the same time, I remained deeply rooted in nourishing soil.

Finally, deep peace emerged dominant in this emotional firestorm, and then a strange and inexplicable joy. At that moment I knew in my bones that the message of Easter was true: that Jesus was resurrected and had truly overcome darkness and death. Mom and Dad were still alive in his presence. I also knew with certainty that he would always be with me, just as he had promised. And, since the shock and agony of seeing the still-burning plane had certainly not gone away, it was also clear to me that this promise did not mean that I would have a trouble-free life, but that Jesus would always be there. Suddenly I understood how "Death has been swallowed up in victory" (I Corinthians 15:54). These things I had believed all my life, but then I *knew*.

Slowly the apparition of Jesus faded. The airport came back to my awareness, but the experience wasn't finished. Almost immediately an inner tape began playing the Easter anthem we had sung in church that morning. I could "hear" it as the bodies were identified, while my sister and I chose the caskets, while staring at horrifying pictures in the newspaper. The music was still there when I went back to school, and when all my friends avoided me because they just didn't

4

know what to say. For the next three weeks this "tape" captured my attention and reminded me of the vision in the airport. It was as if Jesus were saying to me, "Pay attention; this is what I mean when I say I will always be with you."

Intense peace, surely passing all understanding, persisted for months, long after the music had faded. But as marvelous as it all was, the vision and music didn't remove my grief and the necessity for difficult inner work. I missed my parents so intensely I hurt physically. I had trouble sleeping and concentrating at school. Even with such a profound experience of the resurrected Christ that Easter, I still had to wrestle with the terrible, inevitable theological question of "Why did God let this happen?" I now know I suffered from Post Traumatic Stress Disorder – flashbacks and all – though no one used that language back then.

By the next year I was in much-needed therapy. It was wrenching to go back over the accident and its aftermath again and again, letting myself feel the stabbing pain of intense grief and shock, but the process of healing was made infinitely easier by the words of Jesus which seemed to infuse every moment: "Don't be afraid; I'm always with you."[1]

All of this held the seeds for a future call to ordained ministry, for becoming a Gestaltist, and for the integration of the two. I believe it is no coincidence that my life's work is helping people invite Jesus into the worst moments of their lives, and that a great deal of my ministry is with trauma survivors.

When encountering suffering in others as I entered seminary and later in Gestalt training, I experienced immediate feelings of recognition. Terror, horror, abandonment, and grief I knew very well. Anger, isolation, phobic reactions, and anxiety were no strangers either. True, I could not feel exactly what someone else was going through, but I was intimately familiar with the landscape of intense emotion. Furthermore, I was still learning that getting well demanded hard work; I couldn't just expect God to make it happen while I remained unengaged. Most importantly, I knew in my bones that even the worst is healable. I became utterly convinced that Jesus meets people in the depths of pain and is able to transform it. So was born the beginnings of a personal theology of suffering and grace, and a faith in God's continual desire for healing.

---

[1] This story was also told in *Ashes Transformed: Healing From Trauma.*

CLOSED DOORS AND A NEW DIRECTION

The second formative experience that gave rise to Gestalt Pastoral Care was that of being rejected by the church, and having to find a new way to be a minister. It began during my last year at Union Theological Seminary in Manhattan when I was looking for a job. Although I felt a very strong call to parish ministry, it was not to be. Despite my pounding on the door, the church simply was not ready for ordained women in 1966. I was told by one bishop, for example, that he would never ordain another woman, because he didn't know what to do with the two he already had. Another church leader, ignoring the fact that I could barely type, suggested that I start as a church secretary with the hope that a job in ministry would open up someday.

Depressed, angry, and with waning self-confidence, I went into therapy once more, and again God was at work. The therapist I "happened" to pick was Dan Sullivan, a feminist, a former Jesuit, and a Gestalt therapist who had studied with Fritz Perls, the founder of Gestalt psychotherapy. Dan didn't make light of my call to ministry, nor did he see pathology in my desire to enter a "male" profession. I blossomed with Dan's help, and watched others in my therapy group do the same. Quite soon I decided to get Gestalt training myself.

This decision was very much a second choice. I still yearned to pastor a church, but if that wasn't possible maybe I could still help someone a little. It *was* exciting to see how people could make rapid progress in Gestalt work. It was so different from the other counseling I had experienced.

At the end of my Gestalt training I began leading workshops and started a small private practice. Right away I encountered people who wanted to work with someone who was familiar with their life of faith. However, faith issues didn't figure much in my Gestalt work for years; as a matter of fact I was deliberate about not speaking of God unless someone specifically brought up a spiritual issue. I didn't want to influence anyone to change to please me, nor did I want to use a counseling relationship to evangelize. Desperate to be acceptable in this new profession, I was following the rules very carefully. So, faith was simply in the background, but for many people it was enough just to know that I shared their convictions.

CONTEMPLATIVE PRAYER

A third formative experience began about seven years into my private practice, while I was the one-day-a-week Protestant chaplain at South Beach Psychiatric Center on Staten Island. By this time I was feeling increasingly pained by the split between my roles as Gestaltist and minister. For each hat I wore I had separate friends, different assumptions and language, and even different jokes. I well knew that my secular colleagues didn't understand my commitment as a clergywoman, nor did my church friends think much of this Gestalt stuff that was so interested in bodies and had people yelling while they sat on the floor. Being a leader on a national task force on the status of women in the church didn't help either. Constantly confronting ecclesiastical sexism in high places only served to reinforce the feeling that there was no place for me anywhere.

Most importantly, I had split off from the vision of Jesus in the airport. Of course I remembered and treasured the experience, but somehow the light had gone out of it. The part of me that knew direct relationship with God was possible had been encrusted with pain and disillusionment, and with trying to be accepted as a professional.

It was during this bleak time that I was guided to learn a new way of praying. Of course I had always prayed; I spoke to God a lot, and listened very little. But when everything seemed to fall apart, I just didn't have the energy or the will to continue praying in such a talky way. I felt so tired, so beaten up by the church, and so abused by constant negative comments from every corner. I had no words left to speak, and I just wanted to rest from the struggle.

Very late one night I went into my office to pray. I tried to summon words and I simply couldn't. Frazzled and exhausted, I said, "Lord, just let me sit with you!" Almost immediately I felt enveloped in God's presence, and in my mind's eye I saw Jesus sitting on the floor with me. He seemed to be pleased with my request; indeed it was as if he were waiting for it. So we sat together in silence for an hour, like two old friends who have no need to speak. It was wonderfully nourishing.

I began to pray this way nearly every night, for Jesus seemed to be waiting for me. Much pain was healed during these nightly meetings. Most often, however, there was just an invitation to rest in God's presence without words, and later, without images. It was – and is – marvelous. During this time there were no big changes in my outward situation. The difference was that I now had a place of rest and healing.

I suspect that I would never have learned to pray contemplatively if I hadn't needed to. The time in the "desert" was extraordinarily fruitful, and was an integral part of the development of Gestalt Pastoral Care.

I began to understand that sitting in God's presence and letting God be in charge was one of the best things I could do for those in pain. From this perspective it became clearer than ever that I didn't have to figure out how to fix anyone. I didn't need tremendous insight or great wisdom. I didn't need brilliant words. I just needed to allow God to listen and speak and love through me. My job was simply to get out of the way of God's healing work, and also to facilitate the same getting out of the way in those seeking healing.

HEALING PRAYER: AN UNWELCOME DREAM

About this time I had a disturbing dream in which I was talking to Dr. Robert Hall, my teacher at the Lomi School[2] In California. Robert said to me, "By the way, say hello to John." "John who?" I asked him. "John the fourth chapter!" he replied with a grin, and I woke up.

Right away I sensed this was an important dream, so at three in the morning I looked up chapter four of the Gospel of John. As I read there about the Samaritan woman at the well being promised living water, I knew that God was asking me to explore healing ministry. Frankly, I'm not sure how that particular passage triggered ideas about healing. Certainly there are other passages in the New Testament which are more directly about laying on of hands and healing prayer. Even so, somehow I knew I was being called to get involved in healing ministry, despite the fact that it was the last thing I wanted to do.

At the time, healing ministry was not well respected by mainstream churches, and like many others I was deeply prejudiced against it. It seemed to me that it was mostly the realm of T.V. healers who were more interested in their own image

---

[2] Lomi Body Work, an outgrowth of Ida Rolf's Structural Integration, opens a door to increased awareness, emotional/spiritual growth, and relief for aching muscles. Lomi Body Work is a part of Gestalt Pastoral Care as I practice it. The bodywork itself is beyond the scope of this book, but I am indebted to the Lomi School of Santa Rosa, California for many of the insights that have formed Gestalt Pastoral Care. See Ida P. Rolf and Rosemary Feitis, ed., *Ida Rolf Talks About Rolfing and Physical Reality.*

and in getting money from desperate sufferers than anything else. I considered healing ministry in the same category with snake oil sales.

The most honest reason, however, behind my objection to healing ministry was that I didn't want to look weird. I knew my church friends would think I had really lost it, and my Gestalt friends would know I had! Professional rejection was too painful to risk another go-round of it. Every time I remembered The Dreaded Dream it scared me, so I did my best to avoid the whole issue.

More dreams about healing elbowed their way into my sleep, however, and I glumly realized that I really would have to deal with them. To top it all off, these dreams were not classical Gestalt dreams in which every element of the dream is a projection of the dreamer. I knew instinctively that these dreams were not really about projections, but were messages from God. Even so, I did a pretty good job of ignoring them for about a year.

Timid Beginnings and the Word Salad Man

When I finally tackled the dreams with my therapist, it quickly became clear that God was inviting me to put my hands on someone and pray for healing. I dithered and stewed until I figured out that I could try praying for someone in the psychiatric hospital where I was part-time chaplain. If I chose the person right, I wouldn't have to risk very much. Maybe I could find someone who was too out of touch to know or care what I was doing. That way I wouldn't have to explain anything or make any promises.

The patient I chose for this little experiment had been in the hospital for over a year, and in that time had spoken only in the special gibberish known as "word salad." He jabbered constantly, only stopping to eat and sleep. I took him by the arm and led him into an office where no one would see what I was going to do. Plenty scared of crossing my own boundary, my heart was racing as I put my hands on his head and prayed that God would heal whatever had caused such a massive withdrawal. He stopped talking as I prayed, but as soon as I took my hands away he continued the word salad, as psychotic as ever. Relief! It hadn't worked, and I gratefully let the idea of healing ministry slide to the bottom of my to-do pile, with no thought that I might be in for a big surprise.

The next time I was back at the hospital a staff therapist bolted out of his office demanding, "What in hell did you do to that guy?" I was speechless as he told me that the word salad man had started talking normally the afternoon after I had prayed for him. When a psychiatrist asked him what happened to make him talk after all this time, the man explained that, "the Protestant chaplain prayed for me." Clearly he wasn't as unaware as I thought. The hospital staff was buzzing about it and my jig was up. At a nurse's request, I prayed for someone else that day, and absolutely nothing changed for that patient then or later. Still, I couldn't ignore the healing of the word salad man. Backed into a corner, I would have to take healing ministry seriously and see what would happen.[3]

Cautiously and fearfully I began to pray for more patients at the hospital and with some of the people who were coming to me for Gestalt sessions. For some time there were no more dramatic sudden healings, but enough happened to convince me that God was using my prayers to heal.

If the person was open to it, I would pray at the beginning of a Gestalt session that God would bless and use our hour together. Sometimes I would pray at the end that God would strengthen what had happened during the session and open up new areas for the next one. Prayer was not so much integrated into the process as tacked on either end. I had always prayed silently in Gestalt sessions; but when I began to pray out loud even in this tentative way, there was a discernible difference in the results.

Right away the process seemed to move more quickly than I had come to expect for most people. Some people were leapfrogging over steps that I had formerly believed were necessary for genuine transformation. Others were just getting unstuck and getting well. I was also changing; finally I was feeling more integrated in my roles of Gestalt coach and pastor.

It was apparent that prayers in a therapy setting filled a great yearning. I discovered anew that Christians are hungry to have a sense that God really cares about their pain and is responsive to their needs. I became convinced that it is just plain wrong to separate spirituality from emotions and physicality, although both the church and the therapeutic community have taught us to do so. I saw that for me to combine spiritual direction (or spiritual companioning, as I prefer to call it) and healing prayer with Gestalt work was not irresponsible at all; it was irresponsible and unfaithful *not* to walk this path to which God was pointing.

---

[3] The story of the word salad man was first told in *Stretch Out Your Hand: Exploring Healing Prayer* by Tilda Norberg and Robert Webber.

BIRTH

From this shaky beginning Gestalt Pastoral Care was born. Over the next year or two, prayer and spiritual companioning crept into every part of the Gestalt process. I saw that while Gestalt can rapidly open people to their pain, God meets them there and makes all the difference. Although Fritz Perls, the founder of Gestalt therapy, would be outraged at the very idea, I came to believe that his brilliant discoveries and theories fit beautifully with Christian healing ministry and good pastoral care.

In the years since dipping my toe in the water to pray for the word salad man, Gestalt Pastoral Care has expanded a great deal, and now has a number of components. These days it includes not only Gestalt work and healing prayer, but also spiritual companioning. Spiritual companioning in the context of Gestalt Pastoral Care shares the usual goals of spiritual direction: seeking to discern God's claim and call, and finding ways to open more faithfully to a life of prayer. In addition, a Gestalt Pastoral Care minister might share faith imagination prayer with one in need of healing, or witness prayers of confession with one who longs to hear a declaration of God's forgiveness. She or he might help create liturgies of healing aimed at one individual's need. In certain circumstances she or he could pray for deliverance from evil, or for generational or institutional healing. All of this rests on an attitude fostered by contemplation which recognizes that God is active and in charge, so that the Gestalt Pastoral Care minister actually has very little to do.

Gestalt Pastoral Care is attentive to the beautiful intricate dance between body, mind, emotions, spirit, and social context. Thus, an individual coming for help might bring a concern for physical healing, or chronic tension, or an inability to pray. He or she might come with a need to confess sin, or for help in getting angry, or for relief from depression or anxiety. One person might need to explore a painful memory that stunts his growth and blocks him from hearing God's voice. Another might want to deal with a dysfunctional institution of which she is a part, or to pray and work toward the healing of her entire family. Still another might want to claim a "lost" part of herself, such as her creativity or assertiveness. Whatever the starting point, it is almost certain that other areas of growth will quickly open up, for every part of us is related to the whole.

Although Gestalt Pastoral Care is an art, the basics are simple. Instead of analysis, it invites attention to the rich liveliness of each present moment, for it is there that personal discoveries are made, and God is revealed. In place of a treatment plan, it seeks to get out of the way of what God is already doing in each person. Instead of talking about whatever is painful, it focuses on direct experience, suggesting creative experiments that hold the possibility of discovery, revelation, and change. It invites pastors and spiritual companions to claim their healing role more deeply, and therapists to become much more interested in spirituality. It gives a lot of responsibility to the person coming for help, while the minister or therapist becomes less and less powerful.

As this new synthesis became more clearly formed, a few clergy asked me to teach it to them. I began a small training group in 1984; this group became the seed of a two-year training program that has expanded to include advanced theory and practicum courses and an internship program. As I trained more and more ministers – and recently, prison inmates – it became evident that Gestalt Pastoral Care is a simple and natural process which is fundamentally a ministry of Christian healing rather than a spiritualized approach to psychotherapy. Because Gestalt Pastoral Care does not call for diagnosis, treatment plans, analysis, or dissolving resistance, and because God is actively recognized as the source of healing, it is far outside the usual practice and expectations of psychotherapy. However, many psychotherapists have taken the Gestalt Pastoral Care training program, and have integrated parts of Gestalt Pastoral Care into their own modalities.

Ministers can begin to use some of the insights of Gestalt Pastoral Care if they have had some training in pastoral counseling. We ministers who practice Gestalt Pastoral Care full time have had a great deal of training, but we no longer call ourselves therapists; instead we identify ourselves as Gestalt Pastoral Care *ministers, coaches* or *guides.*

Everything is awareness.
Fritz Perls

1

A VERY SHORT COURSE IN GESTALT THEORY

German psychiatrist Fritz Perls (1893-1970), who called himself the "finder" of Gestalt psychotherapy, wasn't always an iconoclast. Trained as a classical Freudian psychoanalyst and later influenced by Wilhelm Reich and Wolfgang Kohler, his work changed dramatically after he came to the United States at age 47. Thoroughly startling his colleagues, he became an analyst who no longer analyzed, bothered with intake information, or spoke in psychoanalytic jargon. Instead, he found a new way to engage people with their therapeutic issues from the first minutes of contact. By simply learning to expand their awareness of the present moment, new patients quickly found themselves experiencing their own depths in a level that was astonishing, particularly to those accustomed to years of talk on the analytic couch. A cranky, rebellious, arrogant genius, Perls supported his theories, not with controlled scientific experiments, but with the evidence of remarkable changes, often after just a few sessions, in those fortunate enough to work with him.

The foundational concepts of Gestalt psychotherapy were radical when Perls first articulated them in 1947 in *Ego, Hunger, and Aggression*. A later book, *Gestalt Therapy Verbatim* (1969), demonstrated how he integrated theory with practice as a nearly magical psychotherapist. Even today, Gestalt theory and practice are set apart from many other systems of psychotherapy.

In this chapter, I will briefly summarize Fritz Perls' basic Gestalt theory; in the next I will discuss how, in my opinion, it all fits wonderfully well with Christian theology and spirituality.

GESTALT BASICS

Gestalt theory is essentially simple and natural. It assumes that each person's being is constantly stretching toward healing and growth. The job of a Gestalt guide is to uncover and make room for this inborn urge to grow. Gestalt theory and the foundations of its practice are based on a few interrelated building blocks:

Gestalt "trusts the process." This trust is based on a belief that a growth process, although perhaps blocked, is already urgently pushing for expression in persons coming for help, and that this inner process actively directs them toward greater health. Put another way, a beautiful innate wisdom encoded into each person guides the way toward uniquely individualized wholeness.

How does this actually work? As you become aware of your lively inner growth process, certain small behaviors suggest themselves. Perhaps you feel an impulse to breathe more deeply, or to make a sound, or to stretch your legs, or to allow a fantasy to push through the edge of consciousness. When you surrender to these impulses *with awareness,* new awareness emerges and other actions present themselves. *Translating this trail of awareness and impulse into action or further awareness is called "working."* Such working is an earmark of the Gestalt process.

Unless the flow is interrupted by resistance, Gestalt work can lead directly, and often quickly, to the next step, perhaps even to the bedrock of your growth agenda. Even more importantly, Gestalt growth work can direct you through pain to its resolution. The Gestalt guide is there simply as a coach who suggests how to actively cooperate with your own constantly surging healing process.

For example, a man becomes aware of the beginnings of a sound pushing up from his diaphragm. Although he doesn't know what kind of sound might emerge, he playfully allows a sound to come forth at the suggestion of his guide. He finds himself sighing. As he repeats his sigh a few times, it becomes deeper and turns into a low moan and then into an even louder cry. As he continues, words form in his awareness that he allows himself to say out loud: "I just can't stand it any more!" At first he does not put his words in context, but as he repeats them several times he discovers that those words are nearly twenty-five years old. Suddenly his present awareness ignites with the memory of himself at fifteen, responding to the unreasonable demands and unsupervised hazing at his boarding school. If he continues to surrender to his inner process, he will likely find a way to forcefully and bodily speak his truth in that school, and thus "metabolize" an experience which has been holding him back for years. Although his metabolizing process regarding this memory might occur quite rapidly – perhaps in one or two sessions – the man may need more time to allow this work to come to closure and become grounded in his life. Whatever the man's personal timetable, his Gestalt guide will trust that the man's inner process will continue to take him toward healing at his own pace.

Gestalt growth work embraces a health model, calling forth the health that already exists in even the most fragmented person. Gestalt work is not so much turned toward what is wrong with a person, but toward what's blocking the health that is surely present. Diagnosis of illness is much less important than becoming aware of where new life is just waiting to break out.

There is a lot of bamboo growing in our yard on Staten Island. It spreads as fast as whispered secrets, sending shoots around rocks, under the porch and even under the siding of the house. We can whack it out one week and it will begin to grow back by the next. The strength of its drive to grow is amazing.

We are not so different from bamboo; deep within us is found a similar astonishing urgency to grow. Gestalt work focuses on this urgency to grow rather than on pathology. Obviously, however, not everyone grows according to an abstract standard of perfection. Like bamboo, we have to grow around our particular obstacles, but each of us, no matter what our stunting handicaps, emotional maiming, age, or physical condition, is somehow striving to be a whole person. Just as our bodies mobilize for healing when we have been physically injured, we can be confident that this same energy for wholeness is expended on wounds of emotion and spirit. In this context, discomfort or pain or anxiety are certainly not imaginary, but are a sign that something is pushing for resolution inside.

Gestalt work is fundamentally and radically holistic, giving lively attention to the exquisite interrelationship between emotions and body.[4] In fact, the word "gestalt" itself connotes wholeness.[5] To a Gestaltist, observation of a person's body is fully as important as listening to what the person is saying; body and emotions are so intertwined that they are separated only by doing violence. Actually, *everything* happening in that person is to be noticed and honored moment-by-moment. This includes what is being said, of course, but also physical sensations, fantasies, thoughts, memories, perceptions, tone of voice, gestures, freedom or frozenness of movement, bioenergy, and so on. This attention to the whole of a person is integral to Gestalt work. Further, it is not just the guide's awareness that is important; even more crucial is coaching such awareness in the person coming for healing.

---

[4] Perls, *Gestalt Therapy Verbatim,* pp. 25-26.

[5] Gestalt: "A physical, biological, psychological or symbolic configuration or pattern of elements so unified as a whole that its properties cannot be derived from a simple summation of its parts." *The American Heritage Dictionary of the English Language,* Houghton Mifflin Company, 2003.

The Gestalt holistic orientation also refers to the goal of integrating split-off parts of a personality. For example, one person may need to integrate his natural exuberance that was forbidden, and later denied, in childhood. Another might need to integrate her pelvis (and the feelings therein) that she was taught to fear, and later to hate. In Gestalt theory, claiming, loving and using all of oneself appropriately is one of the marks of a healthy person.

Gestalt work is based on awareness of the ongoing experience of each moment. Perls called this ever-changing perception of the present the *awareness continuum.* To work with an awareness continuum, we might ask such questions as:

•What do you notice *right now* outside of you?

•What do you hear, see, smell, feel, taste *right now?*

•What is going on inside of you *right now?*

•What fantasies, physical sensations, memories, postures, movement, feelings are you aware of *right now?*

Perls' great discovery was that if a person is able to simply broaden her awareness of here-and-now experience, she gets healthier. Basic awareness of the present moment undergirds every aspect of Gestalt work.

Why is basic awareness so important to Gestalt? Perls rejected the concept of the unconscious as a repository for repressed feelings and memories. Instead, he taught that "unfinished business" is constantly pushing for awareness and resolution, and that this material is always being expressed in some fairly *discernible* way. For example, if a person has spent her childhood in fear of physical abuse, it is nearly certain that she will carry reactions to this experience into adulthood. This is true, of course, even if she does not remember the horror of her childhood. Her tense muscles and rigid posture may hold not only forgotten memories, but also terrified screams. Her clenched fists and constricted breathing may be pushing down roars of anger that were much too dangerous to express as a child. Such memories and feelings not metabolized when they first occurred are still intact, not in Freud's unconscious, but in a person's *body.* That's why attention to bodies is so important, for simple body awareness can lead directly to one's growth agenda. In Gestalt terms, present awareness, particularly body awareness, is the only "treatment plan" necessary. Perls puts it this way:

> Gestalt Therapy is an experiential therapy, rather than a verbal
> or an interpretive therapy. We ask our patients not to talk about

their traumas and their problems in the removed area of the past tense and memory, but to re-experience their problems and their traumas – which are unfinished situations in the present – in the here and now. If the patient is finally to close the book on his past problems, he must close it in the present. For he must realize that if his past problems were really past, they would no longer be problems – and they certainly would not be present.

In addition, as an experiential therapy, the Gestalt technique demands of the patient that he experience as much of himself as he can, that he experience himself as fully as he can in the here and now. We ask the patient to become aware of his gestures, of his breathing, of his emotions, of his voice, and of his facial expressions as much as of his pressing thoughts. We know that the more he becomes aware of himself, the more he will learn about what his self is. As he experiences the ways he prevents himself from "being" now – the ways in which he interrupts himself – he will also begin to experience the self he has interrupted.[6]

As a person becomes vividly aware of her body and lets it "speak", old memories often surface and are re-lived. When this happens, Gestalt work does not urge a person to *remember* what happened; instead the invitation is to *re-experience* it as fully as possible, in the present. In this way, the past is experienced in the present moment. Furthermore, Gestalt work does not aim to explain why someone is the way she is; instead Gestalt encourages broader and deeper awareness of the present.

Not every Gestalt session reveals the gold of a buried memory or a cleansing explosion of emotion, of course. Much of the work of a Gestalt guide is simply coaching awareness. However, coaching increased awareness of the here-and-now is a wonderful way to work with another, for it easily builds a sense of accomplishment into a growth process. Almost anyone can do it when they are shown how. For example, the small awareness that one is breathing shallowly much of the time, can eventually open doors to "more breathing room," both physically and emotionally. Gestaltists are trained to work with physical awareness as easily as an emotion or memory; in fact, there is very little separation made between the two.

---

[6] Fritz Perls, *The Gestalt Approach and Eyewitness to Therapy,* pp. 64-65.

Gestalt work is non-analytical. We are not interested in asking *why* a person is the way she is, or what he thinks about his problem, but rather *what* she is doing and feeling, and *how* she is expressing it. Oddly enough, "why" questions are, more often than not, answered in retrospect and almost by accident. Asking or answering "why" in a Gestalt session is to be avoided because it inevitably pulls people away from feelings and experience of the present.

Not having to analyze makes the job of the Gestalt guide infinitely simpler and easier; she doesn't have to fear trampling over anyone with a wrong interpretation because there is no interpreting to do. This approach implies that people in a growth process are trusted to do their own work. In fact, they, not the guide, are in charge of the process and make the discoveries.

Instead of engaging in analysis, interpretation, or reflection, Gestalt work explores through experiments. Gestalt experiments are truly experimental. They are usually created by the guide and are suggested with the attitude of "would you be willing to try something for a few minutes and discover what happens?" Experiments are usually designed to enhance awareness of what is already going on. For example, if a person says, "I'm feeling so trapped right now!" a suggestion might be, "Would you be willing to close your eyes and be in your trap? What's it like in there right now?"

As each experiment is suggested, the person is free to try the experiment, to modify it, or to say no to it altogether.

In Gestalt work, resistance is deeply respected because it carries the seeds of health. Resistance is seen as a coping skill, learned in childhood. It is rooted in a healthy impulse to protect a young, fragile self, and is usually successful in helping the child feel better – for the time being. Many people owe their emotional, and even physical, survival to their ability to resist experiencing the intolerable. A Gestalt guide does not try to break down resistance; instead she *supports* it by pointing to its healthy origin.

In addition, resistance is honored as a safety valve. When resistance is left alone, it keeps the seeker from being flooded with feelings and memories for which he may not be ready. Letting resistance be is one of the major ways that a Gestalt guide gives up being responsible for the process, and puts the responsibility for the process where it belongs: with the person coming for healing.

Gestalt work holds the belief that each person is responsible for his or her own growth, and that as awareness increases, most people are capable of choosing health. This means that the guide is not the one who knows answers, but is a consultant and coach. The guide is not a motivator or a sage, and certainly is not a treatment provider, but a fellow traveler. It means that the seeker is really and truly in charge of how to live his life, and of course does his own inner work. This radical trust in the one seeking to grow minimizes dependence on the guide (and thus shortens the process) because the seeker is working more with himself than with the guide.

HOMEOSTASIS

All these interrelated concepts come together in Perls' understanding of homeostasis, or *organismic self-regulation.*[7] As a physician, Perls was fascinated with this biological mechanism, and he saw it as a paradigm of how human beings maintain themselves and continue to grow, not only physically, but also emotionally. This process, outlined below, undergirds Gestalt theory and is its organizing focus.

First, every person, and indeed every organism, has a drive toward homeostasis, the state in which every need is satisfied and the person is at rest – until the next need emerges. This drive to deal with our needs is vital in maintaining health and in spurring us to grow. The classical example is that when you are thirsty, this need prompts, and later *drives*, you to drink in order to return to homeostasis. If you break your arm, immediately your body mobilizes to begin healing. If you are running, your body automatically adjusts so that you take in more oxygen. The process of homeostasis occurs even on a cellular level in our bodies, maintaining blood sugar, regulating heartbeat and digestion and so on. We share with animals and plants a drive toward balance, growth and health. We could not exist without it.

Human needs for growth are not just biological, however; they are spiritual, emotional, and social as well. For instance, if we have not grieved the death of a loved one, our whole being stretches toward resolution of this pain. We may avoid working toward its resolution, but in order to do so we must deaden impulses that will be pushing on us from inside to cry and remember the one who died.

Second, this theory assumes that needs emerge one by one, and that the most important need will be experienced as urgent. Perls called this urgent emerging need "the emergency."[8] This wonderful mechanism means that a Gestaltist

[7] Fritz Perls, T*he Gestalt Approach and Eyewitness to Therapy,* pp. 5-9.
[8] Perls, Hefferline, and Goodman, *Gestalt Therapy: Excitement and Growth in the Human Personality,* pp. 277-78.

does not need to figure out what to do next; the emergency will be obvious through awareness and trained observation, verified and clarified by working with experiments. Frequent refrains in a Gestalt process are questions like "What are you feeling right now? What are you aware of?"

Third, a healthy person is aware of his needs, and these emerging needs – and his previous experience of these needs – color the way he perceives the world. Whatever will meet his needs become "foreground" or the focus of awareness, while other things recede into the background. If he is thirsty, for example, he is very aware of faucets, drinking fountains, and ads for sparkling water. If he is thirsty enough, he may even notice puddles on the sidewalk. Once he has slaked his thirst, he won't be as aware of these things anymore, for they have faded into his perceptual background.

Thus, our life experiences and needs shape our perception of the world. This is one reason why two people looking at the same thing can have such radically different reactions. When my daughter Shana was twelve, we made a trip to Birmingham, Alabama, where I was born. I was eager to show her the house where I lived until I was six, and as we drove there I gave her an overheated description of a wonderful tiny Spanish-style villa (yes, I called it a villa) made of yellow stucco. As we approached the house, good memories of gentle lazy afternoons in the Alabama sunshine came flooding back. I could almost feel my mother lovingly rubbing oil on my skin to protect me from the sun. I vividly felt myself jumping into my father's arms again as he came home from work.

Except for the little house now being pinkish brown, it was just as I remembered. Immersed in warm memories as I was, to me the house looked simply beautiful.

Shana, glancing at the house, obviously amazed at my big build-up, said, "Mom, it looks like a *Taco Bell!*" It took me a minute to see it, but darned if she wasn't right. Objectively speaking, the house wasn't even that pretty or unusual. Clearly, my childhood years there had shaped our wildly different perceptions.

In his training groups Fritz Perls liked to demonstrate how differing inner agendas color perceptions of self. He liked to ask everyone in a group to describe themselves as a rosebush. Invariably there would be wildly differing "rosebushes" in the group. One person might say, "I'm a beautiful rosebush. I'm blooming in the sun and giving pleasure to everyone. I'm rooted in the earth and I drink deeply of the rain...." Another might say, "I'm a rosebush, stuck in the ground, not able to move. I'm full of thorns and I'm tired of people picking me for their pleasure. Why can't they just leave me alone?"[9]

Needs for healing left over from childhood, which Perls called "*unfinished business,*" are especially powerful in shaping adult perceptions. For example, if a person has a need to work on the damaged relationship with her father, she will find "fathers" everywhere. If her father was critical of her, she will be likely to interpret criticism in the comments of her friends, even if none is intended. She will also have a tendency to pick critical friends. If she is the pastor of a church, it is quite possible that the entire congregation will feel like a horde of critical fathers bearing down on her. Even God may feel harsh and demanding, ready to pounce at the least infraction.

Unfinished business with the past is constantly being expressed in the present, and comes to consciousness in the ever-changing experience of the present moment. Thus focusing on the awareness continuum can be a remarkably fast way of getting at the unfinished business. In addition, present awareness can open a door to healing, for we tend to notice that which would meet our need. Simply being aware of what stands out for us in our inner or outer environment can lead directly both to our inner growth agenda, and to the next steps in the actual growth work itself. "What is going on right now?" is always the relevant question in Gestalt work.

Fourth, a healthy person mobilizes to get her needs met and to process her unfinished business. She will metabolize experiences as they come. If she is tired, she will sleep; if hungry, she will eat. If she is in an abusive situation, she will get out of it as fast as possible. If he feels tears welling up, he will let them come without judgment or shame. If he is in an environment in which crying ordinarily would not be appropriate (a classroom in which he is the teacher, for instance) he will go out of his way to find the setting he needs as soon as he can.

My son Noah was 18 when he had to make the terrible decision to put his passionately-loved dog to sleep. Buck and Noah had been close companions all their growing-up years, but now Buck had cancer. When the vet said there was nothing more to be done, Noah was devastated. He cried; then he faced the situation with maturity and courage. He decided that he would not let his dog suffer, and that he would spend as much time as possible with Buck before he died. Buck's last days were full of visits to all the places he loved: the park where he

---

[9] For example see Perls, *Gestalt Therapy Verbatim,* pp. 134-139.

chased squirrels, the fascinating duck pond, the woods where they loved to wander together.

We began to sense how deeply Noah was reaching inside himself for his own wisdom when he decided he wanted his 19th birthday to be Buck's last day. As Noah so fervently put it, "I want to spend my birthday doing what's right for my dog!" He asked the veterinarian to come to our house, so Buck could die at home where he felt most comfortable and surrounded by love. The morning of Noah's birthday, he bought Buck an enormous steak, and fed it to him. He held him most of the day, weeping and telling Buck how much he loved him. When the time came, Noah continued to hold Buck as the life drained out of his body. Even though the veterinarian and his pretty, young, female assistant were looking on, Noah let himself wail unselfconsciously, giving full expression to his grief at the death of his good friend.

When Noah was ready, we buried Buck in the back yard, with Noah insisting that he fill in the dirt with his bare hands. He cried with each handful, saying goodbye to each part of Buck's body. Immediately after the burial, he placed Buck's portrait with other photographs on the "family wall". We knew he was finished when, dirty and sweaty, he demanded, "And now I want a cold beer!"

It seemed to my husband and me that there was an exquisite rightness to Noah's actions that was almost liturgical. At each step in the process, Noah allowed his behavior to be dictated by his need to grieve in his own way, without censoring or interference. It is unlikely that Noah could have done what he needed to do at the animal hospital, or if George and I had not been okay with it. With the wisdom and awareness of a healthy person, he set things up so he could do just what his inner process called for. In Gestalt terms, Noah's acute awareness of himself led directly to his effectively contacting the environment in order to metabolize his pain.

Fifth, it's obvious, then, that you can't separate a person from his environment.[10] Simply put, in order to get his needs met a person must have surroundings which nurture him physically, emotionally, spiritually and socially. When this is not the case, he suffers, but it is the environment – family, church, society – which is sick. Although he will work to overcome these obstacles, it is clear that it is his environment that most needs the healing.

---

[10] Perls, *Gestalt Therapy Verbatim*, p. 26.

Although Perls didn't draw out this point very far, there are obvious implications for the relationship between personal transformation and social change. I believe every counselor and pastor should clearly understand that there is often a social dimension to personal pain. Racism, classism, gender oppression, economic injustice and homophobia stunt people emotionally and spiritually. Institutions dedicated to good purposes are capable of blindness, even cruelty. Unexamined attitudes of a society can chew up certain of its members. When awareness of this social dimension is present in a pastoral or counseling relationship, then part of the healing process of an individual can be to address the social problem causing his – or another's – pain. (In Chapter Seventeen I will discuss institutional healing in greater detail.)

Sixth, when her need is met, a healthy person returns to homeostasis until the next need or bit of unfinished business emerges. Naturally, the state of homeostasis never lasts very long, because new needs are always emerging. The urgency to grow never stops. Even when one is dying, there will be urgency to let go, to finish up, and to find meaning in the life that is ending. There will be, however, "rest and recuperation" plateaus in most growth journeys. When these occur, usually after making major progress, a Gestalt guide is content to encourage the integration and enjoyment of the new healing, not pressing for more growth until the need for it emerges naturally.

Perls describes the entire process of homeostasis as the *"ability to form and close gestalts."*[11]

Since the death of Perls over thirty years ago, Gestalt theory and practice has expanded a great deal. Gestaltists have discovered that Gestalt blends quite naturally with other ways to grow. Some have learned to combine Gestalt with family systems theory; others specialize in broader relational issues or in using Gestalt as a tool for conflict management; still others have integrated Gestalt with various forms of Eastern or New Age spirituality. The next chapter discusses my still-evolving integration of Gestalt with Christian spirituality. I believe the two fit beautifully.

---

[11] Perls, *The Gestalt Approach and Eyewitness to Therapy*, p. 9.

The glory of God is humanity fully alive.
Irenaeus, Bishop of Lyon, 2nd century

2

BEYOND PERLS: INTEGRATING GESTALT WITH CHRISTIAN SPIRITUALITY

I first learned about Gestalt concepts after I had experienced them myself in my own growth. With increasing excitement, I read everything I could find about Gestalt. It seemed so natural and right to trust that humans are created with the lifelong drive to grow. If that is so, I reasoned, then the way to encourage personal growth is to pay attention, and in a protected setting to let happen what wants to happen. I saw that there is good reason to refer to Gestalt as the "philosophy of the obvious."[12] Gestalt theory just made sense to me, and indeed seemed consistent with the way I had experienced my own growth. Furthermore, I was captivated with the idea of the counselor not being the explainer of another person's life, and I loved the way Gestaltists schooled themselves to trust another's process. Appealing also was that although Gestalt work is an art, it is really very simple.

What didn't seem so wonderful was Perls' insistence that spiritual matters have no place in Gestalt work. Though most of the time he simply ignored religion, if pressed he insisted that belief in God was nothing more than a fearful and childish projection of our own human power. We need to grow up and claim our power, he would say, and not abdicate responsibility for our own lives.[13]

Perls was certainly not alone among therapists of his time in his antipathy toward religion. Even today many other systems of psychotherapy still have a taboo against a therapist getting involved with a client's spirituality. True, in recent years some therapists have gotten interested in integrating psychotherapy with various Eastern spiritualities,[14] but Christian spirituality still seems curi-

---

[12] Perls, *Gestalt Therapy Verbatim,* p. 74.
[13] Dan Sullivan, a Gestalt therapist and former Jesuit from Princeton, New Jersey, told me that he repeatedly quizzed Perls about the place of religion in Gestalt Therapy. Perls' position outlined here comes from Dan Sullivan's memory of those conversations.
[14] See for example Sylvia Crocker, *A Well Lived Life: Essays in Gestalt Therapy.*

ously off limits, even for some pastoral therapists. For example, one well-respected church-related pastoral psychotherapy training program in New York teaches its students to deal with spiritual issues only if the client insists. Similarly, much current wisdom among spiritual directors emphasizes that they should stay away from anything that smacks of therapy.

In practice it is difficult to draw these lines, since people don't draw them when they reveal their lives to a trusted listener. For example, one bewildered student chaplain reported that her supervisor admonished her for encouraging a dying man's prayer in which he had an image of Jesus with him in "the valley of the shadow of death." Why? Because doing so was therapy! Gestalt is not unusual in drawing a strict line between emotions and spirit, but few systems make quite the same claims to being as holistic as Gestalt.

I never felt Fritz Perls was right about faith; yet when I started to pray with people during Gestalt sessions I was quite anxious about it, feeling that I was breaking every rule I had ever been taught. Although I had no trouble praying with another as a minister, each time I suggested prayer in a Gestalt session my heart would pound and I would get sweaty all over.

Finally, I did some Gestalt work of my own in which I had an imaginary conversation with Fritz the Irascible. I told him that I was praying with people as a Gestaltist, and that I intended to continue. In my vivid fantasy he was furious and called me a terrible therapist, yelling that I was stuck in dishonest, moralistic "shoulds," and that I should grow up. He was plenty scary! Although I was shaking, I was able to shoot back that he had disowned his spirituality that he badly needed to integrate. Furthermore, I snarled that he was irresponsible to ignore such an enormous part of human experience while claiming to be holistic. Surprisingly, in my imagination he listened to my tirade silently, stroking his beard as if he was pondering. I felt I had made my point with him – and had survived to tell about it.

Probably I would not have had the courage to say these things to him while he was alive, but as I did so in fantasy I began to feel more confident in these convictions. In the aftermath of my anger at Fritz, I felt the quiet voice of the Holy Spirit saying, "Go ahead. This is right."

Over the next few years prayer for healing became a central focus of my Gestalt work, and because I was working mainly with church folk, I got bold about mixing Gestalt with Christian spirituality. Further integration occurred as I experienced many small "aha" moments that showed me how to put it all together. I never felt right claiming that I was creating this integration; I couldn't escape the feeling that the Holy Spirit was teaching me this synthesis bit by bit – and I was getting it rather slowly. A few years into this learning process I recognized, to my surprise, that what seemed like small additions to Gestalt added up to a new way of engaging in healing ministry. I named the new baby Gestalt Pastoral Care.

Because Gestalt theory is simple and accessible, I saw that it does not have to be the exclusive realm of psychotherapists. As I began to teach it to ministers, it was increasingly clear that most clergy were able to incorporate a beginning-level Gestalt perspective into their existing ministries of pastoral care.

With more experience, I began to see just how well Gestalt fits with healing ministry and spiritual companioning. Gestalt recognizes emotional and physical healing as a natural process, and a Christian perspective says that the Holy Spirit is intimately and personally involved in this process. Put another way, human nature compels us to strive toward wholeness, and God's nature offers ways for this healing to occur. I have come to believe that Gestalt Pastoral Care invites nothing less than cooperation with the great ongoing Christian story of creation and redemption.

CREATION

First, God created human beings with a wonderfully intricate interplay of spirit, body, emotions and sociability. We experience things on many levels at the same time; everything that happens to us sends reverberations to every part of our being. Surely we are "fearfully and wonderfully made." Gestalt's strong holistic viewpoint is indeed consistent with the way God created us. The gospels record occasions in which Jesus demonstrated his wisdom in this regard. When he asked the man at the pool, "Do you want to be made well?" (John 5:6) it is not difficult to imagine he was addressing the emotions of one who had perhaps made an uneasy peace with his paralysis. Another paralytic, the one lowered through the roof, was told that his sins were forgiven. In this story, paralyzing guilt was addressed before the healing of physical paralysis. Good pastoral care would suggest that we, like Jesus, strive to see and love others as whole beings, in the faith that God is at work in every part of us.

Secondly, humans are created with an innate hunger for God, and God generously finds a home in our deepest selves. Creating the spaciousness to pray in the context of emotional growth recognizes and gives expression to this longing in people of faith to discover and acknowledge God's action in their lives. In Gestalt terms, it is part of our awareness continuum. In recognizing God's presence we are simply increasing awareness of what is, just as Fritz taught.

While Gestalt teaches us to pay attention to gentle inner tugs, Gestalt Pastoral Care suggests that inner nudges are to be received as a gift of God. The integration of matters of spirit with our emotional growth acknowledges our need for grace when we are truly helpless, our need for forgiveness when we are guilty, our need for comfort when we are terrified, and our need for meaning when our lives have fallen apart. It understands that praising God may be the only genuine response we can make when our hearts overflow with thanksgiving. It knows that just being in God's presence with awareness is healing in itself. Thus we pray because it is utterly natural, even organic, to do so.

Third, in Christian spirituality there runs the constant question, "Are you willing to surrender even further? Will you take the next step? Do you say 'yes' or 'no'?" Each person must decide for himself how he will respond to what his life brings, choosing or rejecting God's continual invitation to commitment, growth, and loving service. In Gestalt Pastoral Care the relationship with the minister is not the centerpiece of the process; instead the primary relationship is with God.

Although Perls had little patience with people who repeatedly interrupt their inner process, he was clear that each person has responsibility to consent – or not – to his or her own growth. He wasn't willing to cajole anyone to change, nor would he offer interpretations or advice. Instead, he proposed experiments that could pave the way for discoveries. Those who claimed, "I *can't* do this experiment" were invited to try saying, "I *won't* do this experiment." He was always implicitly asking, "Do you say yes or no to your life? It's up to you."

Although I was excited by the way Perls gave permission for each person to chart her or his own course, I was appalled by his habit of insulting and humiliating those who volunteered to work with him. I instinctively knew that for permission to be genuine, the context must be supportive, hospitable, and accepting. Both Christian love and good sense call for creating enough spaciousness for people to feel safe enough to be themselves, choosing how and when they will grow. In addition, speaking the truth does not need to be condemning. Although Perls would disagree, sometimes we must make room for a few minutes, or even a whole session, of "talk" if that's what someone wants. For some, just telling their story is the experiment that is needed. Others need to talk about ways to pray or other concerns of spiritual growth. In these matters of latitude, permission, and encouragement, Gestalt Pastoral Care and Gestalt therapy part company.[15]

When a Gestalt Pastoral Care minister proposes an experiment, there is clear understanding ahead of time that the person working has the freedom and responsibility to try the experiment, modify it, or say no altogether. If someone ignores, deflects, or otherwise resists an experiment, the minister helps the person say no with awareness, and there are no accompanying judgments or accusations. Instead, the minister *supports* the resistance, sending a clear message that defenses will not be torn away. Paradoxically, when people realize that they truly have the choice to say "yes" or "no," an overwhelming majority eventually chooses to say "yes." In fact, they usually dive into their depths pretty quickly. (I will discuss working with resistance in Chapters Ten and Eleven.)

With its emphasis on freely chosen experiments as a way to grow, Gestalt Pastoral Care echoes the freedom-giving invitational style of Jesus. Always he *invited*, setting people free to respond to the workings of God in their own hearts. Though he asked the wealthy young man to give away all he had, he allowed him to walk away (Matthew 19:16-22). He didn't try to stop Judas from doing his dirty deed (Matthew 26:47-50). He invited, but did not compel, some men to give up their livelihood and come with him instead. Among the earliest disciples there was a continual gracious invitation from the Lord to come, to watch, to learn, to be aware, and to be changed by what they experienced.

Combining Christian spirituality with Gestalt experiments offers many new gifts for inner work. Added to traditional Gestalt experiments, there are "Christian experiments" such as laying on of hands with healing prayer, faith imagination prayer, anointing, Eucharist, confession, and individually-created liturgies of healing. They are experimental in the sense that while we believe that God surely responds to our prayer, we can seldom predict just how. These ways of prayer are avenues that open us to discover what God is doing; we pray, we pay attention, then wait expectantly to see what happens.

When we dive deeply into our need for healing, we inevitably encounter both limitation and mystery. There is just so much we don't know and can't figure out. Although God is revealed in Jesus, we still can't really know God; we are too small. Even so, when we confront suffering and tragedy, we try. We naturally cry out with spiritual questions: "Why did God let this happen to me?" or "Why do

---

[15] In the years since Perls died, many secular Gestalt therapists have also adopted a warmer, more relational and encouraging style. Among them are Gary Yontef, Lynn Jacobs, and Sylvia Crocker.

innocent people have to suffer?" or, "How can God possibly love me after the way I've messed up?" Questions like these, while completely natural, can tie us in knots, sometimes for years. Theological explanations, even faithful and astute ones, might comfort one hurting person but plunge another into even deeper despair.

Spiritual companions learn that the most honest and helpful response to questions like these is to admit that we simply don't know. Although meditative reflection on heartfelt questions can be a good way to pray, insisting that answers arrive on our terms is not. We can rest in the belief, however, that God is able to help us work through such questions, and eventually find answers that satisfy our hearts. Such a shift in focus invites us to discover, rather than figure out, the movement of grace in all of life's circumstances.

In my experience, spiritual dilemmas such as these seldom surface in secular Gestalt work. People just know that they must deal with spiritual matters elsewhere. I believe, however, that Perls has given us some wonderful tools that can be of great value to Gestalt Pastoral Care ministers along with other spiritual companions and those who seek a deeper relationship with God.

Gestaltists believe that focusing on *why* can greatly delay a growth process. "*Why* do you run from intimacy?" is the kind of question that would not be posed by a Gestaltist. Instead, an experiment might be created having to do with changing *why* into *how* or *what*. Returning in fantasy to a situation in which intimacy threatens, a person might be invited to discover what happens to her there. *What* is she feeling? *What* is going on in her body, and *what* is her body saying? *How* exactly does she escape from the scary intimate circumstances in her fantasy? Is she willing to stay there this time and discover what happens? As always, the focus is on the present moment. Important, even life-changing, discoveries are often made through such awareness. Almost incidentally, answers to *why* are frequently discovered along the way too. "Oh, so *that's* why!" can be the surprise ending to a Gestalt session.

This simple Gestalt device of changing *why* to *what* or *how* can be a wonderful help in working with both agonizing spiritual questions and ordinary discernment. Asking, "*How* is God working to redeem this situation? *What* seems to be God's invitation these days? *What* is my reaction?" can open a floodgate of discoveries. Engaging with questions in this way can be a great help to Christians seeking to discover how God is at work.

REDEMPTION

Both the healing ministry of Jesus and the healing ministry of the church attest that God is passionate about healing. It is God's urgent desire that we be whole. In fact, the Greek word, *sozo*, normally translated as "salvation" in the Bible, also means "wholeness" or "healing." When we proclaim that Jesus is our savior, we could just as correctly affirm that Jesus is our healer.

We are not always healed according to our wishes, but according to God's will. True, God sometimes heals a life-threatening condition or a chronic emotional problem in minutes as someone prays. More often healing comes in other ways, and more slowly. Although we can't deny the power of illness or permanent handicaps or growth stunted by another's cruelty, as Christians we can affirm that at every stage of our living – and our dying – God is creating and bringing healing that is consistent with God's vision for each of us. It is in this sense that we can say that healing is still present in every situation, even at death. In faith we affirm that God is able to bring joy out of suffering, order out of confusion, and life out of devastation. Those experienced in healing ministry know to be on the lookout for where health is taking hold in persons for whom they have prayed.

Gestaltists, too, watch for health. Because Gestalt adopts a health model we do not dwell on illness and its diagnosis. Our job is to help another person discover and cooperate with her inner process, trusting that when an inner process is honored with awareness, some kind of healing will emerge. Secular Gestaltists have radical trust in the process; Gestalt Pastoral Care ministers seek to have an even more radical faith in God at work in the process.

Gestalt Pastoral Care rests on the incarnational belief that God's self-revelation is not only corporate, but also personal and somatic. God has surely parted the curtain through Jesus Christ, through scripture and through the example of saintly men and women. Beyond that, God speaks with us in a beautiful way through our awareness continuum and our homeostatic process in our own marvelous bodies. In particular, God whispers the way to healing through bodily sensations, images, perceptions, dreams and daydreams, our breath and heartbeat, the very musculature of our bodies, through what we notice around us and what we ignore – in everything that makes up our experience of the present moment. We can trust our inner process precisely because the Holy Spirit is at work in it, for the drive toward wholeness is written into our very beings by the One who created us. The more I have increased my awareness of *what is* through Gestalt training, the more I discover God "making all things new" (Rev 21:5).

Personally speaking, learning to surrender to my inner process through Gestalt work has been invaluable as I seek to surrender more fully to Jesus.

So when we pray for discernment about how God wants to heal us, the answer often comes by simply paying attention to what is happening to us at the moment. We can trust that both our unfinished business and God's desire for our wholeness are pushing for expression, like a tree growing around a boulder. Just as Perls taught, another step toward wholeness frequently comes just from becoming more aware.

Once at a workshop for clergy I introduced the idea that God really does want to get through to us, and then led a meditation in which the participants were invited to allow God to communicate through their imaginations. In the sharing afterwards one tearful man said that he had so hoped that God would touch him in some way, but he had felt absolutely nothing during the prayer. He said he had been feeling separated from everyone for a long time, and that it was hard to experience the affection of friends, or even his wife's love. Most distressing of all, he was cut off from a sense of God's presence. I asked him whether the whole group could pray for him, and he readily agreed. We gathered around his chair, and putting our twenty-three pairs of hands on him, we prayed earnestly that God would heal whatever was wrong. He continued to weep, but when I asked him what was happening, he replied "nothing, nothing at all." To help him expand his awareness of the present, I asked him whether he could physically feel all our hands. "Yes, sure," he said. To keep him focused on this awareness, I asked, "How do our hands feel to you?" "They're warm – and comforting," he replied. "What is God saying to you now through our warm and comforting hands?" I persisted. "Connected! I'm connected!" was his immediate response, as he wept in relief. It was clear to us as we continued to pray for him that God had indeed opened the man's heart to the web of love that surrounded him. It was also clear that his expanded awareness of the physical sensation of being touched by many hands had a lot to do with his being able to perceive God's love – and ours.

In each life there seem to be cycles of death and rebirth, of crucifixion and resurrection. Gestaltists are not afraid to accompany people to wherever their process leads, including the "deaths" everyone experiences sooner or later, for they know that healing and rebirth are possible. Nor are Gestaltists squeamish about the expression of intense emotion. Working with memories that become present in the here and now, they often follow brave people to vivid scenes of mayhem and terror. They are there when people *re-experience* (rather than talk about) rape, incest, physical abuse and political torture. They accompany anguished

31

parents who again watch their child die a painful death. They sit with a weeping nine-year-old (now an adult) watching his father abandon the family for good. Gestaltists have not only heard it all, but have also "been there." And so, of course, have ministers.

As a Christian minister I have sometimes had the feeling when I'm with a suffering person that I'm watching crucifixion. And just as often, I discover again that God is there with us in a powerful and palpable way; God even seems to be eager to join us in our terrible ordeals. And why not? If I as a minister am willing to go with one who dares to re-experience an ancient trauma, surely Christ the healer goes ahead of me. I believe that Jesus chooses to "go to the cross" again and again to bring emotional healing and resurrection to a suffering person. Those in the healing ministry know that God can heal even the worst traumas and pain. In this sense Gestalt awareness is quite similar to contemplative awareness. Contemplatives are aware people. They stop to savor things, they pause to allow gratitude to gather force and spill over, they are willing to look at suffering and ugliness, knowing it can be transformed. Surely "death is swallowed up in victory" again and again as suffering is redeemed and re-framed.

Ideally, Gestalt Pastoral Care encounters between a minister and a seeker are characterized by a sense of holiness and reverence. The minister has a finely-tuned sense that God is in charge and actively directing the process. As best she can, she has surrendered her own power to the infinite power of the Holy Spirit. In doing so, she has grown strong enough to be powerless. Oddly, when she gives away her power – and is able to see Christ in the one coming for help – she is very powerful indeed; her power is to create room to grow, to create an environment of yeasty freedom and spaciousness which recognizes the presence of the Holy One.

A germ of this profound respect is found in Gestalt's insistence that each person is in charge of his or her own growth. Discoveries are made together. The radical trust in the process in Gestalt therapy points to the more basic faith of a Christian who trusts that God is in charge and leading the way.

Finally, Gestalt Pastoral Care groups provide a context for the gift of Church. I don't mean that these groups *are* a church. Nor are they a substitute for church membership. They become a beautiful, but temporary, *expression of Church* because Gestalt Pastoral Care groups gather in the name of Christ, because together they witness God's power to heal, and because they intercede and midwife one another's growth.

Traditionally, much secular Gestalt work has taken place in groups. Perls taught and demonstrated Gestalt in groups, and many Gestaltists, myself included, still prefer groups to individual sessions. One person's work can be catalytic and give permission for another's. Participants in Gestalt groups learn to accept differences. They learn that helping does not help. They learn that when they feel judgmental of another, they have work to do with themselves. Most have to learn how to stop trying to figure out what's wrong and why. A Gestalt group makes space for each participant to take his or her very own next step and creates wonderful freedom to grow. I believe that this openness, when combined with prayer, creates a fertile climate for an experience of Church.

Typically, weekend Gestalt Pastoral Care workshops take place at a retreat center. A wide mix of denominations and theological perspectives are frequently represented, as well as varied ages, educational backgrounds, and reasons for being there. In the first few hours participants learn that each person is on a unique journey that is to be honored. Most are relieved to find out that everyone has the freedom to say yes or no to anything that may happen, and that no one will be pressured to participate in any way. They see that the group is committed to discerning and opening up to God's particular invitation for each person.

As the retreat proceeds they watch and pray silently as the work goes on. With explicit permission from each participant, they lay hands on each other and pray for continued healing. They learn to trust that they will experience healing grace. The group watches discoveries being made as transformations, both large and small, are received with relief and joy. The group might help create a liturgy for a group member who wants to make new, life-giving vows. They are present as someone contacts his experience of abandonment in childhood and later senses the Holy Spirit present in that tragedy. They might witness a confession for one, and become Christ-with-skin-on for another. They learn how to support the one who decides that he needs to just watch for now. They will be accepting and patient with the one who feels stuck in old patterns and responses, praying that his logjam will dissolve as soon as he is ready. They will see God at work in their interconnectedness as one person's work opens doors for the others. They might wash one another's feet during a celebration of Eucharist. In short, they become an *ad hoc church.*

GESTALT NARCISSISM AND FAITH

Some Christians have objected to Gestalt on the grounds that the emphasis on one's own needs and inner agenda is narcissistic. "What about being able to love as a mark of a healthy person?" they might ask. "What about putting aside one's own needs because someone else needs us? What about prayer, fasting or sacrifice for a principle? What about seeking justice for the poor instead of making an idol of one's impulses? What about prayer that focuses on God rather than our wants?" These objections are supported by the existence of Gestalt "workshop groupies" who spend a great deal of time and money dealing with every little psychological twinge, every quirk of body/mind. They seem to believe that it is possible to make themselves perfectly healthy. Psychological hypochondriacs, they are fascinated with themselves. (Spiritual companions would recommend learning to trust God instead, who loves them even with their foibles.)

It is certainly true that unhealthy narcissism is potentially the great weakness of Gestalt theory and practice. Distortion of Gestalt principles could, and sometimes does, lead people to think that, "Impulses are god. If it feels good, do it. You are the final judge of your life, and you are in control. You can fix yourself."

The well-known profligate lifestyle of Fritz Perls has reinforced these objections, and has kept many away from the gifts that Gestalt has to offer. For Perls personally, desires of any kind were practically a mandate to act. Perls behaved as if his whole life was a Gestalt experiment in which the goal was indeed to express whatever was inside. To be fair, he was committed to ruthless honesty, with no contradictions between what he felt and how he acted. Nor did he tolerate any split between his professional and personal identity. He had very little patience with social fakery, white lies or other niceties. He must be respected for his unwavering commitment to truthfulness about himself.

In my opinion, however, because he made little distinction between the process of therapy and the living of his life, he never integrated impulses with ethics. He was outrageously promiscuous, ignored and publicly berated his wife and children simply because he felt like it, and was rude and contentious with colleagues and friends. He could be cruel or generous, icy or warm, depending on the whim of – what else? – the present moment.[16] Quite a few therapists he personally trained more or less adopted his deliberately disconcerting style. Added

---

[16] See Martin Shepard, *Fritz: An Intimate Portrait of Fritz Perls and Gestalt Therapy.*

to this, Perls' fame was at its height in the freewheeling 1960's. Sometimes there was sexual acting out in early Gestalt groups involving both group members and therapists. None of this has enhanced the reputation of Gestalt for church folk, even though these days Gestaltists are as ethical and responsible as any other group of professionals.

I believe that it is precisely because Gestalt has historically ignored spirituality that there has been so much room for solely focusing on self. However, it doesn't have to be this way. Our impulses don't have to control us, and surely there is more to the awareness continuum of a Christian person than impulses. There is, for example, grace and call and discernment and repentance and forgiveness, and love beyond all imagining. There is longing to serve others and bring justice in the name of Christ. If we are engaged in a lively spiritual journey that is integrated with the rest of our growth, there is a very good chance that the Holy Spirit will confront any unhealthy narcissism or selfishness or arrogance that creeps in. We can trust that God continues to invite us to grow into "the measure of the full stature of Christ" (Eph 4:13).

On the other hand, many Christians sorely need Perls' teaching that it really is okay to love oneself, to be "selfish," to own up to unsavory feelings, and to reach inside for answers. People who have grown up in the church often have great difficulty facing up to what is really lurking inside of them. They have absorbed the Christian distortion that they should never be angry, jealous, spiteful, glum, or overtly sexual. They may be uneasy even claiming their own genuine gifts, because, after all, they should be humble and self-effacing.

I have found Gestalt work to be personally invaluable in this regard, helping me to be more honest about who I am. I have learned that I myself have the impulse toward every destructive behavior I have heard confessed in my office. I am also learning to claim the gifts and power God has given me, and to know that being myself is enough. As a result of Gestalt training, I now firmly believe that nothing human is foreign to me, and I am a better minister for it.

GESTALT PASTORAL CARE IN ACTION

How does the merging of all this theory and theology look in actual practice? What might actually happen in a Gestalt Pastoral Care session? The following account of a rather ordinary session illustrates much of what has been discussed in this chapter.

Henry had been busy and distracted all week, so he had no awareness of his "emergency" when he came for his regular appointment. As we prayed at the beginning of the session for clarity and direction, he became aware of a slight sensation of heaviness pressing in on his chest. Since this heaviness had emerged from our prayer and his awareness continuum, we took this as a possible way in to find out what God was doing. I suggested a simple Gestalt experiment. "Would you talk to the heaviness on your chest?"

Readily consenting to this experiment, Henry closed his eyes and said, "Heaviness, you are pressing on me, putting pressure on me. Your weight drags me down. I feel like you are sucking my energy away. You don't want me to move or breathe." He paused, his face flushed.

"Damn! It's my boss. He is the one putting pressure on me and sucking me dry. I had no idea it was bothering me so much. I really do have something to get off my chest with him." Altering the experiment now in response to Henry's present awareness, I said, "Let your chest talk to your boss, would you?"

Five minutes into the session Henry was well into unfinished business, dealing with anger and helplessness at his boss. Later in the hour the same kind of feelings emerged for his demanding and crotchety grandfather. This important discovery was made after we noticed his voice had changed in timbre and pitch. Suddenly he sounded like a little boy, and his shoulders took on the hunch of a chastised child.

Thus the past was experienced in the present. At that point Henry was not really remembering as such; instead he was eight years old again, feeling cowed and shamed by Grandpa. As Henry, now weeping, sunk further into eight-years-old-with-grandpa, we prayerfully invited Jesus to enter the scene. He saw Jesus come into the room and look straight at him with great love. Then Jesus said, "You are my boy and I want you to have room to breathe."

As this prayer encounter was taking place, Henry's body was visibly loosening up, and his breathing was becoming deeper and less constricted. I asked Henry how his breath felt to him and he affirmed that indeed he now had more room to breathe.

When the experience with Jesus was over, I asked Henry if he would return to his present age and see how he felt. He immediately told me his heaviness was mostly gone. He then allowed himself to imagine that his boss was there. In a strong clear voice, Henry told his boss that he had been confusing him with grandpa, and that he wasn't going to do it anymore. "I have a right to breathe! And I will not allow you take that away from me. I'm your employee, not your child." His voice was that of a mature strong adult. He was not cowering; his energy was centered and clear.

In this session, Henry became aware of unfinished business pushing for resolution through the heaviness on his chest. He let God, through his inner process, direct his work as he surrendered to it with awareness. He returned to homeostasis after coming to a new resolution of the unmetabolized issues concerning his grandfather/boss. His self-identity shifted toward greater health. He experienced first-hand the healing love of Christ. He did all this in one session with minimal interaction with me. In fact most of the interaction was with his boss, grandpa, and, of course, Jesus, who spoke the beautiful healing words.

Naturally, this session did not finish the grandpa/boss issue for Henry. In later sessions, he assimilated the important work he had done, and let it expand. He learned more about his breath and how to let it support his growth, and to let his breath welcome the presence of God. He began to rest on the iconic words of Jesus, "You are my boy..." He experimented with ways to translate his new growth into behavior outside my office; in particular he discovered new ways to speak as an adult to other male adults in authority. In other words, as Henry "lived into" his inner work, the work took root and became part of his life.

3

A CONTEMPLATIVE MINISTRY OF PRESENCE

A Gestalt Pastoral Care minister has a repertoire of pastoral skills that can invite healing; those I will outline shortly. Even more vital, however, is a certain quality of presence and attention that is rooted in *being* rather than *doing.* Her presence is at once powerless and potent, reverent and earthy, and is rooted in loving attention and contemplation.

LOVING

Love is not only the motive for God's healing, but also the method God uses to heal. God loves us into being, and continues to love us into new life. Gestalt Pastoral Care ministers seek to embody God's love as best they can; in fact much of the emotional and spiritual preparation for doing this work has to do with being able to love more fully.

Loving does not mean taking pain away prematurely, covering it up or soothing it away. It does not mean advising, rescuing, or figuring things out. It is not about glossing over hard truth. It is certainly not about taking charge of another's healing process.

Loving means to invite God – daily, hourly – to love through us. Because our own love is incomplete and subject to distortion, we depend on God to fill us with the love we need to journey with another person. With the greatest respect we enter the private world of the one in need of healing, intent on discovering together how God is inviting him to take the next step. As companion and midwife, we humbly suggest ways he might cooperate with God's work. We are willing to accompany him to places of remorse, terror, despair, and tragedy, without turning away to make it easier for ourselves. We stand in awe of the process of growth and healing already set in motion, and of the unique and ingenious ways each person has found to cope with adversity.

Loving is not always easy. We must constantly work to rid ourselves of judgments, agendas, resentments, and fear. We must give up any need for personal power, but we continue to pray that God's power will be active and evident. Then we wait. Oh my, how we wait. Like any good midwife we know there is ordinarily nothing to do until the next contraction comes, except be there.

CONTEMPLATION

Allowing God to love through us is rooted in the contemplative grounding of the Gestalt Pastoral Care minister, who works from a foundational attitude of deep and attentive rest. As we allow ourselves to sink wordlessly into God's presence, we are awed by God's power and love as we watch people being invited to greater wholeness. Instead of trying to make something happen we pay gentle attention, trusting that God will somehow shape our awareness as well as that of the person coming for healing. In other words, as best we can we surrender the other person to God's desire to heal, knowing that God is already at work. Out of that deep rest comes direction and discernment about how to proceed. Naturally, sometimes we fumble or allow our own egos to get in the way, but against all reason God uses us anyway. Again and again we discover that the Holy Spirit seems to give us what we need to help people if we are willing to be quiet enough interiorly.

When my kids were born, I delighted in nursing them. I loved the special communion which developed with each child; I loved being able to make them feel so satisfied; I loved that I was giving them exactly what they needed; I loved my own physical sensations as each baby tugged on my breast.

I nursed my two children a total of five and a half years. Contrary to expectations, I was still producing an amazing amount of milk six months after I stopped nursing. About that time my friend Judith delivered her baby. Both Judith and the baby were quite sick at first, and the baby desperately needed breast milk. For three weeks I nursed the sick baby until Judith was well enough to take over. It was only then that my milk dried up – in less than a week. Both Judith and I had the strong feeling that God had specially preserved my milk for her child.

This experience of nursing the three children has become a parable of loving, contemplative ministry for me. A nursing mother does nothing to create this perfect food for her baby. She must get adequate rest and good nutrition of course, but it is not her job to work at producing milk. In fact, if she strains and gets anxious her milk is likely to decrease. The very best thing she can do to feed her baby is to put her feet up, relax, and enjoy the fact that nourishment is flowing through her. Instead of somehow trying to rise to the occasion if something extra special is needed (like nursing Judith's baby), she trusts that God will empower her.

Just so with Gestalt Pastoral Care. It is God's love flowing through us that is nourishing; we do nothing except say "yes" to it. Our job is to show up on time, relax, pay attention, and trust God to work through us.

Of course the nursing analogy shatters when we think, not of the minister, but of the person striving to be whole. Adults on a growth journey are not helpless babies. They do not need to be taken care of, but loved as they are. They do not need a mommy or daddy to hold them; they are already being held by God. They simply need a quiet, unafraid, prayerful, uncontrolling, and loving companion who honors and respects their process.

WHAT A GESTALT PASTORAL CARE MINISTER DOES

How does this contemplative, loving stance translate into action? What does a Gestalt Pastoral minister actually do? This entire book is an answer to that question. However, below is a brief summary of what is to follow.

A Gestalt Pastoral Care minister seeks to discern with the person what God is already doing, and assists the person in opening to the grace that is surely there. Their work together is actively directed by the ever-present and constantly changing process of the one coming for healing.

She tries to see where health is blocked, and where health is emerging. God seems to meet people in their greatest pain, so she invites people to look for God there. Wherever she sees new life and health emerging, she points to God's activity there as well. Because she focuses on health, there is no need to diagnose what is wrong. Nor is there any need to label, analyze, make judgments, or formulate a treatment plan.

He schools himself to be an acute observer. He focuses not only on the story being told, but also on body language, frozenness or fluidity of movement, tone of voice, gestures, energy blocks, and so on. He trusts that whatever is surfacing is a holistic expression of the person's existence. He also seeks to be aware of how God is speaking in his own inner process: intuition, memories, spiritual quickening, discernment, boredom or interest, and whatever else is in his own awareness continuum.

She coaches the person to become aware of what is happening in the present. Again and again she will ask, "What is going on right now?" Simple awareness is the bedrock of Gestalt – and crucial to Christian prayer as well. She is comfortable even when the person with whom she is working insists that nothing is happening, for she knows that the experience of nothingness is itself creative and fertile.

Along with his own discernment, he uses the material that surfaces in the person to devise experiments. He makes it clear that the person can always say no, or alter an experiment. He can risk being wrong because experiments are just a way to explore. Examples of experiments: "Would you exaggerate the movement in your shoulders a little, and see what you feel?" "Would you be willing to see what happens if you squeeze this pillow instead of squeezing your throat?"

A Gestalt Pastoral Care minister supports resistance by pointing to its healthy origin. This stance echoes both the radical freedom given by God to say yes or no to life, and to God's love that accepts us as we are.

At an appropriate time a Gestalt Pastoral Care minister might suggest that the person invite Jesus or some appropriate symbol of the Holy One into the work. Coaching the person to stay with the encounter, she will continue to offer her own discernment by creating experiments, and very occasionally through simple sharing. Probably she will pray for healing with laying on of hands. She might help create a liturgy of healing, or give assurance that sin is forgiven, or follow some other avenue of prayer that emerges in their work.

Because he is not in control of the process and not analyzing and not confronting resistance, he is content to seem not very powerful. In fact, he actively seeks to surrender his power to be used by God. He remembers that one of the most important skills in Gestalt Pastoral Care is getting out of the way of the Holy Spirit. He also knows well the importance of getting out of the way of the person doing the work. Paradoxically, when he gives up his power, he becomes an increasingly powerful conduit for God's grace.

WHO CAN DO GESTALT PASTORAL CARE?

People often ask whether pastors or therapists are able to do all this without further training. The answer is, of course, no. And yes.

Some have suggested that graduates of the Gestalt Pastoral Care training program be the only ones certified to do any part of this work. Or that even simple Gestalt techniques should be employed only after one has completed a Gestalt training program. Or that any therapist wanting to incorporate spirituality into his practice should first take a course in spiritual direction, or even get a seminary degree. Or that I should not include in this book anything that might give ministers powerful Gestalt tools they are not skilled enough to use.

I have struggled a lot with these cautions and caveats, and in fact my colleagues and I in Gestalt Pastoral Care Ecumenical Associates are in the process of establishing training and supervision requirements for Gestalt Pastoral Care Ministers. We have found, however, that folks who simply participated in a few short Gestalt Pastoral Care workshops were already responsibly incorporating bits of what they experienced into their ministries. They were beginning, for example, to let resistance alone, or to pray more easily with others. They were starting to emphasize discovery more than figuring out. They were timidly coaching others to become more aware of their present experience. They were adopting a more holistic approach in their ministries. They were creating liturgies of healing or teaching faith imagination. In other words, they were beginning to assimilate a Gestalt Pastoral Care *perspective*.

Further, we have seen that there are those without formal credentials who seem innately gifted to companion another's growth. When my Aunt Melva was dying of cancer, my young cousin Kristin emerged as a naturally gifted pastor. Someone told her that the way to minister to Aunt Melva was to "stay close and do nothing." Just that. Although at the time Kristin didn't have a college degree or any counseling experience, she was able to follow this remarkable bit of advice day after day, week after week. She listened, she sat, she spoke little and prayed much. Taking her cues from Aunt Melva, and calling me occasionally for informal supervision, Kristin engaged in an increasingly sophisticated, nuanced, and non-anxious ministry of prayer and presence. Clearly, Kristin's emotional and spiritual readiness and her natural gifts for ministry went a long way toward making up for her lack of training. However, she did not continue to depend on her natural gifts alone. After Aunt Melva died, Kristin traveled to New York every month for two years to get training in Gestalt Pastoral Care. Later she graduated from college, and most recently she began the process to become a lay minister in the United Church of Christ.

For these reasons, I invite you to use this book in your own ministry, but to use it carefully. Gestalt techniques can allow people to open up to their pain very quickly. In just a few minutes people can be experiencing a depth of feeling that can be quite disconcerting to beginners. It is not just the Gestalt component, however, that can pave the way for deep feelings. Various forms of healing prayer, available to anyone, can also enable intense emotions to surface. Faith imagination, healing liturgies, and even simple laying on of hands can open doors to wrenching pain, traumatic memories, and paralyzing fear. Unless this intensity is understood as simply part of the process, it can be frightening to both minister and seeker alike.

If you have not had explicit Gestalt training or training in Gestalt Pastoral Care, do not suggest any experiments to another except the ones for beginners. (Even these few, spelled out in Chapter Nine, can lead to powerful discoveries.) If you are not comfortable with emotions, especially your own, by all means don't encourage their expression in another person, even through prayer.

I strongly urge you to engage in the individual and communal discernment process offered below. At the end of this chapter there are some specific suggestions on how to begin.

ENGAGE IN A DISCERNMENT PROCESS

Your reluctance to plunge into Gestalt Pastoral Care may indeed indicate that you are indeed not ready, so honor your reticence and fear. Sit in prayer with the questions of whether you are called to this form of ministry, and whether it is time for you to begin.

Assess the level of your training and competency in Gestalt, other forms of counseling, or in spiritual direction. Honestly and prayerfully ask how much experience you have had of your own depths. Admit to yourself if there are some matters of emotion or spirit that you keep behind closed doors. Are you comfortable with your anger? Your fear? Your tears and anguish? Do you accept your capacity for jealously? For violence? For lust? Are there some things in your life you refuse to talk about? Are there some kinds of people you just can't stand?

Examine your motives. What needs of your own might you be trying to meet? Do you want to be powerful? Or to seem extra holy? Do you *need* to help?

Know your limits and resolve not to go beyond them.

I'm definitely not suggesting that you answer these questions on your own; much of what makes a ministry legitimate is that the church has called it forth and has recognized God's call in your life. Is your local congregation interested in using your interest or skills in a healing ministry? Will some church board or conference help you get further training? Will they officially sponsor your ministry? Also, ask the opinion of those whose maturity, integrity, and spiritual growth you respect. What does your spiritual director think? Your therapist? Your family? Your close friends?

SOME CRITERIA AND A CAUTIONARY TALE

The following story illustrates what can happen when a minister goes beyond her limits, forging ahead without training, insight or discernment.

I once received a frantic call from Hannah, a pastor who had attended an introductory three-day workshop on Gestalt Pastoral Care. She was greatly moved by the healing she witnessed, and was excited by this new approach. Although the workshop she attended did not constitute training in any way, she decided to try out with a parishioner some Gestalt techniques she had observed during the workshop. She genuinely cared and wanted to help; but even as we spoke on the phone, I could hear the parishioner wailing that she couldn't stop crying.

What should she do now, Hannah wanted to know. Although she truly meant well, Hannah was not ready to be a Gestalt Pastoral Care minister, or even a good listener, for she lacked the necessary self-awareness, training, and experience. Here are some criteria for deciding if you are ready to begin using Gestalt Pastoral Care on a limited basis:

First, a Gestalt Pastoral Care minister must be able to be really present with the one coming for help, and able to love that person freely. One of the most important signs of readiness to do this work is having dealt with your own issues *enough* that you are able to go with people into their spiritual and emotional depths, and not get kidnapped by your own needs, fear, or pain. If you find yourself afraid, turned off, disgusted, judgmental, shocked, trying to control, immersed in your own memories, angry, making an agenda for the person, or wondering every few minutes how you are doing, you are not present. More importantly, you are not able to allow the love of Christ to come through you. You need to engage with your own issues before you can work in depth with anyone.

Hannah, the pastor of the frantic phone call, had never dealt with her lifetime of suppressed emotion. Because she was terrified of her own pent-up tears, she was scared to death when her parishioner began her deep sobbing. Hannah was not able to love her with the love of Christ because she was too preoccupied with her own fear. She had no business inviting her parishioner to go into such depths because she was a rank novice in her own emotional landscape. Thus Hannah violated a cardinal rule: she tried to take someone to an interior place that she herself had never dared to visit.

Second, a Gestalt Pastoral Care minister needs to be able to surrender his need for power. He must be able to be with a hurting person and not need to take away the pain. He is comfortable even though he has no answers of his own, and he has mostly given up the need to be seen as a holy person, a terrific healer or a sage. He does not need power or admiration; in fact he is willing to be a fool for Christ. He is okay even if absolutely nothing happens in a session, and thus he will not do anything to crash through resistance. He will let loose ends be.

Hannah of the SOS phone call was not yet healed enough to be powerless. She had not been valued as a child; and as an adult she still had a great need to prove herself by seeming powerful and competent. As a result, she had taken charge of the session with her parishioner and had set out to break through her resistance. Because the pastor was so clearly in charge, the parishioner relinquished responsibility for herself. She left it to Hannah to stop her tears; she was putty in her hands. Hannah didn't understand that she herself had invited the woman's dive into helplessness by her own need for power.

It was fairly simple to intervene in this pastoral fiasco; just giving back control to the frightened, wailing woman was enough. I asked the parishioner over the phone, "Do you want to stop crying now, or do you want to keep on for awhile? It's OK with me whatever you decide." She stopped crying almost immediately.

Third, a Gestalt Pastoral Care minister needs to be able to rest in God's presence. As attentive to God as she is to the person coming for help, she is willing to allow God to be in charge. She knows that God is already working with the hurting person and is responsible for any confronting, motivating, urging, or prodding that needs to be done. Even though she has skills, she is willing to "not do." In fact, a great part of her skill is getting out of the way of God's healing work.

Hannah did not approach the session with her parishioner from a contemplative stance. Although she really cared about her parishioner, she didn't ask what God wanted, or how God was already at work. Instead she blundered ahead with her caring agenda, full of doing, trying hard to make something happen.

Finally, a Gestalt Pastoral Care minister must be willing to get supervision, refer when advisable and take further training as needed. Even very experienced ministers and therapists make referrals to other professionals and need supervision from time to time. With beginners, frequent supervision is utterly essential. All of us have blind spots, unhealed pain, and unmet needs that can derail another's healing process. Working with suffering people will bring to light all the issues we might prefer to keep hidden guaranteed! In this context, a wise truth teller is a wonderful gift to any minister. To her credit, Hannah realized at last that she was in over her head, and was willing to reach out for help.

I don't want you to automatically conclude from Hannah's story that exploring Gestalt Pastoral Care is inevitably fraught with danger. I simply share her obvious mistakes to stress the importance of prayerful discernment, training, and supervision.

SAFEGUARDS

If Hannah had known a little more about Gestalt Pastoral Care, she would have been aware that though Gestalt Pastoral Care can be rapid, powerful and intense, when practiced correctly Gestalt Pastoral Care carries inherent safeguards. These safeguards are important not only for beginners, but for experienced ministers as well.

- •Perhaps the most important of these safeguards is the Gestalt approach to resistance. When a minister does not push for results or try to break down resistance, then resistance itself can be depended on to keep the sufferer from opening doors he is not ready to open.

- •When there is no preaching, advice-giving, judging, coercing, persuading, or analyzing, the possibility of doing damage is greatly reduced.

- •When the minister is willing to seem relatively powerless, it is unlikely she will impose her own agenda on a sufferer.

•When the minister trusts that God is at work in the person's aware-ness continuum, he knows that assenting – or not – to a growth process is solely the privilege and responsibility of the person coming for healing. Thus the minister will not push for results.

•When the minister is monitoring her own awareness continuum for signs of needing to control the encounter, or for *any* strong reactions such as judgments, fear or anger, she can take such perceptions as a caution light directing her to step back and do her own work first.

•When the minister honestly and humbly asks the guidance of the Holy Spirit before and during each session, there is a very good chance that things will stay on track.

•When the minister takes seriously the necessity of finding a good truth-telling supervisor, she will have not only a safety net, but also an invaluable resource for hands-on learning and insight into her own needs for continued healing.

With these safeguards clearly understood and respected, a minister will not only understand how to avoid doing damage, but will also know how to get out of the way in a healing encounter.

GETTING STARTED: EASING IN

If you have discerned a sense of readiness and call to use Gestalt Pastoral Care in your ministry, and this call is confirmed by those in your church commu-nity, put your trust in God, and get started. Don't imagine that you need to be in *perfect* emotional health and spiritual blessedness. Remember, God can use your woundedness to help others. However, I recommend beginning slowly, gently integrating pieces of Gestalt Pastoral Care as you feel led.

Therefore, I recommend using the material in this book in two stages. First, you might simply explore this approach by adopting a *Gestalt Pastoral Care per-spective,* integrating some of the riches of Gestalt into the work you already do. Many ministers have found that a Gestalt Pastoral Care perspective has crept bit by bit into their pastoral counseling, or has informed a healing ministry project of their church.

You might want to go further to the second stage by seeking training in secular Gestalt therapy or in spiritual companioning, using this book to assist further integration of the psychological, somatic, and spiritual. Explicit training in Gestalt Pastoral Care paves the way to become a *Gestalt Pastoral Minister.* Becoming a Gestalt Pastoral Minister might mean doing this work full time as a resource for the church.

STAGE ONE: A GESTALT PASTORAL CARE PERSPECTIVE

The first stage in claiming our pastoral role in this new way is exercising it from a Gestalt Pastoral Care perspective. A Gestalt Pastoral Care perspective embraces:

•Gestalt's holistic viewpoint

•commitment to surrender power to the one coming for help

•respect for the wisdom of the body

•courage to combine spiritual companioning, prayer, and especially faith imagination, with other types of counseling

•willingness to claim the unique resources of the Christian faith in a healing journey

•belief that God is constantly at work in each person's process and that this work is discernibly evident

•commitment to enter into another's world

•focus on present experience rather than analysis

•willingness to suggest some very simple Gestalt experiments

•resolve to let resistance alone.

A Gestalt Pastoral Care perspective can undergird such healing ministries as spiritual companioning, prayer and laying on of hands, individually created healing liturgies, witnessing confession, declaring forgiveness and helping people forgive. With more experience, a Gestalt Pastoral Care perspective can be helpful in praying for generational pain, institutional healing, or deliverance. These components of a Gestalt Pastoral perspective will be discussed at length throughout this book.

You may be skittish at first, feeling that anything that could possibly take people into heavy waters should be left to psychotherapists. Perhaps you feel that you would be crossing a forbidden boundary. Emotionally, you may agree with the pastor who believes that he just isn't qualified to do much more than "pastoral counseling lite."

Once you have a sense of call to this work, however, I encourage you to be bold. Get training, find a supervisor, and trust that you will be empowered as you go along. Perhaps you could begin by simply praying for healing with laying on of hands. Or by helping create a ritual of healing. Or by trying some very simple Gestalt experiments. Or perhaps you would be able to play an adjunct role in the healing of someone who is already working with a psychotherapist. There are some contributions to a person's healing journey that are unlikely to come from anyone besides a minister. (I will discuss the unique contributions of ministers in the next chapters.) Eventually, you may feel ready to integrate a Gestalt Pastoral Care perspective into counseling or spiritual direction sessions.

Admittedly, it does take a little faith, courage, humility, and perhaps a shift in consciousness to pray and pastor in these new ways. It is hard to imagine, though, how prayers for healing and faith imagination, a holistic viewpoint, spiritual companioning, Christian liturgies, and declaring God's forgiveness in a confidential setting can do any harm – if all is done with gentle respect, good humor, and humility.

The preparation for this stage is, of course, some experience in ministry and a firm commitment to pursue your own spiritual and emotional growth in such a way that you are free to be there with another. As I have already said, you need to be in an ongoing healing process yourself before you can get out of the way of God's love pouring into a suffering person. Most certainly you need to be faithful at prayer, so that the Holy Spirit can love you in the way you need most. Claiming your pastoral role more deeply and valuing your unique calling are really possible when you yourself are relatively centered and clear.

STAGE TWO: GESTALT PASTORAL CARE MINISTRY

The second level in using the material in this book is to become a *Gestalt Pastoral Care Minister*, integrating pastoral functions with Gestalt skills. *Identification with Gestalt Pastoral Care Ecumenical Associates requires completing an authorized training program in Gestalt Pastoral Care.*

You might also decide to explore Gestalt itself before you are trained to integrate the spiritual component. There are many good secular Gestalt training programs in the United States; most will stress learning by experience and will include a requirement that trainees be in Gestalt therapy themselves.

In Gestalt training you can expect:

• to come to understand Gestalt theory in depth, making cognitive, somatic, and emotional connections with your own experience, as well as to learn how to apply theory to psychotherapeutic practice

• to receive direct supervision as students work first with each other, and later with clients

• to work actively on your own issues by entering into your own depths as completely as possible

• to prepare for work with the range and depth of human emotions

• to learn how to design creative and well-fitting experiments

• to gain experience and increasing sophistication in supporting resistance

• to understand and facilitate work with polarities

• to work more competently and artistically with dreams – your own and those of others

• to learn to perceive more deeply and broadly, without judgments

• to learn to work with somatic and energetic realities

• and to be constantly reminded not to take responsibility for another's growth.

Secular Gestalt training programs will probably not include any attention to a Christian spiritual component; as far as I know, there are no Gestalt training programs, besides the ones sponsored by Gestalt Pastoral Care Ecumenical Associates, which combine pastoral care or Christian spiritual direction with Gestalt. Nor is a training program in spiritual direction likely to include attention to Gestalt. It is my hope that this book might be a resource for those seeking to integrate Gestalt with Christian spirituality, particularly healing ministry.

Spiritual direction training programs are blooming everywhere these days and might be of special interest if you are already a Gestalt therapist and want to integrate Christian spirituality with your therapeutic work. It is quite likely that you will find that spiritual companioning fits well with what you already know.

Most spiritual companion training will include learning:

• to trust God more deeply to be in charge

- to maintain the utmost respect for what God is doing in the person, and to stay out of the way

- to experience one's own spiritual journey with a companion/director

- to practice, under supervision, being a companion for others

- to use scripture, not as source of quick and easy answers, but to inform a spiritual growth process

- to become familiar with the wisdom of the church expressed in the writings of saints and others.

PUTTING IT TOGETHER

Whether your current expertise is theological, pastoral, medical, or psychological, you will go through a process of integration as you become more holistic in your approach. In our Gestalt Pastoral Care training groups, participants bring a variety of education, skills, backgrounds, and personal styles. Most identify themselves as lay or ordained ministers; others are primarily psychotherapists, social workers, artists, administrators, teachers or medical professionals. As they become more familiar with the basics, each trainee is urged to discover connections between Gestalt Pastoral Care and what they already know. Each is invited, first of all, to adopt a Gestalt Pastoral Care perspective, finding ways that Gestalt Pastoral Care (or its components) can be used in their particular work. For example, I have a friend, a professional violist, who plays regularly in symphony orchestras and in her own recitals. She beautifully integrates a Gestalt Pastoral Care perspective with her musical vocation. Before and after rehearsals, during breaks and intermissions, she counsels other musicians informally and prays with them on request. Her young students and their families also benefit from her compassionate listening ear, and her training in Gestalt Pastoral Care.

As participants progress through our training they become able to utilize more components of Gestalt Pastoral Care. They become more adept at broadening their attention to another person's psychological, spiritual, physical, and social realities. They become less afraid of the depth of suffering in another, and more creative at suggesting Gestalt experiments. They become more trusting that God offers some kind of healing in every situation. They gain experience in coaching awareness in the one coming for help, and in laying on of hands and prayer for healing. In other words, they become familiar with, and later, skilled in, the various ways of encouraging growth that are components of Gestalt Pastoral Care.

PART TWO

THE UNIQUE CONTRIBUTIONS OF PASTORS, FROM A GESTALT PERSPECTIVE

Part Two invites pastors and other ministers to claim and employ their own unique, specifically Christian resources for spiritual, emotional and physical healing. It suggests how to join another's world, and how to shape healing actions based on the lively inner process of the one seeking help. These resources include spiritual companioning and faith imagination, discernment, healing prayer, confession and forgiveness, help with forgiving, individualized healing liturgies, and entering another's world.

All of this can be done in the context of a Gestalt Pastoral Care perspective, which includes, among other things, a holistic viewpoint, respect for the wisdom of the body, the belief that God is constantly and discernibly at work in each person's process, and the willingness to let resistance alone.

Keep in mind that many ministers already have what it takes to begin learning how to work in this new way. Often all that is needed is interior permission to claim their unique expertise. That, and getting out of the way of the grace God infuses into the healing stream that exists in each person.

...to be human means...
to have a core which longs for God.
Julian of Norwich, 14th century

4

SPIRITUAL COMPANIONING AND FAITH IMAGINATION

CLAIMING OUR SPECIAL ROLES AS PASTORS

Pastors are often the first professionals church folk see when they are feeling ragged and broken. They come in searching, scared, upset, perhaps more ready than ever before to open themselves to grace, more willing to go deeper and more prepared to be honest about their lives. Their vulnerability is a wonderful opportunity for good ministry, and many pastors eagerly try to meet the challenge.

There is, however, a big problem. The needs of individual church members can be overwhelming to an overworked and overtired clergyperson; there is simply not time enough to respond fully to everyone who asks for help. Further, she or he may not feel qualified to do much more than listen with a compassionate ear. If the person's problem calls for a more long-term response or special counseling skill, we ministers can immediately get concerned that we might do damage, or that we will be in over our heads, or that what we have to offer is of secondary importance. These concerns are real and to be respected, especially if we haven't honored our own need for healing. So we refer church members to someone else for in-depth help, recognizing that we can't possibly provide what everyone needs for healing. Clearly, making referrals is sometimes both prudent and necessary.

I believe, however, that many pastors habitually bow out too quickly or too completely. As ministers we tend to devalue what we alone can contribute to people's healing and well-being. We have lost the sense that we ourselves might have an important part to play in personal healing, and that maybe spiritual help is actually what the person needs most. Student hospital chaplains report that initially they scuttle out as soon as any member of the medical team enters a hospital room, even if something vitally important is happening between chaplain and patient. More seasoned chaplains, knowing they make an essential contribution, have learned to sometimes say, "We'll be finished soon. Could you please come back later?"

We ministers need to boldly and faithfully reclaim our role, our experience, and our areas of expertise. Ideally we are part of the team, *a vital part*, along with medical professionals, social workers, teachers, therapists and police, for human suffering is not only physical but also emotional, social, and most certainly spiritual. A process of deep healing is likely to take a sufferer into each of these realms; in fact it is rare when all four areas are not involved simultaneously. Furthermore, no matter what the diagnosis, matters of spirit can be *paramount*. If clergy and other ministers abdicate their role in healing, a suffering person is not likely to receive the spiritual help he needs.

Spiritual Companioning

While attending a large secular professional conference for psychotherapists sometime around 1970, I came across an afternoon workshop called "Sharing Religious Experiences." Intrigued, I went in. There were perhaps fifty people in the room, and for three hours we took turns sharing stories of our encounters with the Holy. Just before the end of the workshop I identified myself as a United Methodist minister and asked if any of them had ever told their experience to a clergyperson. Not one hand was raised. Upon asking why, I was told by several people (with nods from most of the others) that *ministers don't understand these things.* There was agreement all around that they would expect disbelief and even ridicule from the clergy, especially if their experience didn't seem to fit the particular group's creed. In fact, several said that they were pretty certain that a clergyperson hearing their experience would view it as evidence of pathology. Comic Lily Tomlin accurately nailed this attitude when she quipped that if you talk to God it's called prayer, but if God talks back, it's called schizophrenia.

I left the workshop feeling convinced that I needed to do some serious thinking about the subtle messages I might be sending as a minister. Was I projecting a "don't tell me what I don't want to know" attitude as well? In the weeks that followed I began to ask church folk if they had ever experienced God directly, and if so, had they told a minister about it. I was astonished to find that *most* people were willing to admit they had had spiritual experiences that were very important to them. Most had not mentioned them to any pastor. Why? The reason was the same: ministers just wouldn't get it. Oddly, when I, a minister, *asked* them about spiritual experiences, they quite readily shared them and were eager to talk further about how to interpret what they had experienced.

Thankfully, times have changed and Protestant churches are rediscovering spiritual companioning as an important form of ministry. A stream of pastoral thought, both ancient and new, proclaims that the church must be willing and able to help people go beyond peak "spiritual experiences" to discern God's activity in ordinary life circumstances. One indication of the pervasive importance given to this ministry is the number of good new books on spiritual direction published in recent years.[17] Another sign is that many retreat centers are filled with Protestant directees and Protestant spiritual directors-in-training. As Christians, we believe that God wants to be in relationship with us and that God knows intimately who we are and what we need. We believe that God calls each of us individually and personally, and gifts us with talents and desires. We believe that God seeks to transform pain and fear and tragedy. God is actively engaged in shaping us to be more like Christ. We continue to experience call and forgiveness and invitation to deeper prayer. Spiritual companioning assists Christians committed to a serious faith journey to stay on course, and is an important part of Gestalt Pastoral Care.

I prefer the term "spiritual companion" to that of "spiritual director" because it implies a more equal relationship. Although one person's journey is the focus, and the other is the listening companion, both are aware that discernment, direction and discoveries are made together. Sometimes it will feel appropriate to engage in spiritual companioning by talking conversationally: sharing about stages and movements of prayer, or calling on wisdom and lore from the saints, or exploring together God's presence in life experiences. More often, spiritual companioning in the context of Gestalt Pastoral Care will involve more direct action, such as listening together to discern God's call, or praying for healing, or confession and forgiveness. Furthermore, it might involve faith imagination, as explained below, or the creation of healing liturgies, as we will see in Chapter Eight. Naturally, spiritual companioning in Gestalt Pastoral Care will be well interlaced with body awareness and with needs for healing of emotions and relationships.

---

[17] For example, see Margaret Guenther, *Holy Listening: The Art of Spiritual Direction.* Using metaphors of hospitality and midwifery, Guenther beautifully illumines the process of listening to God's invitation with another.

FAITH IMAGINATION

A major way that spiritual companioning enters into Gestalt Pastoral Care is through faith imagination prayer, a wonderful help in opening to healing grace, and a way to become aware (there's that word again!) of our own need for healing and what God might be doing to bring us to wholeness.

One of the most dramatic journeys of faith imagination healing prayer[18] I've ever experienced involved Maria, a woman of great courage and determination. As a child she was nearly destroyed by repeated and sadistic emotional abuse, physical cruelty, incest, rape, and abandonment. Speaking solely from a psychological viewpoint, I would have predicted that she would never be well, even though her motivation to grow was tremendous. She was just too damaged, and the damage had begun too early. In the opinion of her doctors, she was beyond real help, and indeed she had simply been maintained, heavily medicated, in a psychiatric hospital's back ward for over twenty years.

Maria, however, was determined to have a real life. When the overcrowded hospital released her temporarily just before a state inspection, she resolved to never go back. Shaky, scared, but resolute, she asked to work with me. I was greatly moved by her gritty will to get better; even so I agreed with gulping trepidation. What could I possibly do to help her heal from the hideous betrayals she had suffered? I had no illusions that I would be the hotshot who would succeed where others had failed. I knew I would be flying blind. However, I did believe – most of the time – that no pain is beyond God's ability to heal. At least I could pray with her.

She began coming to my office every week ready to open up to her childhood abuse. It was incredibly hard work for her. Frankly, I don't think I would have had her courage. Many of her stories were so utterly horrifying that I was in awe that she had survived. Nearly every week she would remember, and sometimes re-experience, a traumatic incident. Then we would pray together using faith imagination and almost always she experienced some measure of God's healing. We also prayed each week that God would hold the memories she wasn't ready for, and let her experience only those she needed for healing, one at a time. At the beginning of each session we prayed that whatever God wanted to heal that

---

[18] Agnes Sanford seems to be the first to coin the term "faith imagination" and to train others to pray in this way. See her book, *Sealed Orders*.

day would surface in Maria's awareness. These prayers for the ordering and filtering of memories seemed to be answered as we found our way together.

A few months into our work Maria told me how she got the nasty-looking scars on her thighs. She was six years old when one day her demented mother ordered her to sit in the ashes of the fireplace as punishment for wetting her pants. Tearfully she sat down on the grate, but immediately jumped up shrieking, for beneath the ashes were hot embers. Her mother grabbed Maria and held her down, screaming that she do as she was told.

While Maria was allowing herself to face this terrible ordeal, the large scars on her legs became much more prominent, gradually turning bright red. She screamed and writhed in pain, as if the burns were fresh. She was not just remembering; she was vividly *re-experiencing* the trauma in what is known as a "body memory."

Holding her hands and looking into her eyes, I asked her if she would be willing to invite Jesus into that room where the fireplace was. Almost immediately in her mind's eye she saw Jesus come in and push her mother out of the way, saying with great emphasis, "Your daughter does not belong in the ashes!" Picking up six-year-old Maria, Jesus sat down in the ashes in her place. As he gently held her there in his lap, she could feel the searing pain drain from her legs. I could see it too, for the bright red scars faded and then almost disappeared. Later she said it was as if Jesus absorbed her pain into his body. Her sobs gradually subsided, and a great peace came over her as she relaxed into his arms. She basked there in silence for some time, breathing deeply, her eyes closed, a little smile flickering. Then she looked up at me and asked with a little shudder, "I don't belong in the ashes, do I?" I shook my head. "No. Not in any way." She continued with a full-faced grin, "I belong right here, being held by the Lord."

Faith imagination is a way of praying in which we specifically invite God to enter into our awareness in a way that we can imaginatively perceive. As best we can we open our capacity for imagination – our inner *seeing, hearing, sensing* and *knowing*. We wait with expectancy for God to act in some way. We try not to toss out anything we might perceive until we have had a chance to mull it over later. We just allow an experience to unfold while paying attention to what happens to us. If nothing seems to happen we remember that we can't control God, and try again another day. We do this in the faith that God desires to meet us in our growing edge, where we are most vulnerable, hurting, or scared. Truly, God is passionate about healing.

Gestalt Pastoral Care ministers employ faith imagination prayer a great deal, at many different points in a person's healing process. It is an invaluable and adaptable tool, for it gives the Holy Spirit access to our mind, our spirit, our sensory world, our memories, our intuition, and our imagination. Unlike Maria's intense experiences, faith imagination is often quiet, inviting the pray-er to take baby steps toward letting a new awareness dawn. Faith imagination prayer can provide a rudder for gingerly venturing into new emotional or spiritual territory, or it can be a doorway to contemplation as pray-ers learn just to sit with Jesus. Faith imagination might invite a shift in attention, or a gentle settling inside. Faith imagination can be a way to allow God's love to penetrate defenses, or a way to shape a prayer for physical healing. It can be a way to ask God an important question, or to tell about our feelings. Faith imagination surely helps in the process of grieving, or in searching for answers to the aching questions that keep us awake at night. It is a wonderful way to ask permission to express "unchristian" emotions, to discover God's healing agenda, or to find out how Jesus reacts to us at our worst. It opens doors to discernment, communion, and healing, and of course is a great way to learn to pay attention.

Through faith imagination, God's specific activity creates what I call "personal icons." An example of a personal faith imagination icon is Maria's sensate experience of sitting on Jesus' lap; another is her memory of Jesus striding across the room to come to her rescue, with his emphatic words: "Your daughter does not belong in the ashes!" For months Maria returned again and again to these words as she made room for very new feelings about herself, and ultimately a new identity as a person being held by the Lord. Paying prayerful attention to faith imagination icons over time is a natural way to assimilate experiences of faith imagination. Faith imagination icons are powerful catalysts for change; they can reframe, overshadow, or even replace, a painful memory or a fossilized way of thinking. Icons can become lifelong symbols of our particular journey and call, or they can simply be temporary signs of God's presence to carry through the day.

Personal icons that come forth in faith imagination prayer seem exactly suited to the person receiving them. They fit. They address the person in a way the pray-er can take in and are specifically pointed to particular needs for healing. For example, one person who has spent his childhood – and his adult life – trying to take care of an alcoholic parent was surprised to see Jesus taking over the care of his father. Another person with a similar background saw Jesus caring for her as a child while totally ignoring her intoxicated mother. Still another sensed strong permission from the Holy Spirit to be as angry as he needed to be at his alcoholic dad.

OBJECTIONS

My seminary training schooled me to reject this sort of thing. When I was at Union Theological Seminary in New York, theologian Paul Tillich had just retired from the faculty. Still under his brilliant influence, Union students learned to speak of God as "The Ground of Being." God is limitless and beyond our imagination, Tillich would say. As soon as we try to imagine God, we have automatically put God in a box, making God into our own image. Surely anthropomorphizing God is to be avoided, but I translated this concern into timidity at speaking or thinking about God at all. After all, what could I do that wouldn't make God smaller and more limited than God really is?

Many Union students, including me, found Tillich both illuminating and inspiring. His three-volume *Systematic Theology* showed us a beautiful way to *think* about God, but when I strived to *pray* to The Ground of Being, I simply couldn't. Even when I was introduced to faith imagination some years later, I was still trying to be a good Union student. I labeled faith imagination prayer as simplistic, shallow, and sentimental. Paul Tillich wouldn't approve of it.

Now that I'm older and hopefully a bit wiser, I know that I have a little mind, and that God comes to my littleness. *Of course* I can't really know the vastness of God, but because God wants to be in relationship with me, God communicates in a way that I can perceive. Isn't that what the Incarnation of Christ – God visible, touchable, audible, imaginable – is all about? God wants to have a way of lighting up our awareness. It is indeed good news that God is self-revealing. Put another way, God wants to get through to us.

Knowing that cognitive constructs like the Ground of Being don't fit my particularly visual way of perceiving the world, I now let myself pray to Jesus as I did as a child, inviting him to be with me. Most often I "see" him with inner eyes; sometimes I "hear" him speak too. Sometimes I just have a sensate perception that the Holy Spirit is near, inviting me to rest in the presence of God, but there is usually at least a fuzzy image of Jesus somewhere in my awareness. Sometimes prayer seems to dry up and go nowhere, of course, but much less often than before I learned to embrace the incarnation more fully, honor my perceptual preferences, and allow God access to my imagination. (Various ways of perceiving are discussed further in Chapter Eight.)

A second objection is one that many people share upon first hearing stories of faith imagination prayer. "How do I know I'm not making the whole thing up?" they say. "How can I trust that I'm not painting pretty pictures in my mind? Maybe it's just my imagination."[19] Good question. Certainly it is possible to distort faith imagination. Emotional wounds, fervent wishes, guilt, twisted theology, or myriad other factors can color what is perceived in prayer. Even in the best of circumstances our expectations and previous experiences shape our perceptions. This distinct possibility for distortion is one reason to pray with a spiritual companion or trusted friend who can sense when things are getting off track. For example, if God seems to be simply reflecting a pray-er's own self-hatred, then a companion can gently ask whose voice is really being heard. Staying aware that misperceptions are possible in faith imagination is a healthy caution and invites us to careful discernment.

The best way, however, to respond to this second objection is to affirm that despite our doubts, God often works through faith imagination prayer. Things happen. People change and grow. Some are healed in astonishing ways. As Robert Webber and I wrote in *Stretch Out Your Hand,*

> ...it is striking how often the quality of the response from Jesus is not in the emotional repertoire of the one praying. A deeply depressed individual cannot usually dredge up a heart-felt message of hope, no matter how great the effort. One who is terrified cannot find a way to feel safe just by thinking about it. Often a quality of 'otherness' and surprise touches us through the action of God when we pray in this way.

> The most compelling evidence that God is indeed at work in faith imagination is simply that people are healed. Pain that has been present for years may vanish or greatly diminish, and the healing seems to take deep root in the person.[20]

---

[19] In this regard, I once heard Francis MacNutt refer to George Bernard Shaw's play *Saint Joan.* In the play Joan of Arc is questioned closely about her voices, which she claimed were from God. The thrust of the questions was, "Aren't your voices just your imagination?" Her reply was that of course these voices were her imagination. How else would God speak to her?

[20] Norberg and Webber, *Stretch Out Your Hand*, p. 65.

Steps in Faith Imagination

How can a spiritual companion begin to use faith imagination with another person? By trying it out himself. By praying with others. Praying with another using faith imagination is a simple process, which usually flows along the lines of the following eleven steps.

Begin with a brief prayer that God will direct the process and bless your time together.

Listen carefully to the person's story. In other words, hear in detail what needs to be brought to God for healing or discernment.

As the story is being told, listen for the story's setting. If a memory is being recalled, the setting will be obvious: the office in which the damaging words were spoken, for example, the garage where the abuse happened, or the highway where the accident occurred. Sometimes a person may simply bring a hunger for God's presence, and the setting might just be the room in which the pray-er sits.

The story may not so much be a memory, however, as involvement in a confusing or crazy-making situation. It may be about the need for discernment, or it may involve a belief that is not, for now, related to a memory. In these cases the setting may come as a metaphor. For example,

• I'm in a box right now.

• I'm being pulled apart.

• I'm right at a crossroads.

• I'm going around in circles.

• I'm in the doghouse.

• I stay on the edge of everything.

If necessary the minister can just ask,

• Where are you located as you bring all this up?

• As you sink into being scared, how old do you feel?

• Would you be willing to tell it to Jesus and see if you can discover where you are as you speak?

It is important to identify the setting, if possible, because vivid engagement with the setting seems to prime the pump of imagination, memory, and emotions through which God can work.

The fourth step is a bit of traditional Gestalt wisdom, that of inviting the person to go inside and imaginatively put herself in the setting. For example,

- Are you willing to close your eyes and go back in time and be in the kitchen you were just remembering?

- When you go back what do you experience there? What do you see, hear sense?

- How old are you? Who is there with you?

- Would you be willing to tell your father how you feel now in his presence?

If the setting is a metaphor, the invitation is the same:

- Would you be willing to close your eyes and be in your box? (or be at the crossroads, or in the doghouse, etc.)

- When you go there what do you feel?

- Can you see, hear, sense anything? What do you know about yourself there?

Questions such as these are asked in an open-ended way, and only if the person needs help in staying in the setting. Such questions should also be asked in the perceptual language of the person. (Perceptual language is discussed in Chapter Eight.) For now, remember that it is futile to ask a sensate person, for example, to try to imagine visually; the result will likely be frustration for you both. Furthermore, prompting questions should be asked only when periods of silence lengthen. The idea is to give the person a great deal of room to make discoveries on her own. Be patient and leisurely with the natural contours of the person's inner process as she takes her time to explore her setting.

Stay with the experience until the person is as deeply aware of associated feelings as possible. As the setting becomes more distinct and lifelike, try to simply observe widely, intuit deeply and pray silently for the person. It is helpful to attend to such details as the person's breathing, body energy, tone of voice, posture, physical motions or frozenness. Armed with this information and some Gestalt training, it is possible to suggest experiments to help the person connect with the feelings associated with the setting. For example, if a person is holding her breath or breathing shallowly, a simple reminder to breathe can sometimes release feelings that have been held inside for years. Similarly, breathing more deeply might allow a pray-er to take in God's love more deeply. Another experiment might grow out of an observation that the person has her hand over her mouth. "Are you aware that you have your hand over your mouth? Don't move your hand; just get aware…Would you let your hand cover your mouth even more firmly and see what happens?"

Ideally the person will experience the feelings associated with the memory or situation that are available to him that day. Another day he may be ready to go even deeper into the next layer of feelings. Obviously we don't need to wait until all the feelings are expressed in all their depth before praying about them. That can take weeks or months. But it does help if the person has gone as far as they can go for the moment. Generally speaking, if a person is in good contact with her feelings in depth before engaging in faith imagination prayer, she will be much less likely to become sweetly pious or judgmental or otherwise influenced by distorted churchy expectations. We are not interested in what people think Jesus would do if he were here. Rather we are seeking to be receptive to a transforming and unpredictable encounter with the living God.

Invite God into the setting and the associated feelings, using language and symbols appropriate to the one praying. A simple prayer is just fine: "God please be with me when I was six."

Faith imagination seems easiest when the pray-er is able to invite *Jesus* to be with her. Because Jesus lived as a human, he is accessible to our human minds and spirits. It is easy to imagine him. But some people, even devout Christians, may not be able to *pray* to Jesus. For example, a woman who has been abused by a man may fear all men – even Jesus. Sometimes asking her to invite *Christ* to be with her circumvents her fear of the maleness of Jesus. If not, there are many other ways to refer to God: the Holy Spirit, God the Creator, God's Light, God who is our rock and fortress, God who is like a Mother as well as a Father, God who holds each person in the palm of a loving hand, and so on. In addition, some people find that God comes to them in faith imagination in the form of angels or of Mary, the mother of Jesus.

We invite people to pray as they can – not as we think they should. We trust that God wants to enter their lives and will do it in the darndest ways, certainly not always according to our plan, preference, tradition, or even theological training. One woman sees God as a Grandmother who sits at a loom and weaves the fabric of creation; another person knows God as her protector who takes the form of an enormous lion. Still another sees God or Jesus – he is not sure which – as a huge hand that loves, protects, admonishes, and beckons him forward. A fourth person sees colors when she prays, especially reds, blues, and purples. As she gazes at the colors she is often given new understandings that change the colors of her inner life.

As the Holy One is invited into the setting, the obvious task is to discern what God is doing. How is God working to heal and birth new life? Long silent pauses might mean that the person is deeply involved in an experience of God's presence and healing power. A minister will do well to just keep quiet and let God work. When this happens, both of you are on holy ground where most words are unnecessary.

On the other hand, the person may claim that nothing is happening. He may meanwhile discount or minimize what he is in fact perceiving. Discounting and minimizing are the major ways beginners in faith imagination miss what God may be giving. A minister can help by simply reminding the person to be aware of and give weight to what is actually happening. For example:

Companion: *Is Jesus willing to come?*

Pray-er: *No, not really. He is standing by the door, but he's not coming in.*

Companion: *What is he doing?*

Pray-er: *He's not doing anything but looking at me. I don't think he wants to come in. Nothing is really happening.*

Companion: How *is he looking? What do his eyes say to you?*

Pray-er: (after a long pause) *Wow! He loves me. (a little gasping breath) He's waiting for me to really invite him into the room.*

Another dynamic that can stop the flow of faith imagination is trying to fit what is being perceived into an expectation of how God will act. For example, during a rich faith imagination prayer one woman looked up and said, "I must be getting mixed up. Now Jesus is in two places in the room. One Jesus is sitting with me and the other Jesus is sitting on the couch with my mother. I keep trying to figure out where he really is." Her minister suggested that she stay with her perception of Jesus in two places at once. Almost immediately she understood that *of course* Jesus is with both her and her mother. Her unexpected image had reminded her of an important truth.

Keep in mind that a spiritual companion can sometimes be much too helpful. Occasionally it seems that the person seeking healing may not have much sense of God's activity, while his companion has a plethora of images, sensations, and intuitions. When this happens it is tempting to blurt out easy answers or try to impose one's own perceptions on the process. Sometimes what may feel like spiritual discernment actually comes out of the companion's own need for power, admiration, or a compulsive need to help. One pastor I know quickly and routinely takes over faith imagination sessions by commentaries such as, "I see Jesus there. He wants you to know that he loves you and that he will help you. He is taking you by the arm and leading you down a path. He wants to show you something..." And so on.

Such "leadership" robs an individual of his own journey and keeps him dependent on the minister – and the minister's perceptions can be wrong. Ministers don't have to be responsible for helping God to get through; God can do pretty well without their attempts to make something happen. If a minister consistently finds that she is the one offering the images in faith imagination prayer, she needs to take an honest look at herself.

On the other hand, discernment sometimes does come through others. All of us need the church community, and sometimes we ourselves are the channels God chooses to communicate with a suffering person. When we are in the role of spiritual companion, we pray along with the other person, and of course we can expect to receive our own impression of what God is doing in a particular instance. Certainly we must pay attention when this happens. I find that the wisest thing is to keep quiet about it at first. If I wait a bit, maybe the person with whom I am working will have a similar impression of God's activity. Then I can just confirm that the work he has done seems right to me too.

Another way I honor my discernment is to suggest a Gestalt experiment. On one occasion I had a feeling that the woman with whom I was praying needed to lie down on the floor as part of her work. My hunch persisted for eight to ten minutes, getting stronger and stronger. Although it didn't make a lot of sense to me, I have learned to trust this sort of intuition as possible guidance from the Holy Spirit. Knowing I could be wrong, I asked her if she would be willing to lie down and *see what would happen.* She settled herself on the carpet, and immediately felt a lovely sense of release in her abdomen, with little silvery giggles spontaneously coming out of her. She told me later that in the act of lying down she had somehow been empowered to "take off her mother's corset" (mother's constriction and taboos) and to give it to Jesus.

When resistance surfaces – and it will – don't fight it. Instead, suggest the person pray the resistance. For example, a man may have a clear sense that God is saying, "Trust me. I'm here and I'm in charge," but he may not be ready to respond with faith and surrender. Instead, his immediate response may be "Yeah, right!" Or, "I'm scared out of my mind anyway!" Or, "Where in hell were you when I needed you most?" There may be a temptation to get pious and skip over these not-so-nice responses, or to try to talk the person out of his feelings. Remember, when resistance surfaces, a sermon is the absolute last thing anyone needs! Engagement with the heartfelt questions, doubts, and refusals which invariably surface in faith imagination prayer can lead to richer, deeper healing than glossing over or erasing part of a person's process. God's invitation is always to be honest. A good reply from a spiritual companion is, "Tell *that* to Jesus and see how he responds to you."

Suggest ways for the person to take in more deeply what has happened during the prayer. For example, she could be invited to repeat a crucial sentence several times. She could tell the minister once more what God seems to be communicating. She could articulate her new awareness. She might be invited simply to breathe in what has happened.

End a faith imagination session with laying on of hands with thanksgiving for what has already happened and prayer for further healing.

Talk a bit about your experience together. The pray-er could be asked how she feels right now, or what's going on in her body. She can comment on the process. She can discuss next steps. She can receive feedback from the minister. Feedback after faith imagination does not involve advice, analysis, questions or judgments; instead it is sharing what happened for the minister during the prayer. For example a minister might mention that she was moved at a certain point, or that a hymn kept running through her head as they prayed. She might say that she felt angry with someone who had hurt the pray-er. She might briefly share the prayer icons that surfaced for her as she followed along.

Such feedback helps call the person back from the setting and orients the work just done in the present. It is supportive and helps assimilate what can be very new feelings. It can be a good beginning for discernment about the experience. It also sends the message that whatever happened in faith imagination prayer was due to the person's cooperation with the Holy Spirit and not the amazing skill of the minister. In this work both are awed by what God is doing. Both are cooperating with God as best they can and neither is making the experience happen.

THREE STORIES OF FAITH IMAGINATION

One: A Glimpse

In the summer of 1993 the Rev. Miriam Crist, one of my closest friends, lay dying in New York Methodist Hospital in Brooklyn. For years she had fought valiantly against the cancer consuming her body. Many people had prayed for physical healing, and indeed she had lived far longer than her doctors said was possible. Spiritually she had grown tremendously. She had prayed often with faith imagination and had a faith-filled relationship with God. Still, her strong will to live prevented her from peacefully accepting her rapidly approaching death.

A few days before she died, some of her friends and I were with her when she had a spontaneous faith imagination experience. Suddenly she began talking about music that only she could hear. "Don't you hear it?" she asked us. "It's beautiful. It's so beautiful!" All we heard was ordinary hospital noise: carts rolling by the door, beepers going off, a murmur of voices, the intercom paging someone. She said she was hearing a choir singing very beautifully. "There must be a door open somewhere," she said. "It's like a door opens and I can hear it much better. See if there's a door open somewhere, will you?" Obediently we checked the door knowing full well that no music was audible to us.

"It sounds like a door is opening in *you,* Mamie," I said. "I think this music is just for you. Why not just listen to it?" She replied by smiling and closing her eyes. She said the voices were singing the spiritual, "Children, Go Where I Send Thee." She hummed along, and at one point waved her hand as if in greeting.

We glanced at each other, moved beyond words. The presence of God was palpable in the profound silence that surrounded us. Despite a custodian banging his mop against the next bed, we were enveloped in holy space and time. After a long pause Miriam described a greenhouse full of light. It was very beautiful, she said, full of plants and flowers. There was a pretty rug on the floor. She knew she was to go there; it was her special place to bloom and grow.

The scene shifted and she was on a bus, with Jesus driving her to the greenhouse. As often happens when we become aware of God's perfect holiness and majesty, she became aware of her own imperfections. She began to sob, weeping for all that had been wrong in her life. We assured her that whatever the tears were about, God had forgiven. "Whatever?" she asked. "Yes," we said. "Whatever. Everything." She breathed a sigh of relief.

Then, still wet with tears, she gasped, "It's all here. My whole life. Jesus has my whole life, looking at it. He can see everything that's happened to me." "How does he respond to your whole life?" I asked. She answered with a cry of faith and joy that we will never forget: "He wants it! He wants me! He's coming to get me!" Then with a beautiful, peaceful smile, she said, "I guess I'm letting go."

"Yes," we said. "Let go. Let go so God can hold you. You are God's trusted servant, God's beloved daughter, God's child." "God's child," she echoed with a peaceful sigh.

She gazed inward into the greenhouse again and saw an altar with a lamp on it. The lamp had a large blue flame, and was being held up by a dove. In an awed voice she said that the lamp and the dove were signs of the Holy Spirit. She kept exclaiming how wonderful and beautiful it all was, weeping with joy. We were weeping too.

"The angels are singing again! The saints are coming for me! So many! They are singing me into the light! They're singing 'For All the Saints From Whom Their Labors Rest'. They're singing me into the greenhouse. Oh it's so beautiful, so wonderful!"

She rested there a few minutes; then slowly came back to what we usually call reality. We knew that she had been given a glimpse into genuine Reality itself, the truth of God's love for her. We also knew that this vision was not given for Miriam alone, but was a special gift for each of us there as witnesses. Beyond that, it was truly a gift of resurrection to be shared with the church – and one week later, with Miriam's permission, I read the account of her experience as part of my sermon at her funeral.

Two: God Laughed

I had not been faithful to my prayer time. I had been "too busy" and prayer had been difficult when I did manage to sit still for a few minutes. As I confessed all this to God, I had a sinking feeling that somehow I had to start all over and earn my way back into God's favor. I sat for a few minutes in a murky pool of foibles and guilt, not accepting the forgiveness I clearly knew was mine. Moments later I had the sense that God was chuckling at my foolishness, and I heard this startling response: "Stop it! Let me woo you back!" These words seemed to clear my head – and my heart – allowing me to rest in God's limitless love once more.

Three: Faith Imagination with a Failure

A pastor near retirement age attended a healing workshop for clergy hoping his crippling arthritis might be healed. A rather taciturn and dignified gentleman, he was surprised to find himself talking about his inner pain as we prayed for him. He had never told anyone, not even his wife, that as he looked back over his ministry he could think of just one achingly descriptive word: *failure.*

He had spent all his professional life working hard in tiny country churches. Some of the churches remained full of dissention and strife; others were cemented in apathy; one church had closed its doors while he was its pastor. None of the churches had grown numerically, or, it seemed, even spiritually. He sadly remembered starting his ministry as a young man full of zeal and idealism and energy. Now forty-five years later it all had turned to ashes and disappointment, and he was asking himself what his life had been worth.

To help him find a setting for faith imagination, I asked him where he was as he was feeling all this. After a pause, he said he was going out the door of the church that he would serve for a final year before his retirement. Over his head he sensed a "dark cloud of failure." (This man was primarily a sensate perceiver, so his imagination used that language.) "It's true. I'm leaving the ministry under a cloud of failure." As he said these words his voice began to tremble a little and one tear dripped down his cheek.

I sensed that allowing that one tear in front of others was a very great step for him, and that he had probably gotten to the bottom of his feelings for the moment. So I asked him if he would be willing to ask Jesus to meet him on the steps of the church. He had never before prayed in that way but he was willing to try. Right away he sensed that Jesus was there with him under the cloud. Awash in shame, he was only able to choke out a bare-bones prayer: "Lord, I'm such a failure."

Then came the outpouring of grace and healing love that I have come to expect as people invite Jesus into their brokenness. The pastor sensed Jesus coming closer and then reaching his arms around him in a most wonderful hug. In that cleansing and powerful embrace he finally surrendered to his tears and cried and cried. Those of us who were there sensed that he was crying the tears of many different hurts and disappointments throughout his life. Later he told us that this was indeed the first time in his adult life that he could remember crying. It was not for us to know the details, but it was clear to everyone that God was working powerfully.

As his weeping subsided he sensed that Jesus was saying something to him. He was quiet for a few minutes; then a grin spread over his face. "Jesus said, 'I didn't call you to be successful. I called you to be faithful. You have done that well.'"

As a way of assimilating this liberating word, I asked him if he would be willing to repeat what Jesus had told him to each person in the room individually. As he walked around the circle telling each of us what Jesus said to him, he was radiant. Suddenly, halfway around the room he stopped, looking stunned. Then: "Hey! I don't have any pain! I haven't been able to walk like this without pain for years! That cloud crippled me! I don't feel it any more! This is really something."

About a month later he called to say that his arthritis continued to be greatly improved. He also said that he was happier than he had been for years, that his prayer life had become rich, and that he was looking forward to starting some new projects when he retired.

This is what God can do through faith imagination. A man was given a new lens through which to view his life in a process that touched body, mind and spirit. A woman was given the gift of a vision of God's presence as she died. Another was healed of the effects of a terrifying childhood. And the beauty of it was that I as the spiritual companion had only a very small job to do. There was no analysis or advice or spiritual wisdom to dispense. I simply kept quiet and encouraged each pray-er to stay aware of what God was doing.

5

HEALING PRAYER, CONFESSION, FORGIVENESS AND FORGIVING

LEARNING TO BE A PASTOR

One of the most profound shifts in my work had to do with embracing more deeply my unique role as a clergyperson. As much as I felt called to ordained ministry, secretly I wondered if ordained ministry was not just a tad irrelevant. Couldn't medical professionals, social workers, attorneys, community organizers, or psychotherapists, offer more to suffering people? On the other hand, ministry seemed so vital and utterly relevant that I shrank from it, terrified of the awesome authority that comes with ordination. Who was I to "Take authority as an elder of the Church to preach the word of God, and to administer the Holy Sacraments."?[21] A telling sign of my ambivalence was that I didn't buy an alb or stole for several years after I was ordained. Instead I wore a ratty old black choir robe and a glued-together "temporary" stole.

This all began to change when a woman taught me an unforgettable lesson about my role as a pastor. One day she brought a list to her Gestalt session, declaring that she wanted to make a general confession of every sin she could remember. Firmly believing that she was in charge of her own process, at first I just listened. As she continued, I was greatly moved, both by her ruthless honesty and by the unmistakable presence of the Holy Spirit in the room. When she finished I was silent, waiting for a cue from her about what to do next.

She gave me a cue all right. Looking straight at me, she said, "Tilda, you are a minister. You have heard my confession. I need you to tell me about God's forgiveness now." Then she bowed her head and waited.

---

[21] The United Methodist Book of Worship, The Service of Ordination, p. 678.

I was about to say something inappropriately Protestant, until I remembered that she was from a church tradition that firmly believes in confession in the presence of a priest. I simply could not cheapen her confession by telling her she needn't have done it in the first place. Surely I could say something that would be meaningful on her terms. As I stumbled around to find liturgical words (during a Gestalt session!) affirming that she was indeed forgiven, I felt a shift in myself. I had the tremendously humbling sense that I was being used by God as an ordained person maybe for the first time in my life, and that I was born for this role. In a way, that woman ordained me. After her confession I began slowly to understand that pastors and other ministers can make some contributions that no one else can. One of these contributions is indeed witnessing confession; others are coaching people who struggle to forgive someone who hurt them, and praying for healing.

HEALING PRAYER

In the last twenty years there has been a remarkable explosion of interest in healing ministry. These days many churches hold regular healing services, pastors routinely pray for healing as part of pastoral care, and thousands of people can give first-hand accounts of the healing power of God. Good books on healing ministry abound. I have come to believe that healing prayer is one of the most basic functions of Christian ministry. Even if a pastor has no time or talent for in-depth pastoral care, surely he or she can at least pray for those who suffer.

As the ministry of healing is being reclaimed by the church, our understanding of healing prayer has deepened. We have come a long way from the old formulaic theology that would say to a sufferer, "If only you have enough faith, God will heal you." My own journey has led me to an understanding of healing that is rooted in God's desire for us to grow toward wholeness. As Robert Webber and I wrote,

> Christian healing is a process which involves the totality of our
> being: body, mind, emotion, spirit, and our social context, and
> which at every stage of our living and our dying directs us to-
> ward becoming the person God is calling us to be. Whenever we
> are truly open to God, some kind of healing takes place, because
> God yearns to bring us to wholeness. Through prayer and the
> laying on of hands, Jesus meets us in our brokenness and pain,
> and there loves, transforms, forgives, redeems, resurrects, and

heals. Jesus does this in God's way, in God's time, and according to God's loving purpose for each person.

Because the Holy Spirit is continually at work in each of us, pushing us toward wholeness, the process of healing is like removing sticks and leaves from a stream until the water runs clear. If we simply get out of the way of the Lord's work in us, we can trust that we are being led to the particular kind of wholeness God wills for us.

Very often the results of our healing are increased faith in God and a new empowerment to love and serve others. Frequently we find that the very thing that caused our greatest brokenness becomes transformed into our unique giftedness.[22]

I love the image of the blocked-up stream with its inherent urgency to flow; it captures how the Holy Spirit creates this urgency in us to grow toward wholeness. Even if thwarted, the urgency is still there, just waiting to be freed. Although we sometimes have to create obstacles in order to survive, God can help us clear them away when we are ready. A great deal of healing I have witnessed seems to have this "clearing the stream" quality.

Although we can't predict exactly how God will work, I have come to believe that God faithfully meets us in our suffering when we invite God to do so. I have personally seen people healed in body, mind and spirit, but the healing can be different from what was asked in the prayer. In fact, quite often the healing is more complete and involves more of a person than the pray-er expected. When nothing much seems to happen after healing prayer, perhaps we need to go deeper to discover how God intends to bring healing in this instance. Sometimes when we pray for physical healing, for example, God seems to focus on emotions first. Similarly, when we pray for emotional or spiritual healing, often the healing is physical as well. Sometimes healing is instantaneous; more often it takes time. Even at death, God's healing continues.

Gestalt Pastoral Care is rooted in the healing ministry of the church, and the various forms of healing prayer discussed in this book are an integral part of Gestalt Pastoral Care. Rebecca's beautiful story below illustrates how God heals in surprising ways that encompass body, emotions, mind, and spirit.

---

[22] Norberg and Webber, *Stretch Out Your Hand: Exploring Healing Prayer,* 1998, pp. 26-27.

Rebecca's Healing

Rebecca, a student at Lancaster Theological Seminary, arrived for class distraught and in tears. She had just come from the doctor who told her that she had a skin cancer growing on her forehead. She had been suffering from lupus for years, and this latest problem seemed almost too much to bear. In fact, her lupus had gotten much worse just before finding out about the skin cancer; even though she was on the strongest possible medication, the lupus had begun to attack the mucous membranes in her nose.

Rebecca asked the class, "Healing and the Christian Community," which I was co-teaching with Robert Webber, to pray for her. As she told the class about her bad news, what seemed paramount was her anguish about her cancer. As some thirty of us gathered around her, Rebecca began to cry and pray aloud, asking God "Why? Why?" Although she didn't hear a direct answer to this question, she did report that she envisioned Jesus holding her as she cried and telling her that none of this was her fault. The focus of the prayers of the class was to ask that God be with her and calm her fears, and hold her with everlasting arms. We prayed that the cancer be healed. One person prayed that the lupus recede.

As we prayed, Rebecca began to speak in tongues. Although this was new for most of the class, they were able to hang in with their classmate, respectful of Rebecca's way of praying. When we were finished, she reported feeling much less afraid, with a peaceful sense that Jesus was very much with her.

That night, for the first time in four months, there was no bleeding in her nose. In fact there was no bleeding all week. When she returned to her lupus doctor, he examined her nose with growing amazement. He said that her nose was nearly healed and he had no medical explanation for it. Finally, he put down his pen and looked straight at her. "I just don't understand," he said quietly. When she told him that she had been prayed for, her Jewish doctor told her that he sometimes prayed in the operating room, and that, "There is no doubt in my mind that you've been healed."

There was no change in her skin cancer after our prayers, but it was excised easily in the doctor's office. The doctor was confident that it was taken care of. In retrospect, Rebecca felt that the cancer had helped her drop her façade of strength and ability to handle things all alone; it allowed her to be vulnerable enough to ask an entire seminary class for prayer. She had a strong intuition that the cancer had served an important purpose in her healing.

As she told this story the following week, her face glowed with joy and wonder. Then she told us what she called "the best part of all." It seems that as we prayed, for some reason her mind went back many years to her violently abusive first husband. She was in the bedroom with him again, even vividly remembering the wallpaper and the color of the bedspread.

Then the terrible memory surfaced of the night her husband nearly killed her. He had thrown her on the bed, put his hands around her throat, and choked her. Her last terrifying memory before she blacked out was of his grotesque, enraged face inches from hers. She was alone and helpless with a monster.

At this moment I had "happened" to ask her to invite Jesus to be with her in her fear. In her mind's eye Jesus came into her bedroom, at first simply standing in the corner, and later holding her. Soon "the best miracle occurred"; her husband's face was replaced with the face of Jesus. At that moment she knew she was no longer alone and helpless with a monster who was choking her life away, but with Jesus who could transform a horrific memory. He could "cage the monster" – the violent husband–monster and the monster of lupus and cancer. Jesus was in charge. For the first time, she could remember her husband without terror and utter despair. She said she felt Jesus' presence as never before in her life, truly "in her heart."

Rebecca was amazed and joyful. Her story had quite an impact on the seminary class as well. Most of Rebecca's student colleagues found their faith greatly strengthened by this experience. Together they affirmed that direct experience is the best way to learn about healing prayer, and that God had touched Rebecca physically, emotionally, and spiritually. Furthermore, it was clear that God had healed experiences in Rebecca's life that we didn't even know to pray for.

Although the results of healing prayer are not always as dramatic as Rebecca's story, I have come to expect that *something* will likely happen when we pray: a new shift in consciousness, perhaps a lessening of anxiety, a sense of peace, or an easing of physical pain. If you have not experienced healing prayer, I urge you to read a good book or two about healing,[23] and then try it over a period of time. Organize a study group on healing with the possibility of becoming a healing team in the future. Learn how to facilitate faith imagination prayer in yourself and others. I believe you will be convinced of the importance of this ministry by the evidence of God working through your prayers.

---

[23] The best introductory book I know is still *Healing* by Francis MacNutt. Others are listed in the Bibliography

WITNESSING CONFESSION AND PROCLAIMING FORGIVENESS

Another of our unique contributions as pastors is our call to shepherd people through the process of confession and forgiveness.

Health workers, psychotherapists, and community organizers know that unresolved guilt can make people sick in myriad ways. Guilt can make us hate ourselves. Guilt can take away our joy and energy. Guilt can contribute to ulcers and other physical ailments. Guilt can make it difficult to pray. Guilt can make us blind or condescending to the poor – we certainly don't want to feel even more guilty! It can be a reason to hate or avoid certain races or the opposite sex because we've projected our guilt onto them. Denial of guilt can produce personal arrogance and national self-righteousness.

In the light of this, it is not surprising that many psychotherapists see guilt as something to get rid of as soon as possible – a task that can actually take a rather long time. The therapeutic goal is self-acceptance, and of course this is important. However, in a secular context it can be enormously difficult to forgive oneself.

In contrast, the Christian response is to see guilt as a gift of God that leads us to repentance and forgiveness. The presence of genuine guilt means a conscience is in good working order. The Christian church has a very clear position on guilt: "If we confess our sins, he who is faithful and just will forgive us our sins and cleanse us from all unrighteousness"(I John 1:9). We stand firm in the belief that if we sincerely confess our sins, God always forgives. This is one of the few instances in which we can predict how God is going to answer a prayer.

It sounds simple, and it truly is. We repent and God forgives. But in the context of good pastoral care we need to recognize that not all *feelings* of guilt are the result of sin. It is simplistic to imagine that all guilt feelings will vanish as we repeat a few words of scripture. Let's consider three different kinds of guilty feelings.

Real Guilt: I Have Sinned

Easiest and simplest is real guilt. When we have truly done something wrong or have an attitude that hurts another or separates us from God, guilt is appropriate and healthy, for we have sinned. The remedy for this kind of guilt is confession of sin, and acceptance of God's forgiveness.

Most Protestant services include a prayer of confession, a liturgical expression of what may actually need to happen privately with pastoral help. Although most Protestants believe that it is God who forgives and no intermediary is necessary between God and a penitent, in reality, people often have a need to admit their sin to another person. They may need to hear liturgical words of forgiveness that are specific to their situation. Face-to-face confession can be a great relief; people are often enabled to finally let go of the guilt that has been plaguing them.

Some Protestant pastors may be uncomfortable about the idea of witnessing confessions because it seems to edge close to denying that God's mercy flows without need of an intermediary. Certainly I felt this way at first. However, I believe we have much to learn in this area of pastoral care from our Catholic brothers and sisters. Admittedly, it may take courage and a little getting used to, but I believe the benefits are worth the discomfort of stretching our boundaries.

Some also wonder uneasily if it is okay for non-ordained ministers to witness private confessions; however, most Protestant churches have no theological reason to deny this role to a layperson. Further, even members of a church which insists on absolution from a member the clergy, could surely respond to a confession with something like, "I know that God has heard what you confessed, and God knows you are sorry. Whenever we confess our sins, God forgives us. I believe God will forgive you." Even if the penitent goes to a priest later for sacramental absolution, any ministering person can respond in faith to a confession of sin.

Speaking from my experience, no other pastoral activity is so rewarding as witnessing confessions, even though many confessions are simply about the many human failings that all of us know intimately. In these small matters it is wonderful to see God's grace at work first-hand. When crippling guilt has been carried for a long time, it is truly extraordinary to see burdens of many years lift, and to witness tears of joy and relief.

Sometimes such confession brings healing in other areas as well. I know one person who was healed of chronic colitis after confessing what was "eating" her, and another person was finally able to enroll in college once his disabling guilt was out of the way.

False Guilt: Shame on Me!

A second situation that produces feelings of guilt occurs when we blame ourselves instead of accepting our humanness. False guilt, or shame, is generalized guilt for just being alive. Real guilt says, "I've done something wrong." Shame says, "I'm a bad person."

When I was in high school, my physics teacher, Mr. Poulson, was diagnosed with inoperable cancer. He finished out the year before resigning, but his daily pain and flagging energy were evident to everyone. One day in class I accidentally dropped my heavy physics book, and it hit the floor with an enormous thud. Mr. Poulson jumped, then winced with pain. Though I had done nothing wrong I felt terrible, even after Mr. Poulson accepted my profuse apology. That was false guilt in action.

There can be many reasons for false guilt:

- We need to preserve the myth of our shameful selves; we hold onto a specific guilt as proof of just how terrible we really are.

- Turning anger toward ourselves is less scary than expressing it to the one who hurt us.

- We have adopted the attitude of a perpetrator of abuse and imagine that somehow we deserve what we got.

- We have gone against our parent's wishes. False guilt might have almost nothing to do with right or wrong, but rather with parental or societal approval.

- We may feel guilty for not being able to make a difference despite our best efforts. Essentially this particular brand of false guilt is about not being able to save the world. Some pastors may recognize themselves here; this kind of guilt is almost an occupational disease.

- Still others may feel guilty because they are scrupulous. Scrupulous people may look holy at first glance, for they are bent on purifying every itty-bitty thought and action – to the point of paralysis. When they can't do it, they feel terrible. Scrupulousness is really disguised arrogance; it assumes that perfection is possible, and it ignores the call to accept ourselves as loved and redeemed children of God.

So what is a pastor to do with false guilt? Certainly none of this is to be confessed as sin in itself, and a pastor wouldn't be helping to hear a confession of "sins" based on false guilt or shame. In most cases it is deeper healing that is called for. False guilt can provide a natural opening for inner healing prayer.

Just as naturally, false guilt can be an opening for leading people to confession at a deeper level. Surely the real confession here is that of arrogance and of believing that we are somehow able to be perfect, that we are able to live without hurting another. Such an attitude ignores God's abundant grace that accepts us as we are. False guilt says "no" to God. Deeper confession should not be suggested by the pastor in a heavy-handed way of course, and probably not until some inner healing has taken place.

Held Guilt: I'll Never Forgive Myself!

The refusal to receive forgiveness for sin results in held guilt. Every spiritual companion has heard the refrain, "I know God has forgiven me, but I just can't forgive myself." When there is held guilt, pastoring needs to be done with great sensitivity to find out what is really going on. Such a person may indeed need a referral to a good therapist, but just as likely is the possibility that the person needs pastoral counseling. In fact, some people hold onto guilt until they can find the spiritual help they need.

We might gently ask the person if they have confessed the whole story; sometimes there is an angle that has been ignored in previous tellings. For instance, imagine someone is holding onto guilt over badly hurting another person. She may have confessed this sin to God and even to another person, but may never have admitted, even to herself, how much she *enjoyed* inflicting the pain. If this is the case, holding onto guilt is healthy, because there is still something to confess – and the guilt brings her to it. So an important question is "is the confession complete?"

It may also be that the person needs to make amends. Perhaps it is necessary to ask forgiveness of the person who has been hurt. Maybe it is necessary to give back symbolically what was taken away. Or both. When a person's healing journey calls for making amends, it is very appropriate for a minister to help the person listen to God's invitation.

Again, we Protestants could do well to learn from our Roman Catholic brothers and sisters, who expect a penance after confession. I am not suggesting, however, that pastors routinely "give a penance." Repentant actions come from discerning God's call *together*. Even then, penance needs to be dealt with sensitively. One who has lived a lifetime of having to please and earn love from withholding parents may need to experience God's free and grace-filled mercy that requires nothing except asking for it. For such a person, penance might reinforce the same old wounding pattern. However, those who hold onto guilt may well be helped by "doing penance."

Finally, for a sin that looms large, a penitent may be helped by faith imagination prayer. I had confessed a sin many times by myself and to another person in face-to-face confession, but words of absolution never seemed weighty enough. I worked on it in my therapy, and still the guilt remained – until someone led me into a faith imagination experience that allowed me to let in God's grace that had been there all along.

While in seminary I worked in the East Harlem Protestant Parish with a street gang of adolescent boys. My job was to spend time with them, trying my best to be a caring presence in their chaotic and violent lives.

George was homeless, and at 21 older than the rest of the gang, but he fit in because of his mild developmental disability and his willingness to get booze for the rest of them. His family wanted nothing to do with him; the gang and the church were all he had. Despite his terrible life, he was one of the most loving individuals imaginable. If he earned a little money doing odd jobs, he would blow it all on a large bag of donuts and then run to the church to give them away to anyone he could find. He always had a big grin for me and for the members of the gang – even when they were mean to him.

George survived by living in a rusted car hulk on East 101st Street. In the winter he would plug an old electric blanket into an outdoor outlet in a gas station, and wrap himself in it for his only heat. He had no place to shower, so he smelled terrible. He had no regular food, but depended instead on sporadic handouts from people in the neighborhood.

I tried to get him on welfare, but he was not organized enough to maintain a regular address. I tried to get him into a sheltered residence, but George didn't want to go. "I need to stay with my friends. I can't go to no 82nd Street!" (or wherever else I was proposing). I was stymied.

In the meantime, whenever I was in East Harlem I would take him to eat with me. He loved veal cutlet parmigiana, and there was a little diner in the neighborhood that served it. We would go there at least once or twice a week. George would chow down and we would talk and talk. I was privileged to count him as a friend.

The winter of my senior year was severe. Temperatures stayed in the teens for weeks. I was incredibly busy finishing up my thesis and preoccupied with trying to get a job, and I didn't remember very often that George was sleeping outside. When I did think of him, I did nothing about it.

One night that winter George froze to death. There was nothing in his stomach when he died.

I felt awful. I felt *responsible,* with an aching guilt mixed with grief for my friend. The irony of working on a seminary thesis while allowing a serious lapse in ministry seemed particularly painful. In my worst moments I felt unfit for ministry or anything else.

I held onto this guilt for ten years. Finally, someone who knew about faith imagination suggested that I imagine talking to Jesus about my feelings regarding George's death. In previous prayers for forgiveness I just heard my own words. However, in this prayer, it was as if I could see Jesus standing in front of me. Then he spoke just two sentences that changed everything. He said,

> *Didn't you know that George was me?*
>
> *Thank you for taking me to dinner.*

I was stunned. Not once in ten years had I ever thought of George as Christ. I felt confronted, comforted, moved to tears, and, yes, forgiven at last. What therapy or many prayers of confession had not been able to accomplish had happened in a simple prayer that made God's grace real. Obviously, those words were the precise ones I needed to hear. The experience of George's death spoke clearly that it is God alone who heals and forgives. It was also clear I needed a pastor, not a psychotherapist, to show me how to pray so I could open to grace.

HELPING PEOPLE FORGIVE

A third unique contribution of pastors and people of faith is helping people forgive the hurts they have suffered.

Some mental health workers, particularly those working in the area of sexual, spousal or ritual abuse, would say that when there has been terrible wounding, forgiveness is not desirable or even possible. They would argue that forgiving an abuser is tantamount to saying the abuse was permissible. They maintain that when one has been hurt so profoundly, forgiveness is usually dishonest. No one can really forgive without pasting a veneer over their pain and pretending that it wasn't so bad.[24]

They do have a point. I've lost track of how many women with abusive husbands have told me that upon going to their pastors for help, they were told to forgive and try harder to please him. Others, while encouraged to get out of an abusive situation, were urged to forgive right away before they had a chance to face the extent of their hurt, feel anger, or discover their own strength. In my opinion, this cockamamie advice has absolutely no place in good pastoral care.

Certainly the church has had tremendous difficulty dealing with anger, let alone rage. Somehow we have absorbed a blasphemous message: Christians are not supposed to be angry at all. In this context, forgiveness is simply a way of sweeping messy, forbidden anger away with a pious Christian broom. But emotions can't be erased by an act of will; even so, devout church folks often try. Most churches have some tense and achy church members seething under their smiles, often gossiping and sniping instead of confronting or genuinely reconciling.

A woman I once knew insisted she had "forgiven everything" and had "given all my hurts to God." It was clear nevertheless that her anger had simply gone underground. A devout Christian, she had a sincere desire to forgive, but desire wasn't enough; she had tried to forgive much too quickly. Her body was rigid, her arms held tightly at her sides. Her clenched teeth, the angry edge in her voice and the frequent verbal zingers she let fly made it evident that her "forgiveness" was really denial. She needed a minister to show her another way.

Another person who needed a minister's help was a man who didn't have the slightest desire to forgive. He treasured a spiteful grudge, keeping it hot to punish the relative who had indeed hurt him. For years, he did not talk to the person with whom he was angry, but he spent a great deal of energy raking over how badly he was wronged, telling the story again and again. He succeeded in starting a family feud. His smoldering anger never really ignited or burned cleanly,

---

[24] For example, see Chrystine Oksana, *Safe Passage to Healing,* pp. 249-250

and in the end poisonous fumes took over his life. When I met him, he was utterly miserable.

Such a person will probably not listen to a sermon on forgiveness. He may well have rejected the church for preaching at him without understanding his inner world first. This man needed a minister who was not afraid to encourage the direct expression of his anger. He needed someone who could affirm that his hurt was real. Once his anger was discharged, he discovered for himself that long-held grudges most hurt the one who holds them.

Gestalt experiments can help make such discoveries. For example, a Gestalt Pastoral Care minister might invite a person to make a paradoxical list of ten good things his resentment does for him, and see how he feels afterwards. Another experiment might be to close his eyes and find out where in his body his grudge is located. Then he could focus on his stomach, let us say, and become aware of what the grudge is doing to his body. If he is open to it, a third experiment might be to ask Jesus if it is time to let it all go.

Another angry person who needed a minister was a woman who finally discovered her anger after a lifetime of forcing it underground. For someone who has been badly hurt, finally releasing anger can be incredibly freeing, even intoxicating, and this woman was no exception. Suddenly she felt much better as her anger began to surface. It was as if a weight was gone from her shoulders. She had more energy and felt more accepting of herself. Shame seemed to vanish, and a feeling of power began to take its place. She was no longer a person to be messed with; at last she had learned to stand up for herself!

At this point, it was no surprise that it was difficult for her to think of forgiving. After all, anger made her feel wonderful. Why change? She was not yet aware that healthy anger can turn into bitterness and spite if it is held onto. It will no longer bring liberation, but imprisonment. She, too, needed a minister to suggest ways of working with her reluctance to take the next steps toward forgiveness.

For a Christian, healing is really complete only after anger has been honestly expressed in all its intensity, given up, and replaced by genuine forgiveness. We have a *call* to forgive others as God forgives us. We have an example in Jesus who knew how to forgive "seventy-seven times."(Mt. 18-22) As difficult as it is, we know that we must keep working until we can forgive deeply and honestly.

Because this belief is not shared widely in the other helping professions, a person facing a difficult process of forgiveness may have nowhere to turn for help except to a minister.[25] We must not offer stones for bread by simply referring such a person to a therapist who may not believe in forgiveness at all. Remember, some persons need pastoring more than therapy. An alternative may be to work alongside a therapist, understanding that ministers have a vital contribution to make around the issue of forgiveness.

First, three things are crucial to understand. One is that forgiveness is a *process* that may take months, or even years, to complete, especially when there has been major wounding. The second is that forgiveness depends on God's grace for its completion. We can't do it alone. Finally, forgiveness is the *end stage* of dealing with a major hurt. It is not fair or helpful to suggest forgiveness before one has had a chance to work toward it.

I offer the following road map for guiding people through a process of forgiveness:

Steps Toward Forgiving

Getting angry is the first and longest stage of forgiveness. This means facing honestly the depth of one's hurt and the intensity of one's anger. It also means expressing both in some way – not necessarily in the presence of the one who did the hurting – but it must be expressed honestly in all its nuances and intensity. It is a form of confession in which we own up to what is inside us. "I'd like to stomp on her head!" is the kind of thing someone might scream when there has been great wounding. Naturally, a minister who has not faced his or her own rage probably will not be able to sit around for such intense anger. Nor will he be comfortable suggesting its expression.

Praying with faith imagination may help one who is afraid of such raw and "unchristian" emotion. "Ask Jesus if it's okay with him if you express your anger so you can be rid of it," I often suggest. Jesus almost always says yes, and sometimes even the most fearful person hears something positively enthusiastic like "Go for it. I'm with you." Facing and expressing anger can take a quite a while, and it is important to not minimize or rush this important step. Neither is it helpful to get stuck here, allowing anger to forge a new angry-person identity.

When anger has been acknowledged and expressed, and the idea of forgiveness begins to nudge a person, it is time to suggest the person pray for the desire

---

[25] Carolyn Holderread Heggen has a helpful section on forgiveness in her book, *Sexual Abuse in Christian Homes and Churches.* See Chapter 7, entitled "Individualized Healing Liturgies."

to forgive. Humanly speaking, we cannot generate this desire in ourselves. In my experience it does come eventually, after a period of several weeks or months "sitting with" this prayer. Another prayer at this stage is to ask for the grace to see the person who hurt us as Jesus sees them.

Next, the person may need to confess any role she may have played in creating the problem or holding a grudge. If the need to confess is there, it usually surfaces after the desire to forgive.

The next step involves will, and not necessarily emotions. It involves saying out loud or in one's heart the words of forgiveness, again trusting that God will eventually supply the emotions needed. "I forgive you Mother, in the name of Jesus, for all you have done to me." No one who has been deeply hurt can manufacture the genuine letting go forgiveness requires. After we have done all we can, we depend on God's grace to work the forgiveness in us. The prayer at this stage might be, "God, please let your forgiveness and mercy for the one who hurt me come through me. Let me see him with compassion. Help me let go of my anger. Help me to stop trying to change him."

Some people naturally wonder if it is possible, or even right, to forgive if the person who hurt them is not sorry. They may also ask if forgiving means that they should no longer be wary of the hurtful person, who may be completely unrepentant.

When we have been hurt deeply, of course we will be alert to protect ourselves and others from the hurtful one. If, for example, a woman is being abused by her husband, she must get away and take the children with her. She will not allow her children to be alone with her husband, even when she has forgiven him. But, a process of forgiveness doesn't depend for its completion on the emotional or spiritual state of the hurtful one. We do not have to wait for another person to reform before we can taste the freedom of forgiving. The abuser is responsible for his own journey and cannot hold up the forgiver's progress by the lack of his own. Forgiving where there is not much chance of reconciliation in the relationship means being willing to give up poisonous rage so that the forgiver can be healed.

Recognize that even after a great deal of work with these steps, resentment may still be there. Forgiveness can be painful and messy, and may come only after much prayer and hard inner work. In the process new memories may surface, and these steps toward forgiving may need to be gone over again. Helping someone stuck in a morass of rage, guilt, *and* the desire to forgive, involves staying with them in this hard place and not pushing for a quick resolution. It means encouraging and witnessing to God's desire to heal and transform all that is not Christlike. It means holding the belief that surely God is at work in the process that works toward forgiveness as well as in the final gift of deep and life-changing forgiveness. Most importantly it means reiterating as many times as necessary that we need God's help to really forgive. We can't do it alone.

Sin is allowing our juiciness
and greenness to dry up.
Hildegard of Bingen, 12th century

6

DISCERNMENT

I was in my thirties before I seriously encountered discernment as an ordinary part of Christian life. I had always thought that discovering what God wants comes only over time, and with much struggle. Seeking God's will on a daily basis seemed impossible, and to be honest, I didn't want to do it. I was more than a little embarrassed for those who seemed to preface every sentence with "God told me..." After all, you can't just get your pal God on the hotline and demand a daily theophany! Furthermore, it seemed to me that cherished personal opinions were sometimes justified by claiming confirmation from God. History is full of stories in which the illusion of having "God on my side" has led to wacky, and even horrifying, actions.

In seminary I read about discernment in church history of course, particularly in connection with the Wesleyan "Quadrilateral." In the Wesleyan tradition there are four factors to consider in every important decision: scripture, tradition, reason, and experience. This profound understanding of discernment slid right by me; my own reading of it back then was that John Wesley and his followers weighed these factors carefully, rationally, and of course, *methodically,* using logic to figure out the right course of action. I always had trouble making choices that way. Reading about the Quadrilateral just reinforced my idea that discernment is complicated and takes forever.

In my own inner life, I wanted terribly to know God's will for me, but it seemed that the best I could do was to let a conviction or desire grow over time, testing it with trusted counselors and with my best understanding of the gospel. God did not seem to speak in any specific way; it seemed to be up to me to work out what God might be saying.

The longing to know God's will was particularly acute in college when I was trying to decide if I should go to seminary. I certainly felt a strong inner nudge toward ministry, but was it what God wanted? Didn't most people who got a call to ministry have some experience that made it crystal clear? Despite the airport vision when I was sixteen, God hadn't bopped me on the head specifically about a vocation to ministry, so how could I know for sure?

Without understanding what I was doing, I began a discernment process that was to take over a year. Looking back, I see that I stumbled on one time–honored way to discover God's will – the slow way that allows evidence from many fronts to accumulate and finally point to an answer.

That year I searched my heart, trying to decide what I myself felt moved to do. I paid attention to what stirred excitement in me, prayed and read the Bible, talked to friends, teachers, and pastors, took psychological tests, encountered my considerable resistance and fear, and kept the question open as best I could. Out of this wrestling, a half-hearted plan took shape; yeah, I guessed maybe, prob-ably, I would, go to seminary sometime. Still, I dithered and stewed until one summer afternoon sitting on a log in the woods, I simply felt the last of my resis-tance and fear melt. It just wasn't there anymore, and in its place was a gentle sense that *of course* I would go to seminary as soon as I graduated from Michigan State. Looking back, I think that the Holy Spirit gave me the last nudge I needed that day to finally dive into the pool I had been circling for so long.

However, despite the sense of being gently shoved by God into seminary and the wonderful experience of God's direct communication in the airport at age 16, I still couldn't imagine just asking God an "unimportant" question and trust-ing that an answer would come somehow. Discovering God's will seemed re-served for Really Big Decisions, not for day-to-day affairs. I held onto this belief for a long time. Even years later when I began working with Gestalt, I often prayed in a general way that God would guide me as I worked, but I did not have a clue how to stay alive for actual direction of the Holy Spirit in the course of a session.

The important shift in my understanding of discernment came when I tim-idly began to pray for healing. In an effort to sort out an approach to healing ministry that made sense to me, I had signed up for a two-year course at a coun-seling center called The Institute for Christian Healing in Narbeth, Pennsylvania. The class focused on faith imagination and other ways to integrate prayer into various forms of therapy. I was astounded, and I must admit, more than a little turned off by how the teachers, Dr. Doug Schoeninger and Sr. Betty Igo, dis-cerned over just about everything. They asked God who should be in the class, what we should talk about, and what to do next as they worked with a counselee. They reported seeing images in prayer, and hearing God speak as they listened. They had hunches and acted on them.

I was fascinated and appalled. "But how do you know you're not making it up? How do you *know*?" was the string I twanged for most of the course. Later they told me that I was "a pretty tough nut"; but as many times as I challenged them, they were unfailingly patient with me. Of course we can be wrong when we discern," they would say. "We can distort things as well an anyone else. That's one reason it's important to discern with other people. If we get too far off, some-one is likely to call us on it. Even if we must discern alone sometimes, we trust God to correct us eventually as long as we're willing to stay open to it." They were not the least defensive; they just invited me to observe how often careful discernment, even about "little" things, seemed to be helpful or accurate in retro-spect. And, they challenged me to try it myself.

Soon I found myself working with a woman who knew instinctively that something happened when she was about four years old to make her very afraid. She had never been able to connect this intuitive feeling with a specific event. Hoping to spark a memory, she created her own experiment, deciding to walk imaginatively as a four year old through her childhood home. As she went from room to room her childish recall of the house was vivid and detailed and she became increasingly fearful, but she remembered nothing that lit up for her as the source of her growing anxiety. I found myself praying silently for discernment, and in a few minutes I began to have a hazy image of the back yard of the house, along with my own feelings of foreboding. The image and the feeling persisted as I debated with myself about whether to say anything about it. I certainly didn't want to inject anything into her memory (nor did I want to look foolish!), but I did want to be faithful to anything God might be giving. Finally, I casually asked her if she would be willing to check out the yard. She agreed and as soon as she was in the yard, she saw a huge dog threatening to attack her. In her imagination the terrified child ran into her sandbox. For some reason this diverted the dog, al-though he continued to circle the sandbox, snarling and snapping. Hearing her screams, at last the owner of the dog came running with a leash and dragged the beast away.

The recovery of this memory, the accuracy of which was subsequently con-firmed by her mother, proved to be important in the woman's healing. It was also important in mine, as I reflected how my own capacity for intuition had been used by God to help her. How had I known to suggest she explore the back yard?

Actually, I didn't really "know" to suggest it. That is, I didn't rationally conclude that she should look in the back yard because she had looked everywhere else; the back yard just seemed to intrude into my consciousness, along with my feeling of foreboding. Although I "had a sense," it didn't really "make sense" to me even as I suggested looking there.

In retrospect, my timid way of suggesting the backyard experiment seemed just right. I now teach my students that experiments need to emerge from a balance of humility with a bold willingness to be used by God. Creating Gestalt experiments is a wonderful way to honor both hunches and discernment while remembering that both could be wrong.

What Discernment Is – and Isn't

Discerned knowledge has a very different purpose from the information that psychics promise to provide. Christian discernment is never for satisfying curiosity about the future, or for gaining money or power, or for reeling in the object of our romantic desires. It is not given to make the discerner look good. It is not a way to avoid the hard work involved in making our own discoveries as we grow. Most certainly it is not finding out what to do from an "adviser" who somehow "reads" us.

Further, discernment does not concern issues that are more rightly the domain of our own human responsibility and good sense. We do not have to discern if we should stop smoking and start exercising; we know we should. We know already that we are indeed called to love our aggravating next door neighbor, (although we may need to discern just how to do it). We don't need to ask whether we should wear jeans or chinos; God probably doesn't care (unless there are unjust labor practices involved in the manufacture of the pants). Generally speaking we don't need to ask permission of God to take a nap or eat an apple; we can rely on our own bodies to shape these decisions, or more accurately, we can trust that God works through our bodies to show us the way in these small things.

When we discern we make the amazing assumption that God does indeed want to communicate with us, and that really and truly God is concerned about even the daily twists of our existence. Always God is trying to get through to us. In faith, we ask for discernment, and then trust that somehow God will give the sense, the quickening, the image, the words, or whatever else is needed for helping, healing or growth. As best we can, we surrender our human capacity for intuition to God's control – and most of us have more intuitive capabilities than we realize. We ask the Holy Spirit to shape and control our perceptions.

I have learned that openness to God's prompting on a daily, even hourly, basis can lead to a lively ongoing conversation with God. Discernment about the next thing to do, what to say in a particular situation, what to write, how to help, or whether to accept this speaking engagement or that committee responsibility can enable us to order our lives in accordance with God's invitation. When we give our lives in ministry, we can expect that God will show us how to love more fully, and how to grow in grace ourselves.

Through Christian discernment we are given a doorway into God's will and wisdom for our very specific lives. Over time we discover answers to our deepest questions. We perceive God's particular and continuing invitation to grow. We are led to understand how to pray and act in various circumstances. We discover our vocation, and the way it plays out and changes over the course of our life. We learn how our loving God sees us, in contrast to how we feel about ourselves. We begin to glimpse how God is shaping and healing us throughout our lives, in matters large and small. We are directed toward social protest that can be effective because it is rooted in prayer. We may be led to talk to a particular person, to read a specific book, or to attend a certain event. We begin to sense how, even in our little lives, God is still making all things new. We catch glimpses of God's greatness, as God reveals God's self to us.

Thus, Christian discernment makes each of us more whole, helps us to follow Christ more truly, and enables us love others more fully. It is profoundly about healing, and is an integral part of Gestalt Pastoral Care. In fact, one way to describe Gestalt Pastoral Care is that it helps another person discern how God is healing him. Sitting with a gentle, constant discernment process in a session helps us understand more keenly, see more broadly, and hear more accurately what is happening right in front of us. We might be shown how God wants to heal or help this person today. Possibly we get a hunch about suggesting an experiment. We may experience a feeling that the person hasn't yet articulated. Of course most counselors experience these inner impressions, and paying attention to them is an important skill. The difference is that in Christian discernment we invite the Holy Spirit to speak through both our natural intuition and our expertise. The consensus among therapists who discern as part of their work is that there is a noticeable difference when they seek to connect with God's power and wisdom instead of just relying on their therapeutic skills. It is clear that when discernment is part of the process, people are healed more quickly, more profoundly and more holistically.

Obviously to help others with discernment, we pastors must first learn to discern in our own lives. This means welcoming the dynamic – and sometimes disconcerting – balance of trust and testing, of courage and humility, of faith and caution, of waiting and forging ahead that discernment requires of us.

Whenever I lead a retreat on Christian discernment, someone always asks if discernment isn't merely picking up on subtle cues in the environment. In other words, is God really involved in communicating these perceptions, or is it our own human capacity for keen observation combined with natural intuition? This is a good question, and one I struggled with myself. Experience tells me that God works *through,* not apart from, our awareness continuum, including our hunches, our intuition, and our observations. This belief makes it crucial to stay attentive to what we perceive in the faith that God shapes our attention in order to get through to us. Thus paying attention is utterly basic to both Christian discernment and, of course, to any Gestalt process.

CHRISTIAN DISCERNMENT: HOW IS IT GIVEN?

Putting aside for the moment how discernment works in Gestalt Pastoral Care, how does discernment come to one who prays? Faith imagination is a wonderful way to discern; as we have seen in the last chapter, our consent to prayerful, playful imagination seems to offer God an open door. Much of my own discernment comes in just this way. Other times discernment prayer is like a gentle conversation. We ask a question or present a need in prayer, then wait attentively and expectantly to fully experience what happens next.

God's reply can take many forms. We might become aware of a flicker of peace or agitation or excitement that gradually takes firmer root. Perhaps words or images emerge in our consciousness, or our attention is captured by something in our environment, or an idea comes forth, or we become aware of a memory, or our body reacts somehow. Similar to Gestalt work, we seek to be as awake as possible to what is happening in the present. We might discover that there are unspoken words inherent in our present perception; our sense of calm, for example, might carry the sense of "It's going to be OK." Then we react and perhaps discover another response from God in that interior place where God meets us. Back and forth, a communion of attention, words, silences, feelings, images. For now we are not evaluating very much; that will come later. As the conversation unwraps itself, it is enough to just be open to it.

What might happen, specifically? Here are three stories:

A woman asked God to teach her about confession and to show her any need for further repentance. It seemed to her that although she was not perfect, she was a deeply committed Christian and generally acted with integrity. In addition, she worked hard at rooting out such attitudes as arrogance and unforgiveness. She didn't want to beat herself up, but reading the biography of a saint convinced her that she was missing something, and it was this inner sense that prompted her prayer. So she asked her question, waiting with expectancy. In a few minutes her eyes drifted to a to-do pile on her desk. Slowly it dawned on her that on the bottom of that pile was an anguished letter from a friend. The letter, written out of loneliness and despair, had stayed there unanswered and nearly forgotten for many weeks.

A group prayed for discernment about a ministry project in which they were involved. Their ministry was not growing numerically, yet a few people were benefiting greatly. With just barely enough money coming in and some big bills due soon, they wondered if they had gotten off track somehow. They spent about twenty minutes listening to God in silence; then each shared their impressions. One heard the words "Trust me." Another saw their small project bathed in light. Another remembered an old gospel song that began, "There will be showers of blessings." Still another simply felt a sense of peace about it all. Their individual perceptions amounted to a group discernment that all was well.

A pastor asked God what should be his priority for the day. He was pressed for time as usual, and as usual, some important things would not get done. As he prayed he was surprised to feel a tiny stir of excitement about visiting the local nursing home. When he asked, "Is this really what I should be doing today, Lord?" he felt a settling inside. He also felt a vague sense that his sermon preparation, also on his agenda, would be enhanced by whatever would happen there.

Does discernment always come easily? Of course not. We cannot compel God, and sometimes we are too tangled up to perceive anything but our own tiresome inner tapes. Distractions, blankness, confusion, darkness, or a lot of nothing can greet us as we wait for an answer. When this happens we may need to be patient and try again, asking God to cut through our underbrush as we pray another day. We might also ask trusted friends to help us discern, for of course we need the church community. Sooner or later it becomes apparent that we can't have a vital life of prayer all by ourselves.

It is important to note that occasionally our darkness or blankness can be a way God communicates. Nothing is definitely something. Indeed, God may well be speaking through our feeling of God's absence and silence. Although admittedly difficult to live through, the experience of God's "absence" is not related to our unworthiness, or God's desire to punish, or God's abandonment of us, but about God's invitation to trust more deeply. Through it we can learn to have faith in God, instead of in our subjective experience of God. We can come to know in our bones that feelings don't always carry the day. Like a baby must learn that Mommy and Daddy haven't disappeared forever when they are absent from the room, we also must learn that God is at work in us even when we aren't able to experience God's presence.

Learning to discern in the varied circumstances of our lives is a wonderfully rich life-long journey. Generally speaking, as we listen to God over a period of years, our perceptions seem to become sharper, especially as we increasingly trust what we are receiving. The process of discernment seems to happen faster and with less fuss on our part.

However – and this is a big 'however'– we need to remember that our discernment can be off. We can be blind and deaf, or just plain wrong. Our own needs, pain, addictions, and previous experiences, can distort or drown out God's voice. We can wish for something so hard that we imagine that God wants it too. Sometimes we think we have received the five-year plan and all we have gotten is step one, and step two may take a surprising twist. God seems fond of leading us along in small steps rather than revealing the big picture all at once. Always we need to be open to having our discernment change or develop.

Once I was fairly certain that a young man with a fatal illness would be physically healed as our healing team prayed for him weekly; it seemed clear to all of us that we should keep praying for physical healing. At first this conviction, which I kept to myself, seemed born out of real discernment; but the man declined rapidly and less than a year later he died an agonizing death. I think my own liking for this man and my great desire for him to live – and maybe my desire for a dramatic healing to prove to one and all that healing prayer works – colored my ability to discern clearly. Even so, genuine discernment was part of the picture. Over time, the prayer of the healing team changed; we were no longer praying much for a cure, but for whatever healing God wanted to give. It was clear that the man *was* being healed – in a way that we weren't willing to consider at first. Toward the end of his life he was radiant with new spiritual and emotional health, and the healing team had learned a great deal about healing prayer.

TESTING DISCERNMENT: HOW DO I KNOW?

The more we trust what we receive, and the more we take it seriously enough to test it out a bit, the more our capacity for discernment seems to increase. What might it look like to test discernment? Simply writing down what we think God is communicating can be a small but important act of trust. In crucial matters, however, we would not impulsively leap to action on the basis of one discernment experience; surely we would pray about it further and let a conviction grow over time. We can mull things over with a friend or spiritual companion. We can let our discernment rest for a while to see if it is confirmed from other sources. We might try following our discernment provisionally and see what happens. We might ponder some evaluating questions:

- Could my own need for healing or wish for a shortcut be getting in the way of clarity?

- Does my discernment sound like the God of the Bible? Would Jesus agree? The answer lies not in finding a verse to match what we are considering, but asking if the discernment squares with the spirit of the gospel.

- Does my discernment have the ring of common sense? If not, I must wait until my discernment is confirmed from many other sources.

- Is it consistent with the best human wisdom and medical science?

- Does it fit with the traditions of the church's faith and practice over the ages? Clearly, the church has not always been right, but even so God has worked through it. What would the saints – living or dead – say?

- Is my discernment consistent with concern for the poor, the sick, the young?

- Do my trusted friends, family members, spiritual director and others in the church find it plausible and consistent with their own discernment?

•Does my discernment get stronger over a period of time, or does it fade? Is it confirmed from many directions?

•Is there an element of surprise? Could I have thought this up myself? Although surprise is not always present, surprise points to the possibility that the discernment is genuine.

•Does my discernment hold the possibility of making me look good or feathering my nest? If so, I must be doubly cautious.

•Am I putting up roadblocks to discernment? For example, am I already certain what God wants even before I ask? Am I discounting part of my awareness because I think it doesn't make sense? Is part of me unwilling or afraid to receive God's attention? Am I stuck on having *perfect* discernment?[26]

Even with our best efforts, seldom is our discernment crystal clear, and there are times when we will never know if we got it right or not. Sometimes the only way to evaluate our discernment is to consider the results after we have allowed it to shape our behavior. Was someone helped, loved, or healed, or did it just make us look good? Did the situation get clearer, or more confused? Did the discernment reveal what I now know to be true?

There are times, however, when we seem to be invited to act with trust without ever knowing the outcome. I was coming home alone from Manhattan long after midnight when I felt a strong urge to go down to the lower deck of the Staten Island Ferry. There were some good reasons to ignore this impulse. I was sleepy and didn't want to move. More importantly, the lower rear deck is usually isolated in the wee hours. Ordinarily I would not go down there by myself in the middle of the night, but I found myself asking if this impulse was from God. Right away the words formed in my head, "Yes. Get down there immediately!" Wide awake now, down the stairs I went, deciding that I would stay near the door so I could retreat if necessary. On the deck was a solitary man furtively, nervously pacing back and forth near the back edge of the ferry. Between him and the water was a low metal gate stretching across the car entrance. When he saw me his face became anguished and he paced faster. I asked God if I should talk to him, and again the words came immediately, "No. Just stand where you are." After several minutes the man glanced at me again, smacked one fist into his other hand, and shambled up the opposite stairs.

---

[26] Fr. Peter Chepaitis, OFM, contributed greatly to this list of evaluating questions.

Was this genuine discernment or not? Who knows? The rear lower deck is where despondent people occasionally commit suicide, so perhaps God used my presence to stop the man from jumping. Why didn't God direct me to talk to him? I have no idea. I have learned to let such questions rest lightly and to trust that God is astonishingly willing to use my desire to be faithful.

DISCERNMENT IN GESTALT PASTORAL CARE

How does a discernment process play out in Gestalt Pastoral Care? It isn't much different from the process described above. We stretch our awareness to perceive as much as possible, we pay attention to hunches and wispy bits of awareness that creep in from nowhere, we humbly remember that we could be wrong, and we use provisionally the discernment we have been given.

When we discern as a pastoral care minister, there are, of course, occasions in which we ask outside of a session, "Lord, what do you want to heal in John? What do you want me to do about it?" or "Jesus, what am I missing with Steve?" Discernment is also integral in planning for an individually-created ritual of healing. If a need for generational healing or institutional healing arises, there is need for considerable discernment here too, before going ahead. (These things will be discussed in later chapters.)

Most often, however, discernment takes place in a session as the work continues to flow. Occasionally my discernment in a session is quite specific, as it was with the backyard dog. However, my instructions usually run something like this: "Keep quiet, and trust me. Stay out of the way and let me do the work." Such discernment tends to be fairly humbling!

How is it possible to pay close attention to another person and to one's own discernment process at the same time? It is something like learning to play with two hands on the piano, reading two different clefs simultaneously. When each hand is first practiced separately, it is much easier to get everything working together later on. Likewise, Christian discernment in the context of Gestalt Pastoral Care almost comes naturally when the minister has both learned to trust discernment in his own life, and is at ease with a basic Gestalt Pastoral Care perspective.

I have come to trust that when I am sitting with another person for the purpose of helping her grow, eventually one or both of us will be given whatever is needed for the process if we ask for it, and if we don't throw up roadblocks. With experience, it is possible to identify what is emerging, and to quickly and silently ask relevant evaluating questions. We go ahead as best we can, in the faith that we will be corrected by an experiment or by further discernment if we don't get it right.

Let us imagine, for example, that I sense sadness in someone, (or more specifically, when I try to enter the person's reality I touch sadness there). This discernment becomes a context for listening and watching. Following the Gestalt model, I do not say "You seem sad to me. Are you?" Instead, I observe as completely as possible to see if perhaps sadness is being expressed in some way. What a person is saying is often the least important thing to be aware of; gestures, tone of voice, physical positions and the like can be more crucial. So perhaps I will notice that the person's shoulders are slumping, or maybe I will detect a tiny quiver in his voice, or maybe his arm will gesture in a way that conveys to me, "what's the use?" In addition there will surely be other things to notice; sadness will probably not be the only thing being expressed, and the person may not be talking about sadness at all. I hold sadness lightly in my awareness because it is my present discernment, and because I am trying to help the person discover his "emergency" underneath whatever resistance may be there. I ask God silently if sadness is the issue for now, and continue to pay attention.

One of the simplest ways to test discernment in a session is to ask the basic Gestalt question, "What are you aware of right now?" Perhaps the person will actually confirm my perception of sadness – and maybe not. If my feeling persists, I can test it with an experiment. (I will discuss Gestalt experiments in Chapter Nine.) The beauty of a Gestalt experiment is that it allows a guide to fully honor both her discernment and the ever-present possibility she may be wrong. So, for example, in the case of my perception of sadness, I could ask the person if he will allow his gesturing arm to "speak" as if it had a voice of its own. Or I could suggest that he repeat certain of his words while paying attention to how they sound to him. Or I might ask if he would be willing to make a noise with each exhale, while paying attention. And so on. If my discernment is confirmed during an experiment, fine. If not, fine as well.

Suggesting experiments is the most common way to use discernment in Gestalt Pastoral Care, but not the only way. Francis MacNutt suggests using discernment by praying provisionally: "If there is any sadness in Jim, please touch it..." If a person is seeking God's will regarding some particular matter, perhaps at the end of the session a minister might cautiously confirm the seeker's discernment with her own: "As I was praying with you today, it seemed to me that God was pointing in the same direction as you received in your prayer."

When a person is praying with faith imagination, the minister will be following along with her own discernment and might gently suggest redirecting the process if things are clearly getting off. For example, "I wonder if you are actually hearing Jesus because he seems as degrading and harsh as your father. How about praying that your relationship with your father keep out of this, so that you hear only Jesus?" Or even, "Would you be willing to listen again? I don't think that's quite right."

Because the person coming for help may not yet be familiar with discernment, and because it is difficult to have clarity when one is emotionally and spiritually tangled, the minister's discernment might have to carry the process at first. Almost immediately, though, we can begin to encourage discernment in the other person. For example, we could work with faith imagination prayer even in the first session if there is openness to it. We can ask again and again "What are you feeling right now?" or, "How is God shaping your experience of the moment?" When we pray together for guidance at the beginning of a session, we can ask the person what they perceived in the small silence after the prayer. We can be comfortable with generous silence as discernment takes shape. We can even say, "I'm not sure what to suggest next. Let's be quiet for a few minutes and listen a bit, shall we?" I have found that people catch on quite quickly to this and are often awed by God's grace and excited by the new possibilities for change it presents.

Using Discernment in a Session

Beginning a session with prayer for openness is a wonderful way to start. But even before that, from the first seconds of contact with another person, the minister can begin to make a most important contribution, that of *noticing*. As he learns to value and honor his own discernment process, he is less likely to toss out certain perceptions as not important. If he doesn't hear that someone's voice has changed timbre, for example, or if he doesn't see muscles tightening, if he doesn't notice the subtle rocking or the change in energy, if he is not aware of his own inner stream, it is less likely that he can perceive what the Holy Spirit might be communicating through these changes. As we ministers become keener observers, expanding our own awareness continuum, we open the windows for the Holy Spirit to blow in. It is as if God has more to work with if we are more aware in general.

But simple awareness is not the end of it. At any given moment, a Gestalt Pastoral minister may be aware of countless things about the person across from her. She may note, for example, that he is bracing himself by leaning on his elbow, and that he has a slight smile playing but not quite breaking through, and that his slightly twitching eyes look a little glazed, and that his energy is slower and his aura murkier today than usual, and that his toes are moving inside his shoes, and that his voice sounds soft, washed out, and tentative. The word "stuck" floats to her consciousness. She may also note her motherly liking for him and her respect for his desire to grow, and that as he begins to talk she feels tired and sort of waterlogged, and that she senses he is sick-and-tired, and that she flashes on an image of him standing up and saying "I can't stand this anymore!"

How might her discernment continue in this instance? She wordlessly asks the Holy Spirit to filter out anything she herself might be creating, and to let what is most important emerge "bigger" or "louder." "I can't stand this anymore!" captures her attention. She asks, again wordlessly, if the man is ready to experiment with "I can't stand it" or if this is just a context for her listening at the moment. She senses he is indeed not ready, because right now he is feeling so mired in mud. She mentally files her image for later and suggests an experiment to explore feeling stuck, asking him if he would be willing to exaggerate his leaning posture. The man agrees, and puts more and more weight on his elbow, until he is sprawled inches from the floor. When asked to describe his physical experience of the moment, he says, "I'm trying to hold myself up, but I'm so tired. I just can't move." She silently notes that her sense of stuckness seems to be accurate.

As the man further explores the contours of being stuck and unmoving, her attention is riveted on his toes. Aha! His toes are indeed wiggling, seemingly the only part of him that is expressing the opposite of "I can't move." She sits with that observation a minute, checking with the Holy Spirit, and feels a "yes". Following where her discernment seems to be leading, she asks him if he would be willing to take off his shoes and say to his moving toes, "I'm so tired and I just can't move", and then let his moving toes talk back. Let there be a conversation between too-tired-to-move, and toes-in-constant-motion. And off he goes, confronting a life-long pattern that has sapped his energy for years.

As the work continues, the man discovers that his toes are an embodiment of healthy rebellion against the stultifying influence of his rich and powerful family that ordered him to, "Take over the business someday! Make money, and lots of it! Don't ever let your guard down! Don't you dare disgrace us! Fit in!"

His toes speak directly to his family now, cracking and sparking with energy, adamantly refusing to have anything to do with the family business. Indeed he has confirmed her original impression of "I can't stand it anymore!"

In a few minutes he is surprised to find himself afraid. What will happen if this energy gets loose? He will do something stupid! He will go crazy for sure! He will lose everything! His family – everybody – will ostracize him! The minister, discerning that the man is now looking straight into the face of his inner dragon, asks if he is willing to invite Jesus into his fear. As he consents to this prayer work he is, of course, consenting to a discernment process of his own.

Discernment: A Way God Heals

Discernment is not just a technique for deciding what to do, and obviously not just for ministers. Part of our job as Gestalt Pastoral Care ministers is to encourage discernment in those who come for help, for discernment is very often directly related to healing. This is not too surprising, is it? When we consider that God passionately desires our wholeness, then we know that whatever God reveals is about somehow assisting that process.

Discernment sometimes seems so ordinary: the whisper of an urge to make a particular phone call, the familiar prick of conscience, a sense of holiness about a bouquet of flowers. (Is it ever really ordinary when God is revealed?) But sometimes discernment can powerfully reframe the entire life of a person so that what has seemed sorry and useless and futile and full of despair can be newly perceived as pregnant with God's mercy and love. When a suffering person is able to sense, even dimly, how God sees her life, the experience is like looking through a kaleidoscope. Suddenly the light hitting the mirrors explodes a few pieces of broken glass into color, ever-changing and gorgeous, blooming into new patterns with each slight movement. Or sometimes it is like an exclamation point that God puts in a various moments of our lives. It is as if God were saying, "Look here! This is important! See! Taste! Know! Feel! Love! Act!"

There are many stories in this book that illustrate the transforming power of discernment, and now I tell one more kaleidoscopic, exclamation-point story.

Bruce and His Drunken Dad

Bruce was thirty-eight when he began working on his emotional and spiritual growth. Although he was a man of deep Christian commitment, by then he was experiencing nearly constant anxiety. There was a knot of tension in his stomach that never seemed to vanish. In relationships, his tendency was to either hide or become overpowering. He had frequent migraines and was often sick with flu or colds. Worst of all, he hated admitting that he hated himself.

Soon it became apparent that the trail bushwhacked by these symptoms led straight to his father. His mild-mannered dad had been an occasional drunk, and when on a binge was dangerously violent. Dad would drive up in his truck and charge up the porch stairs, yelling and taking off his thick leather belt. As soon as he got in the door he would begin wildly swinging and lashing about with his belt, destroying furniture, glassware, the television, whatever got in his way. Then he would come after any family members in the house.

Bruce learned to dread the sound of the truck. He would run to the window; if his dad was staggering, Bruce would run out the back door and into the woods, staying away as long as he could. Sometimes he even spent the night there, preferring cold or rain to what was waiting at home. In the woods he would weep in helpless rage for his mother and brothers still in the house, and berate himself for not helping them.

Finally when he was 14 he bought a knife, a big lethal knife, and hid it in the woods. Icy as steel, he promised his father that if he laid a finger on anyone else ever again, he, Bruce, would get the knife and kill him in his sleep. The beatings and destruction stopped cold. And from that moment Bruce was burdened with guilt that he had become just as violent as his father, using hatred, anger, brute strength and a weapon to control the household.

Fast forward to Bruce, at age 38 in a Gestalt Pastoral Care process. He is re-experiencing his terror as a young teenager as his father comes roaring up the steps, eyes wild, belt thrashing. Bruce has not been able to get away this time, and has locked himself in the bathroom, trembling and waiting for the inevitable beating. His minister suggests inviting Jesus into the scene. Bruce agrees, and through faith imagination prayer everything changes for him.

He sees Jesus standing in the bathroom door facing his raging father who is trying to push his way in. Jesus does not budge; instead he stands there and receives the blows of the belt, protecting Bruce. Finally Jesus pins his father to the wall and invites Bruce to speak his truth to his dad. For the first time, Bruce tells his father that he is a cruel bully and a coward. He says alcoholism is no excuse; he should have gotten help, gone to AA. Bruce tells him although he fathered children, he was never a real dad. As his anger builds, Bruce screams out his rage while vehemently whacking a pillow with a plastic bat.

Spent, he is astonished to sense that Jesus is proud of him, and to hear his words: "Well, Bruce, I'm glad you've finally got that out of your system!" Then Jesus adds, "Bruce, you stopped it the best you could when you were 14, and now it's really over. Let's go!" And Bruce senses that Jesus is leading him away from that house of horrors forever. As they leave, Jesus grins and says one last thing: "By the way, Bruce, with my stripes you are healed."

In the weeks that followed this prayer, Bruce felt freer and safer than ever before. The tension in his stomach was gone, and the migraines never returned. Relationships with his family slowly improved as he was freed to find new ways to love them. He even began to imagine forgiving his father one day. He learned to cut himself some slack. In fact, he felt the new, fragile sense of actually loving himself, drawing forgiveness and compassion from the Lord's words that he had indeed done the best he could. Bruce cherished his dawning realization that his rage had been appropriate. Best of all was Bruce's wondrous experience of being worth protecting.

In this powerful discernment prayer, Bruce was able to experience first-hand God's healing activity. He saw that the words and actions of Jesus were perfectly suited to his particular story and his need for healing. The shattered glass of his terrible childhood was refracted by God's love into something vividly fresh and astonishingly beautiful.

Authentic rituals grow out of the depth of human experience…
Hoyt Hickman, Ritual in a New Day

7

INDIVIDUALIZED HEALING LITURGIES

It is remarkable that the same healing grace mediated through prayer and laying on of hands seems to come through healing liturgies as well. I'm referring to the familiar liturgies of anointing, Communion, Baptism, and confession of sins, of course, but not only those. Christian liturgies that are specially created around one person's particular need can be wonderfully healing as well. In these tailor-made liturgies we incorporate the raw material of the liturgical tradition of the church, scripture and creedal statements, along with the person's dreams, memories, personal history, and life transitions. I believe it is possible to create a liturgy of healing around almost any special event, need for healing, or growth milestone.[27]

Some Protestants are rightly suspicious of "empty ritual" – rote repetition because "we've always done it that way." I'm definitely not referring to empty ritual, but rather to actions and words that lay bold claim to God's truth. Actions and words of power, which are given to us as we ask the Holy Spirit for them. Actions and words of power through which God heals. Actions and words of power that are rooted in the tradition and wisdom of the church, indeed which use familiar Christian liturgies in new ways.

Such liturgies of healing are yet another unique contribution that only ministers can make. After all, ordained clergy are professionals specifically trained to create and lead worship services, and lay ministers are likely to have had long experience with worship and liturgy as well. Further, we have an exceedingly rich tradition from which to draw, and pastors are likely to know about the many styles of worship through 2,000 years of church history. The prayers, the rites, the many forms of worship are ours to claim.

---

[27] The material in this chapter will be expanded into a book provisionally titled, *At Your Service: Personalized Healing Liturgies.* It is scheduled for publication in 2007 by Upper Room Books.

Personalized liturgies of healing are similar to Gestalt experiments in certain important ways. Both involve discerning what action the person's growth process is suggesting and finding ways for the person to actually do what is necessary in the safe setting of a private session or small group. Both invite increased awareness and discovery. In secular Gestalt workshops participants feel affirmed when other people identify with their inner work; during Gestalt Pastoral Care retreats Christians often become aware of their longing for the church to act as both witness and truth-teller in their growth process. In other words, while secular Gestalt draws on the power of community, Gestalt Pastoral Care relies on God working though the gathered church to pave the way.

WHAT CHRISTIAN HEALING LITURGIES ARE NOT

Individualized Christian liturgies are not a harangue or a pep talk that sends a message to "snap out of it." They are not a way to get someone to change. They are not coercive or condemning; instead they are respectful and gentle. They are never done without the explicit and detailed permission of the person for whom the liturgy is created. As much as possible, the wording and flow of tailor-made liturgies should come from a blend of the church's liturgical traditions and the person's own expressed desire or faith imagination.

It is even more important to understand that Christian healing liturgies are not magic; they do not try to manipulate forces somehow to obtain specific results. Their purpose is certainly not to make God bend to our desires, but to proclaim God's love in a targeted, personalized way. They do not seek personal power; instead they support deeper surrender to God's healing work. It is clear, however, that there is more "doing" in creating personalized liturgies than there is in simply praying for healing. Some planning will surely be involved, and during a liturgy the minister of healing and the congregation may be quite active. In addition to praying for healing they may proclaim gospel truth, they may anoint the person who is the focus of the liturgy, or they may assist with some highly individualized action. With such an important role for the gathered church it is more important than ever to be clear that healing comes, not through liturgical actions, but through God at work in our worship.

Christian healing liturgies are not a substitute for therapy or a "quick fix." In fact, individualized liturgies usually have the most impact when one is well along in a healing process. Occasionally an individualized liturgy will break up a logjam early on, but usually the effect is simply to make it possible for the person to do the hard work required for growth.

Finally, although Christian healing liturgies may take place in a very small group, they are not essentially private. Even two people meeting for a liturgy constitute a congregation of the church, and are always representing that larger reality.

FOOTWASHING

My eyes were opened to the healing power of liturgy when I was chaplain at South Beach Psychiatric Center, a large state hospital on Staten Island. Whenever I led worship at the hospital, I also had to keep order; someone was always doing something disruptive. I knew that these disruptions came out of illness, but I was perplexed as to how to deal with them so that worship might be a meaningful experience. I tried hard to make the services relevant and interesting but nothing I could think of seemed to work. The turning point came after the following dialogue took place during a service for patients:

Me: *The New Testament reading is from the Gospel of John.*

Someone else: *My brother's name is John.*

Another person: *I hate John!*

Someone in the back: *I have to go to the john, right now!*

Suddenly, a man was pounding a metal chair, making quite a racket, and others were shifting in their seats.

Me: *Okay. Let's all try to be quiet and listen to the Bible.*

I had lost them again, and my response was, as usual, puny and ineffective. Discouraged, and with nothing to lose, I decided to try a footwashing service with the patients. The East Harlem Protestant Parish where I had worked during seminary held regular footwashing services, and everyone, from seminary professors to street people, loved it. I reasoned that a more interactive service might channel the many distractions. Then again, such a crazy idea might produce real chaos. Many psychiatric patients react with fear and anger at being touched. How would they respond to the chance to be touched in this very meaningful and tender way? What if no one was willing even to try it? I didn't know, but it seemed anything might be better than what had been happening. So, before the next time they came for worship, I rounded up some basins, soap, and towels and had the room set up for footwashing.

From the beginning, things were different. Instead of reading from the Bible, I told, rather than read, the story of Jesus washing the feet of the disciples. Then I said,

> We are going to have the chance to do what Jesus did when he washed the feet of his friends. Anyone who wants can wash the feet of another person in the room. If you want, you can have your feet washed, just like the disciples did. If you don't feel you want to participate, that's OK. You can just watch, or it's fine if you want to leave. But if you decide to participate, you might experience how much God loves you. You might also find out that God wants to help others through you.

Everyone listened quite attentively. I had the distinct feeling that this approach was getting through, and to my surprise, everyone wanted to be a part of it. Immediately they chose partners and began to kneel in front of each other. I watched them carefully so I could be ready if anyone got upset.

What happened after a few moments was astonishing. Soon from all around the chapel I heard little snuffles and sobs. Many were weeping, not with anguish, but with soft, releasing tears. Faces lined with tension relaxed, and shoulders let go. The chapel was pregnant with hope and relief. For at least fifteen minutes no one did or said anything out of line. God's presence was very evident, and all of us knew it. It was apparent that God was working in us deeply through the vehicle of this simple Christian ritual, calling forth the sanity underneath all the illness.

After this shining experience in the hospital, I decided to try footwashing with retreat groups. I must admit that at first I was daunted by the logistical problems of getting enough basins and towels for everyone, having the water warm enough at the right time in the service, changing the water for each person, and cleaning up soapy water that had sloshed all over the floor. Although the rewards were great, I found such services were lot of trouble. Then one day after a meal in a Japanese restaurant I got the idea of making a pile of rolled-up washcloths in a pottery bowl. As the story of Jesus washing the feet of his friends is read, hot water is poured over the washcloths from a pitcher. Then each person receives a hot washcloth to be used to wash the feet of a partner.

Once the practicalities were worked out, I was enthusiastic about including footwashing along with Communion at each healing retreat I led. I found that many others responded to footwashing in a similar way to those suffering with mental illness; they have a physical and emotional experience of God's love. This simple ritual speaks to our depths, as Jesus meant it to.

I have come to wonder why footwashing never became a sacrament for most churches. Mennonites, Moravians, various Pentecostal groups, and Church of the Brethren have claimed footwashing as a regular part of church life, but to most Christians footwashing is a novelty. Roman Catholics do have such a service during Holy Week, but until very recently only the priests and twelve men representing the disciples could participate. All women and most men were excluded.

I believe that footwashing has all the earmarks of a genuine sacrament, and one that has particular relevance for the healing ministry. In the biblical footwashing story, Jesus made it clear that his disciples were to continue washing each other's feet.

> After he had washed their feet, had put on his robe, and had returned to the table, he said to them, "Do you know what I have done to you? You call me Teacher and Lord – and you are right, for that is what I am. So if I, your Lord and Teacher, have washed your feet, you also ought to wash one another's feet.
>
> For I have set you an example, that you also should do as I have done to you....If you know these things, you are blessed if you do them."

> *John 13:12-17*

I look forward to the time when footwashing might be a regular part of church life, especially in the context of healing ministries. If footwashing ever becomes broadly recognized as sacrament, it will be the earthiest one, certainly the most clearly connected to human shame and plain old dirt. It is a sign that God wants to heal and love the part of us that we find most distressing – that which is painful, shameful, callused, fearful, or dirty. It also shows forth the radically transforming nature of God's love, in which the Lord assumes the role of a slave – or of a mother tenderly washing her children. There are social implications here too. Gender and class and role distinctions are obliterated in this amazing demonstration of God's passionate love. And how interesting to ponder that Jesus may have gotten the idea for footwashing from the woman who washed his feet with her tears and dried them with her hair (Luke 7:38)!

COMMUNION AS A LITURGY OF HEALING

Because my experience with footwashing was so rich I began to explore other Christian liturgies as vehicles of healing. Remarkable healings occurred as I shared Communion in my office, sometimes with just one person, sometimes with a small group called together to pray for an individual. Roman Catholic friends have faith that God's transforming presence is poured out in a special way during the celebration of Mass, particularly in the context of a person's specific need. I am beginning to agree with them as I experience the power of healing Eucharists.

For instance, a woman who had worked with me for three years was moving to another city where she had been promoted to a new job. She asked to have Communion in her final session. Both of us found it a wonderful way to finish together, and to celebrate the next phase of her life. For her the Communion was a special celebration of God's love, thanksgiving for how far she had come, and a sign that she and I would still be connected in Christ after she moved away. It was also a symbol of her need to move on, following a new call.

In another instance, there was a man who never felt he was good enough. Using physical and verbal abuse his parents had drummed into him a brutal and damaging lie. "You're disgusting," they would sneer. "You're nothing but a pain in the butt. You'll never amount to anything." He had so internalized this belief (in Gestalt terms, an introject) that he felt unworthy even to exist. Work, relationships, leisure, faith – every aspect of his life was a shambles and infused with, "I'm just no good. How can anyone stand to be around me?" This introject was so strong that it formed the essential core of his self-identity.

He had worked hard to get beyond his parents' cruelty. He had wept in sorrow and despair at not being loved. He had tried to disconnect from his parents, knowing that they would never be able to give him what he needed. He had expressed rage at them many times, vigorously attacking a pillow with a plastic bat in my office. He had come to believe that his parents were themselves terribly damaged by *their* parents, and he had prayed for their healing. All his intensive inner work had helped somewhat but he still remained angry and depressed. Faith imagination was difficult for him because, while he would see Jesus reaching out to him and even hear his words of love and acceptance, he couldn't let it in. At other times it would seem to him that Jesus was sneering at him just as his parents had done. Despite his keen desire to participate in worship, he had not been to church for a long time because he felt so unworthy.

110

One day he came in and said that although he didn't understand it, he felt a desire for Communion. He had stayed away from Communion for many years because of his deep shame, but now, unaccountably, he wanted to receive it. I am pretty certain he would have had great difficulty in taking this step in a public service because his feelings were too raw and too near the surface. The setting of my office made it much safer for him. Even so he was quite anxious – but willing to take the risk.

As we shared in the liturgy together we could pause as often as he wanted to experience and process his feelings. Several times he asked me to repeat something so he could more fully take it in. He was doing his best to be open, but his shame was so intense that soon he was huddled in a near-fetal position, scarcely breathing as he sat on the floor.

When I said the words "This is my body broken for you," he burst into tears. "for you, For You, FOR YOU, **FOR YOU!**" filled his consciousness like a huge wave. As the words thundered into his heart, they seemed to wash away the terrible messages from his parents. At that moment he experienced the world without disabling shame for the first time, and he took in a new message of God's love for him. God used the familiar words of the liturgy and the gesture of offering bread and wine to let grace touch this man. He left feeling euphoric.

His euphoria only lasted a few weeks, but in its place was a new interior foundation. In subsequent sessions when we prayed with faith imagination, he could receive the grace offered to him. He could get angry at his parents in my office without collapsing into helpless rage and despair. It was as if he now had a place inside to put good feelings about himself, and somehow he was enabled to let go of the bad ones. He could allow himself to be loved, and bit by bit his life reflected this new core identity. He was not "a pain in the butt"; he was cherished. He was not "disgusting"; he had a place around the table of the Lord.

WHY HAVE "PRIVATE LITURGIES?"

As I have told stories of healing Eucharists, some are troubled about what they would call "private Communion." They cite ecclesiastical rules of certain churches that specify in some detail under what conditions Communion can be celebrated. Others have just questioned why it takes a private liturgy for God to heal. Why not just let them come to church on Sunday where there are regular services of Communion and prayers for healing?

This is a good question. It is certainly true that many people report being healed or touched by grace on Sunday morning. That's how it should be, but the problem is that not everyone is ready to open up in a public service. Furthermore, Eucharist is always "public" no matter how small the group, for even two or three are a congregation of the church and are always representing that larger reality.

Pastorally speaking, there are some compelling reasons to celebrate Communion with just one other person or a small group:

- Some Christians struggling to be faithful are so wounded by distorted, or even abusive, theology that the church building itself or the crowds or the candles or the pastor in an alb are angering or frightening.

- Some hurting people may need to slow things down in order to take in what is happening in a liturgy. In a private setting we can repeat, or stop for some quiet, or allow for tears to flow freely. We can "work through" the liturgy if need be.[28] If a song or a bit of scripture come to mind during the service, we can easily add to the planned service as we go along. These small spontaneous additions are often an important part of the healing that takes place.

- In a private setting confession can be specific and can take as long as needed. In fact the whole service can be created around a confession or other personal issue or life transition.

- Some issues needing healing prayer are not appropriate to share with a large congregation, or even with a small healing prayer group. One who is suffering should not be deprived of the gifts of the church because he or she needs a confidential setting.

- For those wounded by the church itself, "private" liturgies can pave the way for return to the larger congregation.

BAPTISM

Ann spent fifteen years in a major clinical depression. She had numerous crisis hospitalizations, had tried every medication and treatment available, gone

---

[28] The Greek root of the word "liturgy" means, "work of the people".

through shock treatments, and had just about given up hope. Although she had prayed daily throughout her suffering, she was convinced that God was against her. Things got even worse when her grandmother, with whom she had been very close, died. Ann plunged into a suicidal pit, prompting her doctor to arrange for commitment to a long-term state psychiatric facility in which she would be maintained indefinitely. She was to be transported to the new hospital the following week.

Perhaps it was the specter of life as a "certified crazy person" (her words) that jiggled something loose in Ann. All she knew was that suddenly she was consumed with the realization that she had never been baptized, and felt an urgent desire to be baptized right away. She talked her pastor into giving her a crash preparation course in the hospital so she could be baptized before beginning her life in the state facility. Despite his belief that baptism should happen only after careful and lengthy preparation, he finally went ahead, largely in response to Ann's desperate desire.

Ann began to feel markedly better the very same day she was baptized. "I was walking on air," she said. "My doctor came by that afternoon to ask how I was doing, and I surprised him by saying 'I'm really doing well!' I never told him that before, believe me." Her pastor was equally surprised and awed. "Instead of a long-term commitment," he said, "she went home, well."

Several months later, her dramatic improvement still held. She had discovered that listening to a favorite gospel song always reminded her of her baptism and helped her to further assimilate it.

> [The song] is wonderful. It's helped me get back to [my baptism] and experience more of the fullness of it. It finished it, deepened it. Now when I think of God I see Jesus with a sort of glow. He doesn't speak. He simply gives his presence. And, I have a much greater appreciation of the sky and trees and flowers. It all speaks of God and his love.

Years later, Ann is still drawing from the well created by her baptism. Recently she said, "I think about [my baptism] often, and it's still vivid in my mind. It still does what it did back then. The memory of it still helps me feel good, especially if I have a down day." Ann's remarkable story underlines once again how God uses Christian sacraments for healing.

Baptism happens only once in the life of a Christian. However, a reaffirmation of baptismal vows can occur as many times as desired, and can also provide a vehicle for healing. One man was empowered to give up disabling and un-healthy ways of relating to women after his baptismal reaffirmation. He heard, as if for the first time, that he was held in love as a member of the Christian family, and was empowered to hold others in love without trying to control them. A woman was able to begin a program of teaching adults in her community to read. For years she had dreamed about inaugurating such a ministry, but lacked the confi-dence to do so. A third person found that he could, through an affirmation of his baptism, finally allow himself to accept God's forgiveness for causing someone great pain.

ANOINTING

> Are any among you suffering? They should pray. Are any cheer-ful? They should sing songs of praise. Are any among you sick? They should call for the elders of the church and have them pray over them, anointing them with oil in the name of the Lord. The prayer of faith will save the sick, and the Lord will raise them up; and anyone who has committed sins will be forgiven. There-fore confess your sins to one another, and pray for one another so that you may be healed. The prayer of the righteous is power-ful and effective.

James 13-16

Anointing and healing ministry seem to go together these days as Protes-tants reclaim this ancient practice so well known to Catholics. Many ministers carry small vials of anointing oil to use as the need arises. People who come to healing services often expect to be anointed as they receive laying on of hands.

It was not always so, but the hunger for the personal, physical contact anoint-ing offers has been with us for many years. In the late 1970's Jim, the pastor of a large congregation, attended a retreat in which he was introduced to the practice of anointing. He found it beautifully meaningful. The next Sunday, quite impul-sively, Jim told his congregation that he had experienced anointing while he was away, and would like to share the experience with them. Anyone who wanted could stay after church for anointing and healing prayer. Jim had not planned to issue this invitation, and during the rest of the service his better judgment told him that he should have paved the way a little. Silently he admonished himself: "I should have introduced it to a study group first, then maybe have tried it on a church retreat after folks had a chance to get used to the idea. Oh well, there'll just be a few and maybe I can head off any flack..."

After the postlude he was stunned to realize that nearly everyone had stayed to be anointed. An hour later he was still praying individually with the people who instinctively realized that anointing might meet the hunger they felt for a concrete and personal sign of God's love.

Anointing seems appropriate in many different contexts. It can be used whenever there is prayer and laying on of hands, or as a part of special healing services of various kinds. It can be a sign of blessing or of sending forth, or of God's forgiveness. It can seal our identity in Christ, or it can be a physically-experienced sign of God's love.

It can also have unique meaning to the one being anointed. One of the most creative uses of anointing I have seen was done with a person who was a survivor of a fanatic sect. This group encouraged emotional public confession, followed by a symbolic punishment of "thirty-nine lashes" with a rope. Though the thirty-nine lashes were administered lightly, each lash was accompanied with dreadful words that underlined how sinful the recipient was. Not surprisingly the survivor was suffering from great shame and a sense of profound unworthiness. The guilt-producing words as well as the shame-filled memory of a ritual public beating, were burned into the survivor's mind and heart and spirit.

' Together a Gestalt Pastoral Care Minister and the survivor decided that what was needed for healing was a liturgy which would bring "thirty-nine of something good." With permission, the minister drew thirty-nine crosses with oil on the face, arms and feet of the survivor. As each cross was made, she verbally proclaimed a different affirmation of God's care and love. For example:

- •I anoint you with this cross as a sign that you belong to God who forgives and loves you.
- •I anoint you with this cross to say that you do not have to suffer to earn God's love.
- •I anoint you with this cross, a sign of your faith in Christ who died for you.
- •I seal you with this sign of your faith and proclaim that there is no condemnation in Christ.

115

The survivor reported that this small liturgy was "just marvelous." God worked powerfully through it to heal this humiliating experience, and to exchange a "new heart" for a shattered one.

PERSONALIZED HEALING LITURGIES: THE HEALING OF A CONCENTRATION CAMP SURVIVOR

Out of Gestalt Pastoral Care work has come some wonderful healing liturgies that combine traditional liturgical elements with intimate knowledge of a personal need. One example is the story of the thirty-nine crosses, using the traditional practice of anointing. Another is a Liturgy of Lies and Truth, described below. The framework of this liturgy echoes the Sermon on the Mount where several times Jesus says "You have heard that it was said… But I say to you..." (Matthew 5:21-48).

Kathy's family was European, and living in Japan when World War II broke out. Kathy, along with her mother and sisters found themselves in a concentration camp where they remained for much of the war. In the camp there was very little food, and the guards were unmerciful. In this desperate situation it happened that Kathy's mother had the chance to send her starving children out of the camp to live with a community of nuns. It was a terrible choice. She knew she would not see her children for months, maybe even years, but they would have enough to eat. She agonized between their need for motherly comfort and their need for physical survival. In the end she chose to send her children away.

As it turned out, these nuns were not kind to the children in their care. In fact, they were cruel, and Kathy bears many scars as a result. One memory Kathy carries is that of The Box, a form of punishment in which children were placed for hours inside a closed wooden box. They would be put in The Box for crying, not obeying instantly, bedwetting, and other natural behaviors of upset children. When Kathy's little brother was inside The Box, Kathy would try to comfort him by hugging the outside of The Box and speaking softly to him. She would be punished for this as well. She was told often that she was a very bad girl.

No wonder Kathy had a fear of nuns and convents as an adult. Any exposure produced dreaded flashbacks to the horror of her childhood. Kathy worked hard and long in therapy, and had experienced much improvement. She also prayed with faith imagination and experienced Jesus, very present, weeping with her in the concentration camp and the convent. Even so, the phobias and flashbacks continued.

Then Kathy signed up for a two-year training program in spiritual direction. Her excitement about the program soon turned to despair when she found out that this United Methodist group was going to meet in a Roman Catholic retreat house run by an order of nuns. Bravely, she stuck it out, trying her best to control her fears. But because of her severe reaction to being in a convent, she was not getting much out of the course.

When I was scheduled to make a presentation to the class on individualized liturgies of healing Kathy welcomed the opportunity to be the focus of a healing liturgy. In preparation for the actual liturgy, the class and I worked with Kathy to identify the lies she had been taught by the awful experience of her childhood. She listed the following lies:

•All nuns are cruel and sadistic.

•I'm not lovable enough for my mother to have kept me with her.

•God forgot about me when I was a child.

•It was OK with God that our family suffered.

•I'm a very bad girl.

It is important to understand that Kathy knew very well that none of this was true. She had no trouble identifying these lies as lies. She also recognized that emotionally and spiritually she believed them.

Notice that the lies did not deny the actual events. We did not say that it was a lie that she was in a concentration camp, nor was it a lie that her mother sent her to the convent. None of the lies concerned what someone else felt either. For example, we would not have called it a lie that her mother didn't love Kathy enough to find a better way; not even Kathy could know that for sure. The lies had to do with only three things: what Kathy herself concluded, (or was taught) about the world, about God, and about herself as a result of these experiences.

When it came time for the liturgy itself, with Kathy's permission we invited two nuns from the convent to join us. To our surprise, the sisters raided the convent attic, donned the outdated long black habits of their order, and walked into our meeting room looking very nunny indeed. Immediately Kathy visibly shrank, but bravely repeated her permission for them to be there. Their participation was to be a crucial part of her healing liturgy.

The class, now understanding itself as a congregation of Christ's church, was invited to participate in proclaiming the gospel to Kathy in a special, personalized, and structured way. Although I explained about healing liturgies in general and the basic flow of our service ahead of time, we went ahead without detailed planning. With the list of lies on newsprint, we prayerfully relied on the Spirit to empower us to speak the gospel to Kathy in a personal way.

We began by asking the Holy Spirit to speak through us to Kathy and the little girl inside her. Then each member of the tiny congregation had a turn in anointing Kathy by drawing a cross on her forehead. Then each person proclaimed that one of the lies that had gotten inside Kathy was indeed a lie. Each person ended by speaking the gospel response to the lie, and quoted or paraphrased scripture to underline their personal proclamation to Kathy.

Notice as I describe what happened, how the truth-telling did not have a condemning or preachy tone. No one told Kathy that she shouldn't feel that way, or that she should remember that she was no longer a little child, or that she should forgive and forget. Proclaiming the gospel to Kathy meant accepting her as she was, and announcing the gospel truth in the name of Jesus Christ. We paused often to allow Kathy to assimilate what she was experiencing, and after each turn we asked her permission to continue.

> First person: *Kathy, you learned that you were not lovable enough for your mother to keep you with her. In the name of Jesus, that is a lie.*
>
> Congregation: *Amen!*

At the church's fervent amen Kathy began to cry, and she continued to weep softly throughout the liturgy.

> First person: *As a member of the body of Christ, I speak the truth to you now. The truth is Jesus loves you passionately and tenderly. You are lovable enough for him. Just as Jesus held the children on his lap, he held you when you were in Japan. Remember that God has promised to never leave you or forsake you.*
>
> Congregation: *Amen!*
>
> Second person: *Kathy, you decided as a child that God forgot about you. We understand why you would think so, but I proclaim to you that that is a lie.*
>
> Congregation: *Amen!*

Second person: *In the name of Jesus Christ I tell you the truth. God never forgot you. Remember you are carved on the palm of God's hand. We in this church believe that Jesus wept with you in that camp and in the convent. Jesus helped you survive.*

Congregation: *Amen!*

Third person: *Kathy, you have been taught by your experience in the concentration camp that all nuns are cruel and sadistic. That is a lie!*

Congregation: *Amen!*

Third person: *The truth is that most nuns are wonderful members of the church, and have dedicated their lives to living out the gospel in a very special way. Even when your nuns treated you badly, God was there saying "I am the Lord your God who takes hold of your right hand and says to you, 'Fear not, I will help you.'"*

Congregation: *Amen!*

At this point there was one lie not yet addressed, the one that told Kathy "You're a very bad girl." Spontaneously the two nuns came forward, and instinctively knowing the power of liturgy, solemnly knelt in front of Kathy. One brought her a small gift, a cross she had made. She said she wanted Kathy to have it as a sign of her respect and care for Kathy. As the nun gave her the cross she sang a special song just for Kathy. Kathy does not remember the song itself, but she clearly remembers how that song soothed the bereft, lonely, and fearful little girl.

The other nun spoke the truth against the lie of being a bad girl:

Kathy, what those nuns told you was a terrible lie. You were never a bad girl, just a lonely, afraid, sad girl. You were God's daughter then and you are God's daughter now. Remember that God loves you with an everlasting love. That is the truth, and I proclaim it to you as a member of the church and as a nun.

In the silence which followed our "amen" Kathy wept harder. It was clear that something was shifting inside her. The nun continued, inspired to offer herself as a ritual representative of those nuns of Kathy's childhood:

On behalf of my sisters in that convent in Japan, I repent of cruelty. I'm sorry we did that to you. It was very wrong for any-

> *one to hurt a child, and it certainly wasn't how nuns are sup-*
> *posed to act. I ask God to forgive and heal any nuns who treat*
> *children with cruelty. And I pray that God will heal you.*

Wisely she did not demand that Kathy forgive, knowing that she might not be ready yet. The important step of forgiving her tormentors more deeply would be for another day.

As the church responded with "amen," something old and painful melted in Kathy. As she wept, one of the nuns crooned another healing song to her. Shyly through her tears Kathy reached out her hand. The nuns did not rush in with smothering hugs. Again they waited until Kathy was ready. Finally Kathy hugged both sisters, whispering to each, "Thank you."…"Thank you." The service ended with prayer and laying of hands for Kathy, followed by a reflection time in which the group spoke about what had happened for them. Clearly, it was not only Kathy who was affected. Many of the group felt they had been on holy ground.

Kathy felt much better after the service, but she knew that there was one more step the group could take on her behalf. Accordingly, a few group members walked with Kathy around the convent later on, stopping where Kathy was particularly reminded of the Japanese convent. Statues, shrines, and the chapel were places where they sprinkled water. At each site they proclaimed that the convent belonged to God, and that Christ was present there.

That night Kathy called her husband; she joyfully and with great excitement announced the change she felt. "I hugged some nuns today!" she exclaimed to her startled mate. A month or so later she told me that she was fully able to go to her class in the convent without fear or flashbacks, and that the nuns had become her new friends.

I have come to believe that God often heals through such simple liturgies of declaration. As I describe Kathy's ritual, it might seem that all we did was assail Kathy with a kind of holy pep talk. But somehow, as the church speaks the truth in this way, God enables hearts to embrace what minds already know.

Others have reported life-changing healing as a result of this Liturgy of Lies and Truth first created by Kathy and her class. They have addressed lies such as:

•I have to punish myself.

•I can't let myself feel better if my family is still messed up.

•I'm not allowed to surpass my father.

- If I really let myself get creative, no one will like me, and God will think I'm proud.

- Women aren't supposed to be assertive.

- I was born bad, and I'm still bad.

UNDOING DAVE'S CHILDHOOD VOWS

One day when Dave was six and walking alone on a railroad track, he made two vows, not that he knew what a vow was. That day something shifted in him that added up to a lifelong promise to himself, and he finally gave in to the despair that he had been fighting since he was very tiny. All his short life he had tried hard to get the love he so desperately needed. After the day on the railroad tracks he simply stopped trying. Although he couldn't have articulated it then, he vowed, first of all, that he would never love anyone again. Second, never again would he let anyone love him.

At the time, his vows made a lot of sense, for his loveless childhood was full of devastating losses and rejection. Making these vows made it possible to insulate himself from pain and helped him survive as he grew up. After a time the actual vows were forgotten, but by then they had become a way of life.

At age forty, he entered a Gestalt Pastoral Care growth process. He spoke of how his relationships never worked out, especially with women. He wept over his loneliness. A devout Christian, he very much desired to love others without deadening fear. As we worked together for many months things did get better, but we both knew that there were some deeper steps to take before he would be free to love with joy and abandon.

One day the memory of walking along the railroad tracks surfaced, and with it Dave was able to name the vows he had made so long ago. He realized that his childhood vows had powerfully influenced his whole life. Together we decided to create a liturgy for him to renounce and *undo* his childhood vows, and to formally take new faith-filled and life-giving vows.

The liturgy itself was very simple, and was set in the context of a celebration of Eucharist with his Bible study group. At the appropriate time he told the story of the six year old who made vows on the railroad track, and how the vows had helped him survive. He also told how these same vows later kept him from meaningful adult relationships. He was now trusting God through the prayers of this group to set him free.

Then Dave, with the help of the small congregation, formally turned away from that which had ruled his life:

> Congregation: *Dave, when you were a child, you decided never to love again. Are you ready now to embrace a different way?*
>
> Dave: *Yes I am, with God's help.*
>
> Congregation: *Dave, you also vowed never again to let another love you. Are you ready to give up this vow, and open yourself to the joys and risks of intimacy?*
>
> Dave: *Yes I am, knowing that God's grace calls me forward.*

As the Bible study group stood in a circle of support, Dave made his new vows:

> *My greatest desire is to love and be loved, and I firmly believe that God wants that for me. For my part, I promise to turn away from a way of death, and, as best I can, to embrace the life God gives me. I promise to pray for courage and discernment whenever I feel myself shrink in fear from an opportunity for intimacy. I promise to trust that God will shape my life in ways that will be a blessing to me and to others. Amen.*

Then the congregation laid hands on him and prayed for the healing of his fear and of the terrible experiences that created the fear in the first place.

Although not dramatic on the outside, the results of this liturgy were immediately obvious to Dave. It was as if a door opened which enabled him to meet his crippling fears in a new way. It seemed clear to him that God's grace was indeed at work, and slowly the fears decreased. During this time the support of his Bible study group was crucial. Several months later he was able to point to his special liturgy as a pivotal point in his growth. He is now happily married to a wonderful woman and has several children in whom he delights.

CLEANSING

A natural opportunity for an individualized healing liturgy occurs in survivors of sexual abuse, who can feel dirty, polluted and guilty because of what was done to them. Ritual cleansing with water can be a powerful experience of God's power to transform. It can be quite freeing to hear a congregation affirm that they are not guilty for what happened, nor does their body belong to anyone else, and that they are cleansed by God's living water. Survivors have reported much healing as they allow the church to minister to them in this way. After her cleansing liturgy in which she was splashed with water by the specially-gathered congregation of eight, one woman said, "Oh my gosh, I can't believe it. I feel new, like a baby. I'm not dirty any more! I really am clean!"

VOCATIONAL DEDICATION AND BLESSING

A woman felt that her spiritual journey was leading her both to be baptized and to dedicate her musical career to God. A small group of friends gathered at her house one evening as a congregation to support her in taking these important steps in her spiritual life. After her baptism she publicly thanked God for her music and made a formal act of dedication in which she promised to play for God's glory. Then we laid hands on her, asking for God's blessing and guidance for her as a musician. Following Eucharist she joyfully played a beautiful mini-concert for us, and we ended the celebration with a delicious spaghetti dinner she had prepared. Six years after the liturgy in her home I ran into her in a store. She reported that the effects of the liturgy were still with her. "It really makes a difference in the way I make music," she told me. "That was a wonderful evening."

We church folks say that we believe in the ministry of the laity and that God calls Christians to many different vocations. Yet it is unusual for the church to recognize liturgically any other vocation except those that have to do with church-related jobs. I believe that ministers of healing need to develop liturgical counterparts to ordination for those who are most surely called by God to so-called "secular" vocations.

LITURGICAL ACTIONS PREPARING FOR NEXT STEPS

A woman buried a rock in the woods while friends supportively sang hymns and prayed for her to be empowered to "bury the hatchet." After much inner work, her desire was to finally let go of the resentment that had poisoned her relationships and made her miserable for years.

Another woman planted flowers in a bare and desolate place as a sign she was embracing God's promise of hope and new life – even in desolation. As the flowers were placed in the ground, friends sang hymns and prayed for her. Then they anointed her and affirmed their own faith that God would be with her through thick and thin.

CELEBRATION OF GROWTH

At a celebration of Eucharist with close friends, an Episcopal priest formally added the name "Francis" to his birth name. He wanted to symbolize the new man he was becoming after a two-year period of turmoil and rapid inner growth, and he wanted the church to bless his journey. He, too, took new vows to live his life more faithfully and joyfully. He felt his special service was both a prayer of thanksgiving and an affirming benediction for work already done.

HEALING AN OLD GRIEF

Another healing liturgy took the form of a funeral for a baby who was stillborn 30 years before. The mother, June, never saw her child. She came home from the hospital five days after the birth to find that well-meaning friends had cleaned the house in her absence and had taken away all reminders of the baby. The tiny clothes, the cradle, the shower gifts were all gone. The result was that June, already numbed to her feelings, just stepped back into her old routine without ever grieving her baby's death. There was no funeral, no recognition of her tremendous loss, nor was the baby given a name.

Thirty years later June was in weekly Gestalt Pastoral Care when the memory of her daughter's death surfaced. Along with the memory came old feelings that were still intact, and June finally wept for her daughter. "She didn't even get a name," she sobbed. "She at least deserved that much."

I suggested that even now she could name the baby and that we could have a funeral for her. June loved the idea. In preparation for the liturgy June wrote a poem to her daughter and named her. She baked the bread for Eucharist, picked out some hymns, and arranged flowers from her garden.

The funeral itself was attended by June's grown children, her husband, and two close friends. Although some found it all a little strange, they loved June and wanted to support her. The funeral followed pretty closely a traditional liturgy for the death of an infant. June read her poem and shared the name she had chosen.

As we prayed that the child be committed to the care of the Lord, June saw an image of Jesus tenderly holding her baby and baptizing her. In this small intimate setting June felt free to tell the others what she was experiencing, and together we gave thanks for this grace. This image, more than anything else, set June's heart at rest that her baby was with God. The liturgy enabled June to find closure for her grief. She was finally able to let go and move on with renewed energy and joy.

Sophie doesn't want to talk like us,
so we are going to learn how to talk like Sophie.
Louise Norberg

8

ENTERING ANOTHER'S WORLD

Perls didn't specifically teach his students to enter another's world, but he did teach them to pay exquisite attention to another's homeostatic process. Again and again he demonstrated that a person's moment-by-moment body/mind process held all that was needed to guide Gestalt work. In that sense, he had profound respect for the people who asked to work with him.

A Christian perspective bids us not only to respect other people's healing processes, but also to love them as human beings. I believe this means that we must learn to appreciate another's unique spin on the world without judging, controlling, or trying to be impressive. We must pray to be compassionate no matter what someone tells us. We must be willing to try on someone else's existence in an effort to genuinely be with that person. I call this willingness "entering another's world."

My Mother's Lesson

My mom showed me how to enter another's world when I was eight years old. She was a third grade teacher with a reputation for being able to get through to the most difficult kids. After school and on weekends she "tutored" some of these children in our living room as I played nearby. Although Mom was not formally trained as a psychotherapist, I now know that I grew up observing a natural-born, intuitive, warm, and perceptive therapist at work.

One of her tutoring kids was Sophie, a four-year-old Down Syndrome child who didn't talk. Actually she did talk, but her one and only word was "ocky-pooky." Ocky-pooky meant anything Sophie wanted it to mean.

Mom: *Sophie, do you want to look at this picture?*

Sophie: (with eagerness) *Ocky-pooky!*

126

Mom: *It's time to pick up the toys now and go home.*

Sophie: (with distress and anger) *Ocky-pooky!*

Many people had tried to coerce or persuade Sophie to talk, reasoning that if she could say "ocky-pooky," she could say other things. Sophie never responded. After Sophie had come for tutoring the first time, Mom told me that Sophie didn't want to talk like us, so we were going to learn to talk like Sophie. She began to imitate whatever Sophie did – the repetitive motions, the crazy postures, the tone of each ocky-pooky.

One day I walked in on a particularly bizarre scene. Mom and Sophie were both lying on their backs on the living room floor with their legs and arms stuck straight up in the air. They were conversing, sort of, but the only thing either was saying was "ocky-pooky," back and forth, back and forth. As if this were perfectly normal, Mom said "Hey Tilda, come lie down here and ocky-pooky with Sophie." So I lay down on the floor and joined in; a few minutes later my little sister Evelyn got in on the game.

Soon we were helping Mom ocky-pooky with Sophie every Saturday. We found it great fun; Sophie *loved* it. She was always the leader, and we took all our cues from her. We took whatever position Sophie was in; if she was upside down with her head hanging off the seat of a chair, Mom, Evelyn, and I did the same. Then we tried to imitate exactly the way she said ocky-pooky. If Sophie snorted or whispered or yelled we tried our best to sound just like her. If she was quiet we didn't make a peep.

Evelyn and I were never allowed to laugh until Sophie did, but sooner or later Sophie would find the whole thing very funny, and she would start to giggle. Our own pent-up giggles would explode then, and usually the sessions would end with all four of us laughing on the floor. Then one Saturday Sophie was ready. She sat up, looked Mom in the eye, and said loudly and distinctly, "I want a cookie!"

My sister and I, schooled to repeat whatever Sophie did, parroted her request, and then completely lost it. "Sophie talked! Sophie talked!" we yelled. Mom, who ordinarily parceled out cookies very sparingly, gave us the biggest cookie bonanza ever, the whole bag.

Sophie kept repeating, "I want a cookie" each time she took a bite. Now happier than ever to be of service, Evelyn and I responded with, "I want a cookie too" as we scarfed cookies with her. Sophie left proudly that day with cookie mush smeared all over her face, and a little smile of triumph.

Under Mom's expert and compassionate direction we had entered Sophie's world enough for her to risk entering ours. She was the host and we were the guests, and all of us knew it. Furthermore, we *enjoyed* her world. It was fun to be goofy and talk gibberish and assume zany postures. It was a new and freeing experience for Sophie to be directly in control of things; and it was an interesting novelty for Evelyn and me to let a much younger child control us.

I believe Sophie decided to talk that Saturday because she finally felt safe. I'm certain she felt loved and valued for herself as she was, for she was not pressured to change in any way. Instead, it was our challenge to taste the delights of her world.

LOVING

Our only real starting point with a person is right where they are. God doesn't ask for change before pouring out love; we must offer the same acceptance to others as best we can. If we are willing simply to allow the love of Christ to flow through us, even before we pray for healing or do anything skillful or wise, we are already being used for healing. Loving in this way helps create a safe healing environment in which people feel free to push beyond old boundaries.

It sounds simple and even trite: just love people for who they are; but anyone who has tried it knows that genuine acceptance does not always come easily. Judgments, labels, self-righteous advice, or comparisons easily creep in.

A young woman came to her first session with me complaining of being tired and grouchy all the time and wanting help to be "more cheerful and energetic." As she told her story, it became clear that her husband was pretty demanding: he expected her to keep the house spotless, iron his shirts, fix his meals and take care of the kids while he relaxed. The fact that she also worked full time didn't matter; "Women's work is women's work," he would say. Actually, neither spouse seemed to question this division of labor. When I asked what was stopping her from telling her husband she needed a fairer arrangement, her reply was "But I *like* to keep the house sparkling!"

At that moment, I left her world and landed squarely in mine. My inner voice protested loudly, "Good grief! Where is your backbone? Why don't you tell this bozo to get off his fanny and pull his weight around the house? And why are you not claiming your identity as an equal partner in this marriage?" Of course I knew better than to say this aloud, but with that tape running in my head, I had surely failed to stay with her. Instead of loving her, I judged her harshly, and her husband too. I let my own anger about having been put into confining niches by the church get mixed up with what she was feeling about her marriage. Instead of seeing her as a woman with an important issue to work on, I judged her as a woman who was wrong for not reacting as I had.

She didn't come back after that day, and I don't blame her. Quite likely she was getting ready to come to some conclusions of her own about her situation, but she must have sensed that I wasn't with her in her just-dawning awareness that something was not right. If I had been able to enter her world, I might have asked her tired, grouchy self to talk to the part of her that liked to "keep the house sparkling." That experiment would have been close to where she was that day.

The challenge is to learn the texture and appreciate the riches of another's world even when a part of us is busy with judgments and labels – for we will never be able to love perfectly. As we confess our inability to love, however, we are enabled by grace to be more and more compassionate. As we become more aware of our own desires for control and power and admiration, we can give them up as our own healing becomes more complete.

Thus we must enter another's world asking, "What is it like to be this person? What is it like to have experienced things the way this person did, to believe the way this person does? To have the body of this person? To have these particular obstacles, this pain? To pray as this person does? How has God's call, intermingled with desires and talents, shaped this person? We listen closely for the perceptual modalities the person uses, and try to respond in kind. (I'll explain perceptual modalities below.) We listen carefully to the names of the players in a person's life so we can use their names too. As best we can, we try to join the person in their cultural, ethnic, and sexual identity.

We must begin to pick up cues about the nature of this other world as soon as we have contact with a person. Does he seem relaxed and easy? Then we can search for that attitude in ourselves. Is he tense, and if so, what is the nuance of that tension? Jittery? Anxious? Angry? Full of dread? Haunted? Self conscious? As we begin to sense his existence, we can begin to be a true guest, experiencing the world from his point of view.

One individual will have a direct let's-get-right-to-it style as she opens up to her healing process. She may easily involve her body as she does inner work;

she might smack her hands together for emphasis, get angry, curl up in a ball, or sob. We will have little trouble knowing what is going on with her; it will all be right out there.

Another person may do none of these things. Everything may seem muted, softer, slower. He may cry or get angry, but it will have little of the outward drama of the first person. Yet he is moving inside. He is making progress. Things are happening. Somehow we know that he is not resisting, but simply working in his own style.

It is up to us as ministers to stretch to meet the style of whomever we are working with. Sometimes we must work with vivid colors and noise; other times we will be working in pastels. With one person we can be rather formal and rely on the language of ritual; with another we can lapse into a laid-back familiarity. Obviously if we are trying to enter another's world, we will not try to get that person to do things in the style that is comfortable for us.

Jesus certainly entered into the world of his friends and followers. The incarnation does not only mean that Jesus became human, but that he participated in the reality of actual lives. In contrast to some Christian groups of our own time, he treated different people differently. He spoke their language: to fishermen he promised "Follow me and I will make you fish for people"(Matthew 4:19). He spoke to the woman at the well in the language of her own Samaritan theological heritage (John 4:7-26). Honoring local custom, he asked lepers to bathe themselves in the river and to show themselves to the priest, who would confirm the cure (Luke 17:11-19). He sternly called the Pharisees and Sadducees to repentance (Matthew 23:1-39), but with Zaccheus the tax collector he was gentle, and invited himself to his house to spend the night (Luke 19:2-5). With the rich young ruler he made a terrifying demand to sell everything and give it to the poor (Matthew 19:21), but the influential and well-off Nicodemus, a "leader of the Jews," was invited to the spiritual renewal of being "born of water and Spirit" (John 3:5). He invited some people to travel with him (Mathew 9:9), but at least one person who begged to come along was told, "Return to your home, and declare how much God has done for you" (Luke 8:39). Some he sent out two by two to spread the gospel (Luke 10:1-9), but Mary, the sister of Martha, was simply encouraged to sit with him (Luke 10:38-42).

DIFFERENCES IN WORSHIP AND PRAYER

As ministers strive to enter another's world, they may find the most difficult challenge in matters of piety and devotional style. What may be very meaningful to one person may be dismissed as sentimental and shallow by another. A person who speaks in tongues, prays spontaneously, and sings loud choruses may be misunderstood or judged by one who responds best to rich liturgy and classical sacred music. And most certainly vice versa. There are many differing styles of Christian worship and prayer, and most of us have chosen to participate in just a small portion of the heritage we share.

Clergy in particular, with our theological sophistication and consciousness of what makes for "good worship", often find it really hard to enter into the way God may speak to someone who is simpler and maybe purer in heart. We may roll our eyes at styles of prayer foreign to our own tradition or culture or personal style. However, it is up to us to find a way to be comfortable with the particular ways people in our care experience God. Here especially we must learn to speak new languages and value differences, even if we can't join in.[29] In the process, it just might happen that our own prayer is enriched by the gifts inherent in another style. This spiritual flexibility[30] is one of the marks of a Gestalt Pastoral Care minister.

This means that I, as a United Methodist clergyperson, have had to learn about and *appreciate,* for example, Roman Catholic devotion to Mary, the richly complex Russian Orthodox liturgical system and its tremendous awe of God's holiness, the teachings of the saints about contemplation, the Mennonite focus on community, and the noisy, joyful enthusiasm of Pentecostals. With Jewish people, I have encountered the rich concepts of God from the Hebrew Bible: Yahweh of the burning bush (Exodus 3:1-6), the still small voice speaking to Elijah (I Kings 19:11-12), the God of the Psalms who is "my rock and my fortress" (Psalms 31:3).

In short, we share a basic commandment to love God and others, and there are myriad ways to live our response. All Christian traditions have gifts to give as well as problems to overcome. Pastoral care is not an arena for making clones of ourselves; instead we must seek to let God shape people as God wants. And, it is

---

[29] For example, one who does not have the gift of tongues cannot pretend that he has this gift.
[30] Author Kathleen Norris (*Dakota* and *Cloister Walk*) is one who has this kind of flexibility. She is a Protestant who attends a small, ordinary church in a farming community. She is also a Benedictine Oblate, and periodically goes to a Roman Catholic monastery for extended periods. Both experiences have shaped her unique spirituality.

always possible that we ministers might be shaped too as we discover the gifts of traditions not our own.

PERCEPTUAL SYSTEMS

An important way to speak the inner language of another person is to learn to adapt to the unique way he or she perceives the world. Joining another in a perceptual system may sound a little daunting, but with some awareness and a little practice it can become a natural response. There are four basic modes of perception that people use to take in the world: visual, auditory, sensate and cognitive. These perceptual systems also affect the way they imagine, remember and pray.

Visual

Most people are visualizers, and perceive the world through their eyes. They tend to form mental pictures, even when thinking abstract thoughts. I am a strong visualizer; when I was in seminary I couldn't understand or even remember theological concepts until I was able to form some kind of picture in my mind. People like me will often prefer to pray with images – they will "see" Jesus sitting with them for example, and will have no trouble seeing visual details in a memory. Even their language will reflect this preference. They might say, "I see" when they understand, and might refer to a bad experience as a "horrible scene."

Auditory

Others prefer to take in the world with their ears and may need to muse out loud so that they themselves can know what they are thinking. In prayer, they tend to hear words from God with their inner ears, but may not have images at all. In their childhood memories, sounds will be vivid to them. Language patterns will tend to have many auditory references such as "Sounds good to me" or "I hear you."

Sensate

Sensate people are those who experience the world through body sensations. They will remember things through the sensation that accompanied the original experience. They will talk about how "my stomach just dropped when that happened" or perhaps they will mention, "I just don't feel good about it." In prayer, they may sense the presence of God, and that sensing may be full of meaning and communication, but they may not hear or see anything.

Cognitive

Finally, cognitive perceivers, or thinkers, are the ones who truly need to have rational understanding before they can take something in. They must analyze and categorize before they can change. In their prayer, they may get a new idea or receive a revelation that transforms everything. It is *ideas* that light up the world for them. Their language is laced with thinking referents such as, "That makes sense to me" or "I think that's right. " One thinker I know said, for example, that it was only when she *understood* how patterns were being repeated in her family for generations that she was able to break from them.

Thinkers in a growth group may be accused of resisting because they are "in their heads," but thinkers really must approach the world this way. In doing so, they are just being themselves. Intellectualizing, though, is often used by non-cognitive people as a perfect way to avoid dealing with feelings. It takes some skill and discernment to determine whether a person is avoiding her feelings or is truly a thinker.

Identifying Perceptual Styles

If I'm not sure what a person's preferred perceptual modality is, I like to ask him to go back in time and be in the kitchen of the house he lived in when he was 10 years old. Then I listen carefully to how he talks about the experience.

- A visualizer might say, "I see the kitchen sink and the old yellow mixing bowl."
- A person in auditory modality might say, " I hear my mother mixing something in the old mixing bowl.
- A sensate person might report a memory of warmth, love and anticipation and something good to eat.
- A thinker might very well explain a concept that puts a frame of meaning around the memory such as, "The kitchen was an expression of the tension in my parent's marriage."

Remember that most people are comfortable with a mixture of these four modalities, but will usually prefer one over the other three. Memories of the childhood kitchen might be, for example, mostly visual with some auditory and sensate components, or strongly cognitive with a bit of sensate perceiving. Keep in mind, too, that nearly all of us have the capacity to experience things in our non-preferred modalities, and we may even switch modalities from day to day. Or perhaps we will experience prayer in a sensate modality, for example, but will become visual if asked to remember something from the past. When a person switches modalities, it is important for the pastoral guide to switch also.

When a minister identifies a person's perceptual system, he can begin to use that language and can suggest experiments and ways of praying which fit the person's system. For example, asking a sensate person to visualize in faith imagination can be frustrating and guilt-producing. If instead, a pastor says, "feel yourself in the presence of Christ" something may happen.

Obviously, a minister working with the perceptual system of others must know what her own system is in order to consciously leave it and shift to what may be more unfamiliar territory. It is well worth the effort. People report feeling very understood when a minister is willing to work within their perceptual systems.

Bioenergy

Bioenergy is the energy field or "aura" that surrounds all living things. Perceiving the bioenergy of another person is not really all that difficult; mostly it involves giving yourself permission to have this awareness. In fact, it is likely that you unknowingly respond to bioenergy already. As you become more adept at sensing bioenergy, you will be able to discern areas of "deadness" or "aliveness" in a person's body. You will perceive whether a person's energy is "murky" or "clear." You will know to be cautious with one whose energy is permeable, absorbing whatever is suggested. Increasingly, you will know without being told when someone has shut down emotionally or spiritually. You will begin to sense when a subtle inner shift has occurred in someone. You might find yourself assuming a similar physical posture as the person with whom you are working, using her gestures and even breathing with the same rhythm. With increased awareness of bioenergy you may discover how to match your own bioenergy with that of someone in your office, speeding yourself up for a "speedy" person and slowing down for someone who isn't so fast. I realize all this might sound a little strange to many Western readers, but those who are familiar with acupuncture or other kinds of bodywork will find it quite familiar. (I will discuss working with energy in more detail in Chapter Fourteen.)

CULTURAL DIFFERENCES

Entering into the world of people from a culture different from our own is sure to stretch us. Asian young adults, for example, separate from their parents in a very different manner from the way American young adults go about it. Conflicts are resolved differently, with less direct talk. The elaborate Asian politeness that may seem stilted to an American conveys deep respect and honor to an Asian. In their world, courtesy must remain even when strong anger is present.

Language itself reflects these differences; some concepts are almost impossible to translate. That is why from time to time I have asked a person whose first language is not English to describe important aspects of his growth process in his own language. Then I just watch what happens to his voice, body and bioenergy, and work with that. A Swahili native-speaker who was struggling to put into English his feelings of abandonment as a child, found he was able to *experience* the feelings only when I suggested he express them in Swahili. As he spoke in Swahili to his father who had left the family when he was very young, he wept for the very first time in his adult life.

Entering the World of an African Village

Years ago I led a retreat on healing prayer in which the whole group was able to enter into the world of an African village. One of the participants was a young African nun who brought to the retreat her pain concerning a cruelly abusive cousin. This cousin, older than her by ten years, made life miserable for her when she was a child. He frequently hit her, pulled her hair, and scratched her with thorns. He ate her food, and threatened to really hurt her if she told. Starting when she was a first-grader, he made her carry his heavy school books on her head. He called her names and told her every day that she was worthless. His daily tormenting became more intense as the years went on. Several times she told her grandmother and her parents; each time the boy was scolded, and each time he punished her severely for getting him in trouble. She was terrified of him, but he was impossible to avoid in her small village.

Despite his harassment she shone academically, and when she was in high school she received a thrilling invitation to go to Brussels to be educated by the same order of nuns who ran the village school. She was so excited she could hardly sleep or eat, but she was beside herself with anxiety about whether she would get permission to accept the offer.

A decision of such tremendous magnitude could only be made by the male elders of the village. The Men's Council allowed no women to speak, not even the one being discussed. During this important meeting, her cousin slandered her, telling terrible lies. On the strength of his testimony, The Men's Council was on the verge of saying no. Finally, pulling rank because of her great age, her grandmother burst into The Men's Council and gave an unprecedented speech. She demanded they let her granddaughter go to Brussels, not only because she deserved to go, but also because her education would be a great honor for the village. In the end, the Men's Council gave their permission.

The young woman had been in Brussels for less than a year when she was called home. Not only was her mother dying, but everyone believed that someone had deliberately caused her grave illness with a death curse. These suspicions were confirmed after the mother died a few days later; a man of the village confessed that he and the cruel cousin had paid a conjurer to unleash the curse.

The nun fully believed that the death curse had caused her mother to sicken and die. As she told her story she was weeping with sorrow, anger, and helplessness. She lamented that she had tried, and failed, to forgive. She also mentioned that she had never once told her cousin or even her immediate family what she was feeling.

I sensed that she would never be able to bridge the chasm of culture to confront this abusive man by herself, even in fantasy. Nothing in her African upbringing or in her formation as a nun had prepared her to speak for herself or to be angry on her own behalf. Nor was the American retreat group familiar with the world of an African village. I sensed, however, that if the retreat group could enter her world even a little, we might be able to support her growth.

In her world, every important event and decision, every major change is experienced and dealt with by the village as a whole. Individual preferences and feelings, so important in American culture, are much less important than the life of the group. With this in mind, I suggested that the nun choose some women from the retreat group to sit next to her, forming a "Women's Council." Their job would be to feel along with her, support her in speaking her truth, protect her from her cousin's wrath, and to pray for her. She loved the idea, and immediately asked every woman in the room to be part of it. As the women moved to sit near her, she asked the men in the room to be a "Men's Council of the Church." She asked that they hold her cousin down and compel him to listen to her, making sure that he couldn't retaliate.

Everyone agreed to this psychodrama, and suddenly it all became startlingly real, as four large men tightly held a pillow representing the cousin, and ordered him to listen and keep his mouth shut – or else! Then she began to speak, haltingly at first, but then visibly drawing strength from the women clustered around her, she told her cousin off for the first time ever. She told him that he was a bully and a coward, and an evil person. As she spoke, the women repeated her words, loudly and forcefully. Stronger now, she drew a verbal, public picture of exactly what a worm he was, and the group's response of outrage at her treatment was profoundly healing for her. In some way, we really had become her childhood village. Of course we were also the church, her "new village." As the church, we carried authority to speak the truth, and for her, the presence of a Roman Catholic priest as one of the village men was of particular importance. Like everyone else in her new village, the priest was indignant about the way she had been treated, and how no one had seemed to notice. He wholeheartedly joined in as we confronted the death curse itself saying, "In the name of Jesus Christ we break any curses directed at any of the —— family, and declare them null and void."

As we prayed for her, the nun felt herself letting go of the familiar, painful knot in her stomach, along with most of her anger. In its place was a renewed faith in God's grace, and a new sense of being safe and loved by her community. When I called her a few weeks later to get permission to tell her story, she repeated how very much the work had helped her. She felt so differently about herself, and was now hopeful that she would soon be ready to forgive her cousin. She also spoke of how grateful she was that the group had been "church" for her by "coming to Africa with me."

QUESTIONS

When I talk about entering another's world, there are always questions that arise quite soon in the discussion:

> *But shouldn't a minister confront people with what holds them back? What about speaking the truth in love, as Paul writes in Ephesians 4:15?*

Our first and most important job as Gestalt Pastoral Care ministers is to love in the present moment, without demanding or pressuring for any change at all. This is not to say that there is no pressure for change in a healing encounter. As a matter of fact, the person is likely to feel pressure aplenty at some point in the process. In a Gestalt Pastoral Process it is *God* who urges, nudges, shapes, invites, and speaks the truth. Very seldom does the Gestalt Pastoral Care minister preach or confront in the context of pastoral care. Our job is to help to "prepare the way of the Lord" (Isaiah 40:3) and then to get out of the way of what God is trying to accomplish.

> *Does this mean that we give away our own faith or ethics or identity in order to join another? Do we just become someone else?*

Of course not. We can't erase what is essential in ourselves even if we wanted to. However, we are ambassadors for Christ, and like a good ambassador, we strive to enter in. When someone issues an invitation to his or her very personal world, we must enter that world respectfully as a guest. It is as if we are in another country where we must learn to communicate in a new way. Language patterns, theology, history, family roles, fears, likes, dislikes are different from ours. Even the manner in which a body is expressive is unique to the one who has issued the invitation. We can stretch pretty far to live in this personal country, but we don't give up our own citizenship. Surely we can set aside such preferences as language, style and piety, without giving up our essential faith and identity.

Entering another's world is not the same as chameleon-like merging. We are there as a guest and companion, not a clone. My mother was still Mrs. Norberg, third grade teacher, no matter what wacky thing she did in someone else's world. She brought her compassionate love and good sense with her wherever she was. She did not merge with anyone, but she was passionately willing to visit.

Thus two caveats should be clear: first, we can't do anything in another's world that we think is wrong. I would not, for example, become involved in astrology with anyone, because I believe that astrology represents the antithesis of trusting God. I would try hard, however, to understand the place of astrology in another person's world. Second, we can't just take on someone else's problems. Letting ourselves be awash in someone's confusion and anguish only compounds the problem. Instead, we can do our best to feel into another person's experience, tasting but not swallowing, while being a steady, unafraid, hopeful presence.

How can we see what's wrong with a person without judging?

Getting rid of judgments does not mean we stop observing. In fact one of the most important things we do is observe keenly and sense accurately what is going on. We might note the rigidity of a woman's verbal responses, for example, and we see the tension of her body. We might feel the truncated, narrow, and perhaps moralistic nature of her spirituality, but we make these observations in the context of loving her. We don't label her a rigid person; we see her as a person needing to be rigid for now. We understand that rigidity has had a genuine purpose in her life, while recognizing her healthy desire to be looser and freer. We admit there may be similar rigidity in ourselves. We strive to see all of her with the eyes of Christ, who loves her just as she is right now.

PART THREE

USING GESTALT TECHNIQUES
IN PASTORAL CARE

Part Three goes beyond a Gestalt Pastoral Care perspective to discuss how the traditional Gestalt techniques of creating experiments, supporting resistance, working with polarities, and playfully exploring dreams can be used in the service of pastoral care and healing ministry.

Of particular relevance to pastoral counselors, Part Three also gives important background information to pastors and ministers of healing who will begin to work with a Gestalt Pastoral Care perspective.

...change can occur when the patient abandons, at least for the moment, what he would like to become and attempts to be what he is.
Arnold Beisser,
The Paradoxical Theory of Change

9

GESTALT EXPERIMENTS

Perhaps the most brilliant idea of Fritz Perls' is the use of Gestalt experiments. Even if he had produced no other innovation, this remarkable tool alone would have made his name.

Experiments are powerful because they can offer access to inner worlds and facilitate work with the material found there. They can dramatically and quickly increase awareness because they invite the discoveries that can come from direct experience. They can provide a way to listen to the wisdom of the body. They enable people to find their own answers at their own pace. They can greatly enhance the growth that is already occurring. They enable the re-living of memories, rather than just remembering and talking about them. In short, experiments create a "safe emergency"[31] in which to explore new reactions, awareness, or behavior. Although it takes practice to learn the skill of designing experiments, I believe the use of experiments makes a Gestaltist's job much simpler than that of a traditionally-trained counselor.

Good experiments, always rooted in the present, ideally reflect the whole of a person: behavior, tone of voice, physical positions, gestures, bioenergy, spirituality, verbal sharing, and so on. Remember, there is always discernible evidence of unfinished business pushing for resolution. The Holy Spirit is always nudging us toward wholeness, and quite often evidence of these nudges can be perceived by a Gestalt Pastoral Care Minister even before the person coming for healing is aware of them.

An experiment is usually a creation of the guide, who listens, watches, intuits and discerns, and then designs some action, or "work," based on the present moment. A good experiment catches and intensifies the seeker's experience of

---

[31] Polster and Polster, *Gestalt Therapy Integrated: Contours of Theory and Practice*, pp. 234-235.

the present, thus encouraging both greater awareness and deeper feelings. In other words, an experiment invites the person coming for healing to experience her process with awareness, rather than merely talk about what is bothering her. A Gestalt Pastoral Care Minister always makes it clear that the person coming for healing is in control; she is always free to consent to an experiment, to change it, or to say no altogether.

- •For example, perhaps she would be invited to make a figure of speech explicit: *"Let yourself be a pain in the neck, would you? Speak as if your painful neck has a separate voice."*

- •Maybe she would allow her past to be part of the present moment: *"Would you let yourself be eight years old for a few minutes instead of just remembering and talking about that time? What do you experience?"*

- •She might be invited to let an action flow from an interior place: *"Would you let your sadness have a physical motion? How about a sound as well?...What are you aware of now that you've done it?"*

- •Almost certainly she will be asked simply to broaden her awareness of the present: *"Are you willing to be aware of your chest? What's happening there right now?"*

Out of such simple experiments, important discoveries are made. A Gestalt guide does not pull these experiments out of the air, nor can she plan ahead for them. Instead, good experiments are closely based on what is happening right now. In the course of a session, one experiment leads to another as the seeking person follows her awareness continuum. Experiments seize each moment as it is unfolding and invite more awareness to emerge. Because experiments are based on the present moment, work with experiments can start within the first minutes of contact.

Because experiments are such a powerful tool, awareness can come quickly; doors can open to intense feelings; forgotten memories can flood in. For this reason, training in the use of Gestalt experiments is vital, even for experienced counselors. Gestalt training in the use of experiments consists of theory, supervised practice, and, most importantly, personal work with experiments in the student's own growth process. Generally speaking, no one should work with experiments unless he or she has had Gestalt training. At the end of this chapter, however, I outline a few simple experiments that those with a Gestalt Pastoral

Care perspective can try even without Gestalt training. Even such elementary experiments can greatly enrich a healing process.

FOLLOWING THE PROCESS

Usually a Gestalt Pastoral Care session will begin with brief verbal sharing. Perls the Purist would seldom allow such easing-in talk; he demanded, even from those working with him for the first time, an immediate dive into personal issues. I feel, however, that it is important to offer welcome and hospitality to one who is suffering. Why not? A bit of talking, a shared prayer, perhaps even a cup of tea, humanizes the experience. It reduces the expectation that the minister will be in control, and will do something clinical and wise to rescue the one in pain. It helps establish a feeling of comfort and safety from which to explore feelings that may be frightening, and sends the message that it is not the minister's techniques but the seeker's experience that is paramount. From the very first moments, however, the minister is already listening and watching closely, monitoring his own feelings and reactions to inform the suggestion of an experiment.

Sometimes it will be important for the person just to share news: the interview went well, my parents are visiting, the dog died. Or, she may need to report how the work of the previous session has settled. Maybe she needs to say that she has a headache, or that she has trouble praying these days. Perhaps she already knows what work she needs to do, and of course would share that as well. This beginning time usually takes less than five minutes; but in fact, verbal sharing may occasionally occupy many hours with someone who is not quite ready to try Gestalt experiments. Again, why not? If we trust people to do their own work, we must also trust them to know how long it takes to get ready to take the plunge.

EXPERIMENTS AND AWARENESS

Why not just ask the person what she is feeling, or what she is aware of in the present? Why make up complicated experiments when all we need do is ask? Sometimes, in fact, asking is all that is needed. Just asking, "What's going on now?" can indeed help the seeker stay with her process. However, especially in the beginning, this may not work at all. Why? The answer is rooted in our complex culture in which we learn not to feel. When asked, "What are you feeling right now?" many will say with complete sincerity, "I'm fine." "But what's going on right now?" a Gestaltist might persist. "Nothing," may well be the honest, but oblivious, answer.

Many of us have been conditioned to be unaware of feelings, perceptions, memories, intuitions, thoughts, and sensations that constantly lap at our shore. When we succeed in blocking out what seems like internal static, we believe we are learning to concentrate. We learn to focus on that which is outside of us in order to do a task, to meet the expectation of another, to anesthetize ourselves against pain or boredom, to fit in. So many jobs that pay the rent involve nearly robot-like activity, both mental and physical, with our attention directed almost exclusively outside ourselves. "Self-control," consisting of suppressing personal reactions, is highly valued.

It is impossible to deny that in our complex, technological world we must, in fact, learn to focus on particular tasks. As we continue to turn outward, how-ever, our own nuanced internal reactions can get lost, even to ourselves. We learn to ignore our tears and helplessness as we watch the news. We tune out whatever triggers our own fears. We lose touch with body sensations. We ignore our hunches and subtle feelings, and in the process, we miss our inner riches, the yeasty bub-bling of the life inside of us. We forget how to be delighted with the outrageous smell of an orange, or with the holy light that radiates from a loving person, or with the brave and astonishing color of a wildflower.

A Gestalt Pastoral Care minister assumes that, contrary to what a person might say, there is *always* something going on. There is always something surfac-ing; there are always feelings and sensations of which to be aware. This constant dance of awareness is profoundly about growth and health, for it is in the aware-ness continuum that the Holy Spirit whispers. Even when it really feels like abso-lutely nothing is happening, when awareness is nil, nothingness itself can be iden-tified and explored. "Would you sink down into nothingness and be in it? What's it like in there?" is one possible suggestion.

Over time, experiments teach how to maintain awareness of the present, and how to live in it. A person who has learned to be aware can, to a large extent, begin to design her own experiments and direct her own work. (In fact, Perls taught his students that the goal of therapy is to become your own therapist.) Just paying attention can suggest the next thing to do, and the thing after that. Being aware that a foot is moving in a particular way, for example, can suggest letting the foot "speak," i.e., putting full attention on the moving foot and talking as if the foot itself was speaking. For example:

> *I'm Tom's foot and I'm sort of jiggling. I'm impatient. I want to*
> *get on with it. I want to move, but Tom here is stuck in inertia.*
> *He can't believe that anything is really gonna change, and I'm*
> *sick of it!*

In this instance, the push toward growth and health is clearly being expressed by Tom's foot, and the foot's "speech" has suggested a new experiment:

> *Would you let your foot talk to the part of you that's stuck in*
> *inertia, and let your inertia talk back? Start with "I'm sick of*
> *being stuck."*

Sometimes just one experiment can open up awareness enough for the seeker
himself to know what to do next. A Roman Catholic man involved in full time
pastoral ministry asked to work with another student in the Gestalt Pastoral Care
training group on some issues regarding his witty, brilliant and distant mother. He
began by saying that he wanted to get closer to her, but what he really yearned for
was for her to acknowledge and enter into his spiritual and ministerial life. Then
he made this extraordinary statement: "By being born, my mother killed her own
mother, who died in childbirth." The student suggested a single experiment: "Be
your mother talking to her mother, would you?"

Immediately he exploded with his mother's anger at his grandmother for
abandoning her as an infant. This anger blew itself out after a few minutes, and he
sat in silence, allowing new awareness to surface. Wisely, the student kept quiet.
Soon the man began to weep softly as he said, "I'm me again, and I need to tell
my mother that God forgives her." Grace was palpable in the room as he spoke to
his mother as a pastoral minister, telling her that she was forgiven in the name of
Jesus Christ for any guilt she carried for causing her mother to die. He also spoke
as a son, forgiving her for being distant and guarded with him and releasing her
from his expectations. It was a profound moment; all of us could feel the shift in
him as he did this work. His session ended with prayer and laying on of hands.

In this session the man followed his awareness continuum and the nudging
of the Holy Spirit. Agreeing to the student's suggested experiment, he allowed
himself to express his mother's anger, which he had carried as if it were his own.
Because he was familiar with Gestalt Pastoral Care he was then able to create
some experiments for himself. He let himself wait expectantly for the next movement to surface in the brief homeostasis that followed his anger. He followed his
impulse to be his pastoral self, addressing his mother as if she had confessed a
sin. He shifted into his role as her son as he forgave her for what she lacked as a

mother. He did all this with almost no interaction with the student Gestalt Pastoral Care guide, for he was alive to God's continuing invitation to grow.

If he had not been so self-directed, the student's job would have been to keep calling his attention to what he was experiencing in the present and suggesting experiments to turn the man's awareness into some sort of action.

HUNCHES

Gestalt experiments can be shaped according to the hunches or discernment of the minister. In fact, willingness to follow her intuition may separate a really good minister from an adequate one. The Holy Spirit often whispers in intuitive hunches; some of the most creative and healing experiments emerge from intuition. Respect for intuition, however, must be balanced by the clear knowledge that the minister's hunch could be dead wrong. Experiments offer a wonderful way for a minister to keep the balance, and to give the control to God and the person who is seeking to grow.

A minister does not have to have a hunch about where the process is heading to suggest an experiment. All she may know is that something she is observing about the person has captured her attention. These actions are not called experiments for nothing; they are really and truly exploratory. This implies that the minister must be unattached to a particular outcome. She must always remember that experiments enable people to make their own discoveries, and these discoveries could send the work in a different direction from even the strongest hunch.

EXPERIMENTS AND DEPENDENCE

Working with experiments gives much more power and control to the one seeking healing than to the minister. This is a good thing; a Gestalt Pastoral Care Minister is in the business of becoming as powerless as possible. When a person is working with experiments, he is focused on his own process. He is making his own discoveries and attaching his own meaning to them. He corrects and modifies suggestions according to his own inner wisdom. He may spend very little of the session talking to or even looking at his guide; interaction between the two may be minimal. If he is a person of faith, there is often a sense that God, not the minister, is guiding the process.

As a result, dependence on the guide is greatly reduced. The Holy Spirit has much more room to work, and the seeker becomes more trusting and dependent on God. Increasingly, God is looked to as the one who supplies guidance, answers, structure, meaning, and love. Surely this is appropriate dependence, for it is on One who is absolutely dependable.

THE NATURE OF EXPERIMENTS: TERRIBLE AUNT MAY

A man began his session by describing his tempestuous relationship with a special woman. He said he loved her and was thinking seriously of marriage. They were wonderfully well-matched and genuinely respected each other. Their sharing was easy and honest. The problem was that from time to time he felt so annoyed with her that his only impulse was to get away as fast as he could. Suddenly and seemingly without reason, during these "grouch attacks" (as he called them) everything she did grated on his nerves. Sure enough, as he described this dynamic, his voice had an angry edge, and his fists punched the air.

Designing an experiment for him was straightforward. "Would you be willing," I said, "to visualize her here on this pillow and tell her how you feel during a grouch attack? Keep punching your fists and let them talk to her, would you?" This very common Gestalt experiment was based on my observation of his fists, his tense shoulders, his shallow breath, his angry-sounding words, and the fact that he was talking about his woman friend. I expected that he would express some anger toward her that might clear the air enough for him to discover what else was going on.

What actually happened was very different. As soon as he visualized her on the pillow, he looked up, puzzled. "I see her there", he said, "and right behind her is my Aunt May who lived with us when I was a kid. She was a terrible old lady who made my life miserable. I can't seem to get her out of the picture."

Now a modification was called for. Because his last sentence lit up for me, I asked him if he would be willing to tell his woman friend, "I can't seem to get Aunt May out of the picture." He willingly parroted these words, but with no real awareness of what he was saying. I asked him to say them again, and yet again. Then the discovery was made: "Oh fuck! I can't get Aunt May out of the picture *with us!* I've been confusing you with her. She drove me crazy when I was a kid, and it looks like she has weaseled her way into our relationship. I'm really pissed at her."

Now the obvious experiment was for him to tell Aunt May just how pissed he was. In this final experiment, he yelled at Aunt May and beat his fists on the pillow, expressing anger that was at least 20 years old. In his fantasy, his future fiancée and Jesus watched supportively and lovingly as he released the rage that had poisoned his relationships for years. The immediate result was that Aunt May was no longer "in the picture," i.e., no longer confused with his woman friend.

This man's work illustrates many of the characteristics of Gestalt experiments.

Gestalt experiments are always firmly based on the behavior or being of a person at the moment. Usually a good experiment won't represent a very big jump from where the person already is, and as the process unfolds, experiments are modified according to what is happening in the present. Obviously, the more a pastor is able to observe, the better the experiment is likely to be. Therefore Gestaltists train themselves to perceive as much as possible about every aspect of the person. (In Chapter Fourteen I will discuss some simple ways to broaden perception.)

Gestalt experiments are designed to enable the person to move from remembering to re-experiencing, from talking to doing, from explaining to discovering. The man's work in the above example might have had a very different outcome if he had simply talked about why he was irritated at his woman friend. His openness to direct experience made it possible to discover something new and important about the effect of Aunt May.

Gestalt experiments are designed to respect resistance. In presenting an experiment, the person's consent is always asked. "Would you be willing to...?" and "Is it OK with you if...." are frequent prefaces. If a person says "no" or wants to modify an experiment, we design a new experiment around the refusal or accept a modification. If a person says, for example, that he feels foolish "talking to a pillow," a new experiment might be to ask him to teach you, the minister, how never to feel foolish. Similarly, a man who resists by intellectualizing might need to let the intellectualizing part of him speak to his own just-budding tenderness. The intellectualizer will probably try to stamp out the new growth, and it is important to let this pressure find expression, since obviously it is there.

If, however, someone refuses to do several experiments in a row, I take those small refusals to be tantamount to a general refusal to work. Some people are genuinely not ready; others have the challenging attitude, "I bet you can't get through to me!" Whatever the person's reason, I believe it is important to increase awareness of what is happening without setting up a power struggle. The goal here is not to trick the person into working when he or she doesn't want to; *in-*

stead we hope to assist the person to stop working with awareness and choice. A Gestalt Pastoral Care Minister might say, "I'm aware that you didn't want to do the last three experiments I've suggested. Are you willing to say no to me some more and see what you feel? How about making a list of everything you choose not to do today?" Or the minister might simply say, "Would you be willing to see how you feel if you just tell me straight out that you don't feel like working today?" When someone exercises his choice to stop working, and his choice is honored without recrimination, it is likely that sooner or later he will decide to work without any urging.

A good Gestalt experiment indicates that the minister has entered the world of the person. It takes into account the person's emotions, body language, worldview, theology, worship style, culture, race, and sex. Suggestions for experiments must certainly be expressed within the person's perceptual preference. For example, the man who was angry with his woman friend was a visualizer, so I suggested he visualize her. In addition, his salty language was accepted and echoed; and his assessment of terrible Aunt May was received without question for the moment.

EXAMPLES OF EXPERIMENTS

1. *Repeat with awareness.* One of the simplest experiments is suggesting the person do, with awareness, what he or she is doing anyway. Some examples:

   - *Are you willing to say that again in the same way, only this time to listen to your voice? What does your voice sound like to you?*

   - *You're talking about such a sad thing, and yet you're smiling. Would you be willing to tell the story again, but this time add after every sentence '...and I'm smiling'? Are you willing to feel your smile each time?*

   - *Would you wring your hands some more? What are your hands saying? Are you willing to let your hands talk?*

   - *Breathe like that again, would you?*

   - *Would you continue to rock back and forth like that, and describe yourself as you do it? You might begin with, "I'm rocking and I feel..."*

Such experiments, although utterly simple, can be extremely helpful because they foster awareness, and can lead directly to the unfinished business of the day. The person who agreed to the rocking experiment made some discoveries in the following way:

> Seeker: *I'm rocking and I feel my body sort of pulsing forward and backward. I like to rock; it's soothing and it's sort of a habit. It makes me feel better. I'm making myself feel better. I have to make myself feel better, because there's no one else to do it.*

> Minister (sensing that a younger voice may be emerging): *How old do you sound right now as you rock?"*

> Seeker: *(voice breaking) I'm really young, maybe about two. I'm all alone and really scared. No one will come, so I'm rocking myself.*

2. *Do what you are avoiding.* If the minister notices that the person working is avoiding eye contact, she can say,

   > •*Would you be willing to see what might happen if you look at me?*

One of the most fruitful experiments along these lines is to remind someone to breathe. When a person gets close to disowned feelings, he may stop breathing for a few moments. Without breath, there is a good chance that the feeling pushing to the surface will be tamped down again. Sometimes all it takes is for a minister to say softly, "breathe," for the stream to resume its flow.

Another promising experiment is to ask a person if he is willing to repeat a breath:

> •*Breathe like that again a few times, will you, and see what you were just breathing out of you. See if there might be a sound that wants to come out on your breath.*

(Breath work will also be discussed further in Chapter Fourteen.)

3. *Exaggerate*

A variation on repetition is to ask the person to exaggerate what is already happening. Just a little exaggeration can easily ignite new awareness. Also helpful is to suggest doing the exaggerated opposite of what is happening in the present. So, for example:

> •*Could you make that gesture again, a little bigger this time? What is your hand saying as you do it?*
>
> •*Are you willing to repeat those words a bit louder?*
>
> •*Would you be willing to fold your arms around your chest even more tightly? You might even let the rest of your body respond as well. What happens to you if you allow this? What do you feel?*
>
> •*Now would you try opening your arms instead of holding yourself like that, and see what you feel in that position? Find out what happens if you shuttle back and forth between opening and closing, would you?*
>
> •*Are you willing to see what will happen if you put your hand more firmly over your mouth as you speak?*

The person who inspired the last experiment was re-experiencing how her uncle had warned her never to reveal that he raped her when she was small. "If you tell, I will kill you," he had said. She believed him. Now at last she was fearfully telling her terrible secret; but as she did so, her left index finger played around her mouth, as if she were saying "shhhh!" Unaware of her finger until the experiment was suggested, she willingly clamped her entire hand over her mouth, and almost immediately began to speak louder against the pressure of her hand.

At once her work became much more focused and intense. Suddenly all of her energy was caught up in the tension between speaking the truth and feeling her terror. At this point she could have chosen to let herself return to the present – and to a calmer state – just by taking her hand away and opening her eyes. She hung in, however, and was rewarded with a powerful body memory. Her own hand became *his* hand over her mouth, holding her down, choking her. It was very, very real. It was as if she was a child again, but not quite, for she was also an adult woman. A powerfully enraged adult woman.

Her reaction was to shriek, "You bastard! I'm not gonna let you throttle me any more. I'm gonna tell the truth, and I'm gonna get free of you! The truth is gonna set me free!" She picked up a plastic bat and hit the pillow where she visualized him. With that, she saw him begin to shrink in size. The more she yelled and hit, the smaller he got, until at last he disappeared into "a puddle of gunk." She sat for some minutes in sweaty silence, breathing heavily. (This process is called "work" for good reason!) Then opening her eyes she announced, "I took my uncle's hand away from my mouth, and I shrunk him down to a puddle."

This woman, who was pretty experienced in Gestalt Pastoral Care, was, to a large extent, able to direct her own work. The little experiment of covering her mouth opened her up to a mighty healing stream. Then all she had to do was reach inside and follow her own inner process, letting her actions flow as she went along. She did not have to be invited to talk louder against her hand, or to express her emerging anger, or to articulate the work she had done when she was finished. It all just happened naturally, and since she didn't stop herself, some important healing occurred. The minister's role was simply to suggest the experiment, then watch and pray.

After the woman announced that she had shrunk her uncle, the Gestalt Pastoral minister suggested she tell this news to Jesus. This she did, and was greeted with an image of Jesus looking at her with love and pride. His expression seemed to say, "Good for you! You've reached another milestone. I'm with you always."

She had finished her work for the present. She had reached a resting place, a brief stop to catch her breath, confident that the Holy Spirit would continue to push her from the inside to grow to be more like Christ. A month or so later, work with her uncle took another leap as she was given the grace to pray for her uncle's healing. A year after the uncle-shrinking day she began the work of uncle-forgiveness in earnest.

4. Make resistance more explicit.

Of course this work is not always easy. Fear, embarrassment, apathy, fatigue, and a host of other things can stop the process. However, unless the person wants to stop, there is always another experiment to suggest based on the resistance itself. Valuable discoveries are made by getting aware of one's objections. For example:

- •A person who says that he feels stupid talking to someone not in the room might be asked if he is willing to talk to himself, and make himself feel even more stupid. The idea here is that the person is already making himself feel stupid, and the experiment might bring this to awareness.

- •Another person might be invited to make a verbal list of all the things he or she *won't* do in a session.

153

- Still another might be invited to warn himself of the awful things that might happen if she followed the suggestion of the Gestalt Pastoral Care minister.

- Another idea might be to invite the person to say no, not only with his voice but also with his body.

Sometimes a person will say, "Look, I don't want to do any experiments. They all seem contrived and fake to me. I just want to talk to you." I believe it is important to honor such demands; and when someone is clear about it, I stop proposing experiments for a time. Actually, "just talking" could itself be an important experiment, for some stories cry out to be told to a trusted listener. If there is no pressure to work in any particular way, often the person will eventually decide to experiment with experiments.

5. Involve the body.

Another way to design an experiment is to suggest that the person embody, or physicalize, what is happening in the present. For example,

- A person who says she is "feeling pulled apart" by conflicting demands might be asked to allow members of a retreat group to pull her arms gently in opposite directions.

- One who is "going around in circles" might be invited to do just that, physically.

- Another person who reports "feeling jumpy" might be willing to actually jump around, or at least make jumping gestures with his arms.

- Still another might make the sound her tense stomach would make if it could make a sound. She might allow her whole body to tense up for a few minutes, the better to become more aware of her stomach's tension.

Whatever a person is feeling is likely to become more intense if he is willing to allow his body more freedom to express it. Of course, every feeling is expressed through the body in some way, so giving the body more permission to be involved can be a revealing experiment in itself. Some further examples:

- *Would you let your clenched fists do what they'd like to do right now?*

•*Would you let this pillow be your baby? See what you'd like to do with her.*

•*Are you willing to let your whole body respond to the helplessness you feel? What do your shoulders and arms want to do?*

•*Would you be willing to let your anxiety make a sound?*

•*You say you want to hide right now. How would it be if we covered you up with a blanket, so you can really hide? Would you be willing to see how you feel?*[32]

6. Re-experience, rather than remember.

Another very common Gestalt experiment is to ask a person to go back in time and re-experience that which is being remembered. If a person says, "I recall an incident when I was seven..." the minister might interrupt with,

• *Would you be willing to close your eyes and be seven years old right now? Let yourself experience the incident again. Tell it to me as it happens, would you?*

In designing experiments, the push is always toward direct experience. Paradoxically, memories of the distant past can be experienced in the present. This experiment is often the prelude to faith imagination prayer.

7. Try a fantasy.

Work with fantasies can offer a way to face a worry by allowing the worst to "happen," to explore what the person knows intuitively but is unable to fit into a rational framework, to try out a new identity, or to simply uncover a person's imagination and creativity. For example:

•A man is afraid of growing old. He might be asked, *Would you be willing to imagine yourself 30 years from now, and see*

---

[32] With suggestions like these, a Gestalt Pastoral Care office needs to be set up for vigorous and safe physical movement. People can get pretty active when invited to express what's inside. My office has a thick rug, and lots of pillows of differing size, color and firmness. There is a plastic bat and an old tennis racquet in the corner. There are two foam rubber couches, although most of the work is done sitting on the floor. There are several blankets to wrap up in, and in the closet there are old towels to tear up. (Sometimes the impulse to tear something up, rather than hit or stomp, say, is quite important in anger work.) The space is light and airy, and full of plants and art. I always try to keep some fresh flowers on the shelf, as much for me as for those who do their work there.

how you feel? ...What do you, as an old man, want to say to yourself as a younger man?

- A woman who is in despair because she cannot conceive might be asked, *would you imagine yourself tiny enough to fit into your own uterus? Would you go in there and explore a little? ...What do you see? Feel? ...Is there something you need to say to your uterus? ...Does your uterus want to speak back? ...Would you invite Jesus to go in there with you?*

- Someone finding it difficult to lose weight might be asked, *Imagine yourself being really thin, would you? ...How do you feel? What's good? What's scary? How do other people feel about you? What happens to you when you go into a bakery?*

- A person with a headache might be asked, *Would you find out what color is your headache? What does it sound like? Do you want to make your headache a different color? Or teach it a different sound?*

- *You said you want to fly away from all your burdens. Imagine yourself actually flying, would you...What do you feel? ...Where do you go? ...What do you do when you get there?*

8. Talk to the person you are talking about.

The person doing inner work can be invited to imaginatively place someone he is speaking *about* on an empty chair or pillow, and speak *to* him or her. He can let the other person reply as he physically moves to sit on the designated pillow or chair. On either side he can talk directly, and perhaps honestly, with awareness. He can, for example, let both his tense jaw and his tender heart speak to his son, and he can be his son responding. He can discover what it might feel like to break off a friendship with someone who is using him. He might hug or hit or weep – or all three. He might turn away, or throw a symbolic pillow out of the room.

A variation on this type of experiment is having a conversation between different parts of himself. For example:

- *Would you let the part of you that wants to break off this destructive friendship have a conversation with the part of you that hangs on?* (This inner conversation is called polarity work and is discussed in Chapter Twelve.)

9. *Dramatize patterns of metabehavior.*

Sometimes a guide will notice patterns of small behaviors that, over time, add up to larger "metabehavior." Being habitually late for everything or sabotaging oneself just when things start going well are examples of metabehavior. So are always acting helpless, playing the clown, or collecting grievances. Metabehavior is not all negative. If a man always feels delight when he thinks of a certain woman, surely this reaction is worth exploring. If a woman feels excited and unusually alive when she volunteers at a tutoring center, this metabehavior may be the basis of important discernment about her life's direction. When patterns of metabehavior are being played out in the present moment, they are pure gold as the basis on experiments.

- The habitual latecomer could be asked to see what happens to him if he joins the guide or a workshop group in reciting, "Mary Had a Little Lamb"— only he chimes in one sentence behind everyone else.

- The self-saboteur might be willing to be her sabotaging voice and threaten the rest of herself with constant sabotage, no matter how hard she tries to get ahead.

- The man who lights up at the thought of his girlfriend might say her name slowly a dozen times with a long breath between each repetition, and discover how he reacts.

- A person who characteristically plays helpless can be offered a chance to try starting every sentence with "I won't" instead of "I can't." Or the opposite: deliberately act even more helpless while staying aware of what happens.

- The clown might say, "I'm laughing again," or "I'm being funny even though nothing is funny right now" every time she is doing just that.

- The grievance collector might list his grievances and after each one repeat, "Everybody does me wrong!"

Obviously these experiments are not designed to ridicule, but to suggest ways of increasing awareness, making discoveries that pave the way for growth. Remember, experiments are never presented with the attitude, "If you want to get well, you should cooperate with me!" Always, the detailed and freely given assent of the one who will do the experiments is paramount.

EXPERIMENTS, FAITH IMAGINATION, AND HEALING PRAYER

I had been working with Gestalt experiments for years before I learned about faith imagination and healing prayer from Dr. Doug Schoeninger and Sr. Betty Igo at the Institute for Christian Healing in Narbeth, Pennsylvania. It slowly dawned on me that this new way of praying seemed just a short step from Gestalt work with experiments. In fact I wondered how I hadn't thought of it myself, but so rigid was the separation between psychology and spirituality in the early seventies that very few people, even people of faith, ever mentioned God when we were supposed to be doing Gestalt work. This separation was in me too. Although I had suggested countless times that someone use her imagination to put her mother, father, spouse, kids, boss, or friend on a pillow and talk to them, I had never thought to ask anyone to invite Jesus or the Holy Spirit or Mary to be there.

At first I thought of faith imagination as a powerful kind of Gestalt experiment, and indeed that is true. The reverse is also true; Gestalt experiments can be a kind of prayer, for in Gestalt Pastoral Care work there is always the hope that we may discover what God is doing to make the person whole. Even when we do not explicitly recognize God's presence, God is surely there. In this context, faith imagination and other kinds of healing prayer do not represent an added-on practice, but are the heart of the process.

At any point in the process, awareness of the presence of the Holy Spirit can, and often does, break in. We can deliberately shift our focus to become more aware of what God is doing. Any experiment can be greatly enriched if the seeker is willing to be aware of God's presence. For the person of faith, acknowledging the presence of God in her growth process just acknowledges what is. It is a way to experience the present moment more deeply.

If a growth process is bogged down in some way, or if there is uncertainty about how to proceed, prayer often helps. In answer to the prayer, "Lord, what should we do right now?" the seeker may suddenly remember an incident which turns out to be an important key as we work with it. Sometimes Jesus himself will suggest the next bit of work. He may communicate something like, "You don't have to carry that alone. Give it to me." Then the pastor can suggest a way to experiment with physical surrender. She might say, "Would you be willing to put the burden you are carrying on this pillow, and physically hand it to Jesus? See if you're ready to do that, would you?"

When there is resistance and fear, the Holy One is there to help untangle things and give courage to go on. Just knowing that she does not have to re-experience traumatic memories alone frequently gives the seeker enough safety to keep going. Very often Jesus gives permission to feel emotions that may have been disowned for years.

Haunting questions naturally surface out of great suffering; one of the most familiar is, "Why did God, who is supposed to be loving, allow this to happen?" The obvious way to work toward answers is to ask God for them. What better "experiment" could there be in the face of a tragedy? Such a process can make room for mystery, for not knowing, for faith, or for peace that we cannot generate by ourselves. It can help us find purpose, meaning, and vocation. It can show us how even our worst nightmare can become a gift.

In other words, God willingly enters into our growth. God seems eager to work in these small experiments as we bumble along. Even after observing for years how wonderfully God works when we get out of the way just a little bit, I am still awed by it. What good news it is that God is indeed with us!

CREATIVITY WITH EXPERIMENTS

I have given only a very few examples of some common experiments. There are countless others, for experiments are limited only by the experience of the person working and the creativity of the minister. Those with Gestalt training are taught to devise experiments that push beyond the basic ones. There are examples of creative experiments throughout this book. Consider also the following:

- A woman punctuating her verbal story with graceful motions in her arms was invited to stand up and dance her story without using words.

- A man attending a Gestalt Pastoral Care workshop said he missed out on being a child because of early responsibilities. He was invited to sternly admonish himself-as-a-boy not to waste time in silly play, echoing the message he heard all his life. Then the man was invited to be five years old and be as noisy and rambunctious as he wanted with his "play group," i.e., other workshop participants who volunteered to be five years old for a few minutes.

•A woman in her late seventies wept that she had married too early and had never done what she really wanted to do with her life. Now it seemed as though her wasted life was nearly over and hope was gone. After she had cried herself out, she was invited to ask the Holy Spirit to help her express the wisdom she had garnered in 78 years of living. She was then asked if she was willing to play at being an elder, a wise woman. She was invited to reach deep inside and teach the younger people in the workshop group.

•A woman who was abused as a child by her music teacher was invited to work with her Gestalt Pastoral Care minister to plan a liturgy of "Cleansing and Consecrating the Clarinet."

•A man became aware that he was not yet ready to give up "carrying the weight of the world," although he fully recognized that this pattern was neither faithful nor healthy. His Gestalt Pastoral Minister suggested he carry an actual 10 pound weight around for a week. The suggestion was to never put it down, even taking it into the shower and to bed.

A GESTALT PASTORAL CARE PERSPECTIVE: SIX EXPERIMENTS FOR BEGINNERS

At the beginning of this chapter, I stated that no one should attempt to work with Gestalt experiments without explicit Gestalt training. Essentially that is true. There are, however, a few experiments that can be suggested by those who are Gestalt Pastoral Care beginners. I am assuming, of course, that there will be no attempt to persuade, coerce, control, or break down resistance, as I will discuss in detail in the next chapter. Although the following experiments are quite basic, even these utterly simple experiments can open the door to discoveries that heal. Since I have described them already, I merely list them now.

•*Say that again. Do that again, would you?* When words or actions are repeated a few times without any suggestion that they change, often that repetition alone is enough to lead to new awareness.

•*Would you be willing to exaggerate that a bit?* This experiment can also lead to new awareness, for the message of a particular posture, a tone of voice, a gesture, a breath, or a few words can light up when exaggerated.

•*Breathe.* A gentle reminder to breathe can sometimes pave the way for the release of long-held feelings and memories.

•*Would you let that part of your body have a voice?* Playfully becoming an aching back, a queasy stomach, tense shoulders or whatever part is calling for attention, can not only lead to new awareness, but can also provide a direction for healing prayer and laying on of hands.

•*Would you talk to the person you are talking about as if that person were here?* This simple experiment is a Gestalt basic.

•*Would you be willing to engage in faith imagination prayer?* Related "prayer experiments" for beginners are praying for healing, planning individualized liturgies, or even simply speaking with honesty to a spiritual companion.

The sick man answered him, "Sir, I have no one to put me into the pool when the water is stirred up; and while I am making my way, someone else steps down ahead of me." Jesus said to him, "Stand up, take your mat and walk."
John 5:7-8

10

RESISTANCE: INTERRUPTING OURSELVES

John came to an *Opening to Grace* Gestalt Pastoral Care workshop to "learn how to help others." A candidate for ordination, he was eager to become a good pastor, and sincerely wanted to become familiar with the range of human emotions and suffering. Ministry was a later-in-life vocation for him, and he knew he needed to gain some new skills and awareness before taking over a church. The real urging to attend such a workshop, however, came from the denominational committee which would approve him – or not – for ordination. The committee said he needed to be more comfortable with emotions.

John began by telling us that he had been very fortunate. His life had been good: no traumas, no deaths, no major disappointments. He had a rich and vital relationship with God, and he was married to a woman he loved very much. He went on to say that "the only dark spot" in his life was his relationship with his father, but even that was pretty okay these days.

When invited to converse with his father as if he were there, a different story unfolded. He revealed a childhood full of cruel verbal abuse, put-downs, and outright rejection. Over and over his dad had predicted that John would flunk out of school and that he would never amount to anything. Imperious and sneering, he ordered John around and called him humiliating names. Although no one in the family escaped his father's sick hostility, John, as the oldest son, got the brunt of it. At age seventeen his father kicked him out of the house, and, "the day I left home was the happiest day of my Dad's life."

As he told this story John's voice shook with tears and anger. It was obvious that it was still terribly painful to him and that his pain was located in his abdomen, which was visibly knotted and trembling. In contrast, he kept a boyish grin on his face, and whenever he began to feel the pain of his first seventeen years a little bit, he would jump back to the present. *Now* he was fine – and truly he was – in a way. He had done well in college and had a good job that used his considerable leadership skills. He had shown his old man to be dead wrong. Much of the time he was able to put aside feelings of inferiority and fear of criticism, and act with assertiveness and charm. He wasn't sad or angry anymore; God and his wife were giving him all the love he needed. As an adult he was even able to tell his father to "cut the crap" when his father started ordering and criticizing. He said he had forgiven his father, but as a Christian, he wanted to *like* him, and was working on that.

All was not great, however. John still had to battle feeling inferior. He dreaded the day when his father would first hear him preach. In new situations, he worried whether people would like him. He was afraid that if he ever had a son he would repeat his father's behavior. He was surprised that one ordination evaluation called him "superficial." From time to time the familiar, trembling, knot in his stomach would surface, reminding him that things were not as good as they seemed.

All in all, though, he had figured out a wonderful way to cope. It was as if he had grown an emotional cyst around the pain of his boyhood, and had then been able to function quite well in spite of his father's criticism. John was good at choosing health. He deliberately focused on himself as a competent adult, and was pretty much able to ignore how he had been brought up. It was a marvelous job, really. By almost any standard he was a success.

But here he was on a healing retreat, a good opportunity to open his pain to God's healing love. He did explore it a little – and then decided to not go any further. "Why go into all that?" he said. "I feel OK!" He made his decision to stop with awareness and clarity.

With a little coaching, the retreat group was able to support (yes, *support*) his resistance. They did not preach at him about what he should do. They did not tell him that he would feel a lot better if he got it all out. Instead, they were able to give him the freedom to shut down if he wanted. While sharing their own reactions to his abusive father, they sincerely complimented John on making the very best of a bad situation. They said they were impressed at how well he was able to draw boundaries for himself in a group. They prayed for him, thanking God for his wonderful ability to survive. He ended the session feeling appreciated and cared for even in his resistance, and with a lot to think about.

THE GIFT OF RESISTANCE

Not so many years ago resistance had a bad reputation. Therapists saw resistance as counterproductive and ornery, with the implication that a truly motivated person would not harbor resistance for long. These days, however, most counselors believe that a practice that treats resistance as something to be quickly eliminated, reveals a mindset focused not on health, but on pathology. Current thinking says that attacking resistance head-on can destroy not only needed defenses but also autonomy and self-respect. Smashing down resistance, rather than allowing it to melt naturally, is positively harmful. Fritz Perls was a major teacher in this new way of approaching resistance.

Remember that Gestalt Pastoral Care is based on a health model. We assume that there is a drive toward wholeness in even the most wounded person. Further, we assume that each person's inner process actively directs her toward this wholeness. Resistance is there for a good reason. Resistance does not indicate stubbornness or reluctance to grow. Instead, resistance is to be respected as an attempt to survive and reach for health.

On the other hand, resistance does put growth on hold. Because resistance interrupts a healing process, these days some Gestaltists prefer to call various kinds of resistance *interruptions.* In the language of Gestalt Pastoral Care, interruptions often reveal fear or unreadiness to follow the Holy Spirit's invitation to greater wholeness. This does not mean, though, that interruptions are intrinsically bad. Far from it! Interruptions are natural, often healthy, and are an important part of a healing journey.

Lifelong habits of interruption are usually formed quite early. We adopt specific patterns of interrupting ourselves so that we can survive our childhood. Since no parent is perfect and no life is without pain, all of us must learn to interrupt our own healthy process at times. That is, we must learn how to shield ourselves from feelings or experiences that are too much to handle. True, interruption stops the process of homeostasis, but it is an effective way of not feeling so awful. Interruption shields us from pain, from dangerous feelings, from terror. It helps us shut off that which would overwhelm us or would be unbearable. It helps us disown in ourselves whatever will be unacceptable to others. It helps us go on when things have fallen apart. It allows us to put off working on painful issues until a better time. All of us, even adults, need it. Thank God for interruption, for without it we would be in deep emotional trouble.

164

Imagine that you are a child and your parents slap, kick, or punch you whenever they are upset. As a battered child it is dangerous for you to protest or talk back because you'll only get hurt more. It is even dangerous to feel as angry and abandoned as you really are, for then you might truly give up on life. Battered children often just become numb, but nearly all of them have well-guarded time capsules of anger, fear and despair sealed in their bodies. They erase their natural reactions as best they can, because these reactions are utterly dangerous, painful, and terrifying.

In a less extreme environment, a child might get enthusiastic approval for neatness or being quiet or getting good marks in school. The unspoken message is that if you want your parents to love you and think you're wonderful, you better not be messy, boisterous or noisy. You better do all your homework every night and put other interests on the back burner. This child, too, learns early on to squash, or interrupt, his unacceptable tendencies. Whether a home is abusive or basically loving, each child learns ways to get the greatest possible parental approval that is so crucial to emotional health.

The result of childhood interruptions is that over time, desires, feelings, impulses, and even natural talents, gifts and personality characteristics are split off and disowned. The splitting may be so complete that the disowned component cannot be called forth even when appropriate. If playfulness has been disowned in childhood, for example, an adult may find it difficult to play, even on vacation. If sexuality has been disowned, it may be impossible to enjoy sex even with a deeply loved spouse.

Thus interruptions forged out of childhood necessity may well put a ceiling on growth as an adult. Even though interruptions are a God-given means of survival, habits of interruption can become a prison. Adults cling tightly to childhood interruptions that worked, even minimally. We make strong inner boundaries that carefully guard habitual ways of interrupting our inner process. We come to believe that whatever is inside our self-identity, or "contact boundary,"[33] defines who we are; whatever is outside our contact boundary is simply "not me." Thus, an adult who has disowned playfulness might say with complete sincerity, "I'm just not a playful person." Childhood interruptions can stop us from being the persons we could be, because so much of us is split off and disowned. They

---

[33]See Polster and Polster, *Gestalt Therapy Integrated: Contours of Theory and Practice*, pp. 98-127, for a discussion of contact boundaries.

can keep us from processing old childhood feelings. They can stop us from taking risks, from trusting and loving, and from growing up emotionally and spiritually.

It is not just childhood habits of interruption, however, that curb adult growth. Normal adult suffering that is simply a part of every life can also be an impetus to construct new ways of survival. When formerly bright hopes turn to ashes, when dear ones die, when money is scarce, when jobs are stultifying, when friends disappoint, when terrible mistakes are made, when tragedies occur, somehow we must keep going. Adults as well as children must find ways to shut down when necessary, and if old habits of interruption don't work, we must find other ways to cope. The inmates of the prison in which I volunteer offer many good examples of how adults find it necessary to construct new ways of responding to painful realities. The men tell me that every inmate must find a way to fully face the enormity of his crime and the suffering he has caused without going truly insane with guilt, or becoming steely with self-justification. They must discover how to live with constant danger, unremitting noise, lack of privacy, acute longing to see their wives and children, and the burden of so many wasted years. Each man seems to have forged his own way in these matters, but their lives attest that in order to survive, adults must continue to defend themselves from suffering.

THE CATASTROPHIC EXPECTATION

According to Gestalt theory an important mechanism that keeps interruptions in place is the "catastrophic expectation,"[34] an unrealistic fear that if interruptions vanish, something terrible will happen. When we honestly ask ourselves what might happen if all the sandbags were to fall off our balloon, we will likely encounter our catastrophic fear. Even though most people gripped by a catastrophic expectation know full well it is not real, the imaginary impending catastrophe feels very real indeed. Statements such as the following are expressions of the catastrophic expectation:

- If I'm a success my friends will be jealous and hate me.

- If I start to cry, I'm afraid I'll never stop.

- If I get angry, I'll destroy something, go berserk, or have a heart attack.

- I just won't be me any more if I'm no longer depressed.

---

[34] Perls, *Gestalt Therapy Verbatim,* p. 52.

•If I really let myself be assertive, no man will ever find me attractive.

•If I become an artist, my family will think I've lost my mind.

Catastrophic expectations work beautifully to keep familiar ways of coping firmly in place, often for years.

THE GOOD NEWS ABOUT INTERRUPTIONS

However strong or long-standing the interruption, ancient feelings and experiences do not simply go away. They are, in fact, very present, constantly pushing for resolution. Habits of interruption may keep feelings from being expressed overtly or from even coming to awareness, but the feelings are there all the same, sometimes preserved intact for decades. It is never too late to contact them. The stream may be dammed up, but the water pushes mightily against the dam.

By paying careful attention to physical bodies, one trained in Gestalt usually has no trouble spotting evidence of the urgently pushing water. (See Chapter Fourteen for information on reading bodies.) Healthy impulses toward metabolizing unfinished business are constantly manifesting themselves, along with the interruptions that continue to squash them. Muscle tension, shallow breathing, disturbances of posture, movements, body energy and tone of voice point to an exquisite dynamic of interruption and the urge to grow. A person who is insisting aloud that everything is fine may have a jaw and shoulders full of tension from holding everything back. Someone who seldom cries may have chronic sore throats or observable redness around her neck. A person who is fiercely independent might frequently take a leaning position when he sits, suggesting a need for at least occasional nurturing. Simultaneous with the interruption there will also be evidence – seeable, discernible evidence – that disowned parts and unfinished business are struggling to get through. As Perls was fond of saying, "The body never lies."

RESPONDING TO INTERRUPTIONS: WHAT NOT TO DO

A Gestalt Pastoral Care minister will never attack an interruption or try to break it down, either with benevolent persuasion or pressure or judging. If there is coercion present, the encounter will have a "you should" quality about it. An arrogant attitude of knowing what's right for someone else has no place in good therapy or pastoral care.

Those who lived through the turbulent 1960's and 70's will probably remember how some irresponsible leaders deliberately structured therapy groups to shatter resistance, perhaps by depriving participants of sleep, or by not letting them go to the bathroom, or by haranguing each person in turn until each gave way. To add to the damage some even used these techniques in the name of Jesus, using Jesus as a club to intimidate and to control.[35] Obviously none of this is in the spirit of Jesus – nor does it work very well. People don't grow well under the gun, and most will wisely dig in their heels in the face of such blatant coercion.

Most psychotherapists, however, are caring, responsible, and genuinely want to help. They would argue that while resistance should not be yanked away, it can and should be carefully melted by skilled therapeutic intervention. Furthermore, they add that allowing people to sit in resistance (and not having a well thought out treatment plan) is tantamount to not doing one's job as a therapist. Finally, they remind us that in this age of insurance-driven psychotherapy, there is no time to waste waiting for people to decide for themselves to move off dead center.

I believe they do have a point, particularly regarding addiction to alcohol or drugs. Denial is such an enormous part of the picture in addictions; and given that some addictions are potentially fatal, an intervention that actively seeks to break through denial is perhaps justified.[36] In addition, it is obvious that there are many wonderful therapists who do skillful, sensitive, and even remarkable work with resistant clients. Clearly, there is more than one way to work with resistance.

On the other hand, I would argue that taking away a person's freedom to choose what is right for her surely doesn't help anyone grow up. If a person is forced into childish dependence on someone else who is cajoling and persuading her to take the next step, how will she grow to recognize the prompting of the Holy Spirit in her own heart? Further, there is a good possibility she will feel emotionally invaded if an interruption crumbles under coercion, even the most well-intentioned. She may feel she has revealed more than she intended. She may well lose trust, and it will be twice as hard to open up the next time. For these reasons I believe that not attacking an interruption actually saves time in the end.

---

[35] For example, see the review of Ian Davidson's *Here and Now: An Approach to Christian Healing Through Gestalt*, (Darton, Longmoor and Todd, London, 1991) published in the *British Gestalt Journal*, 1991, vol. 107-109.

[36] It is important to note that while interventions for alcohol and drug addicts are often staged to the surprise of the addict, they are carried out without anger, and express caring of the one confronted. Participants simply point out what they have observed in the behavior of the addict and express the hope that she will go into treatment, and what they will do if she doesn't. Then the decision is left to her.

Finally, if an interruption is protecting something that the person is not yet strong enough to handle, taking away the protection an interruption offers is truly destructive. Inexperienced counselors are the most likely to do this, and they are the least equipped to deal with the aftermath. On the other hand an inexperienced counselor – and minister for that matter – can depend on interruptions as a safety net. People who are not pressured to overcome resistance before they are ready will rarely venture into realms they are not strong enough to handle.

INTERRUPTIONS: WHAT TO DO

When Jesus encountered resistant people he was respectful of their choice to say yes or no. He accepted them even before they were ready to change. He didn't coerce people to grow; rather he issued invitations that tugged at their hearts. The rich young ruler was *invited* to give away everything he had and follow Jesus. Martha was *invited* to stop fussing so much with hostess duties that she lost sight of her Guest. Jesus *asked* the man at the pool what he wanted done for him. Even when he confronted various hypocrites he was forceful in truth-telling, but did not force his listeners to heed his words. Always he invited, giving opportunity for real choices.

I believe it is a holy thing to be invited close to a person's pain. When interruptions come – and they will – they are to be approached with as much respect as possible. We can trust that the Holy Spirit is doing the nudging from the inside. Truly, it's not our job to urge anyone to grow.

When I begin a healing retreat, I always try to set ground rules which give as much control as possible to participants. I make it clear before we start that I will not attack resistance. For example, I might say:

> Nothing will happen to you here that you don't want. You don't have to share anything you're not ready to tell, and you can stop anytime you feel like it. When I suggest an activity for the group, ask yourself if it feels right for you. If it doesn't, claim your right to sit out. When it's your turn to work as the focus of the group (if indeed you do want to work) you can modify or say no to anything I suggest, and there will be no argument.
>
> I believe the Holy Spirit will nudge each person here, so keep in mind that maybe you are called to something quite different from

the rest of the group. Perhaps you'll need to take a nap or go for a walk or write in your journal instead of coming to a session. That's just fine. Do it. Please feel free to leave the room at any time, and you don't need to explain your absence to anyone.

This is not the kind of group in which everyone gangs up on you until you break. Part of my job is to make sure that you will not be persuaded to open up in a way you don't want. If you decide not to participate in some way, you might discover something if you ask yourself what your objections are. Regardless of your reasons, your decision will be honored as something you are doing to care for yourself.

I believe that God will offer each person here an invitation to grow a little bit – or maybe even a lot. Perhaps you will get in touch with a next step. Or maybe now is the time to experience some feeling or memory you've been avoiding. Maybe you will get in touch with an inner shift of some kind, or a new awareness. Maybe you will discover some new parts of yourself. Whatever it is, it's up to you and God how far you go during this retreat. I already said you can stop whenever you want. You can also go as deeply as you want into anything that surfaces for you. I'm not afraid of intense feelings, so even if some people leave, I promise to hang in.

By the time I finish, most people have begun to feel fairly comfortable. Some will need to wait and see if I really mean it, but when they find out I do, they usually feel permission to be themselves, resistance and all. Occasionally someone at a retreat will hardly say a word the whole weekend or might spend considerable time away from the group, and I will continue to coach the rest of the group to keep offering that person spaciousness and permission. Typically, however, most people in these retreats choose to stay in the room and work at a depth that often astonishes me.

When someone comes for private sessions, my introduction is similar. Again and again I discover that when people feel safe enough and loved *even in their resistance,* they can risk looking at the world in a new way. People who have genuine choice in a safe environment usually choose to allow resistance to melt eventually.

Siding with Interruptions

By no means, however, are interruptions to be ignored. Instead of attacking interruptions, side with them. Support them; cheer for the role they have played in the person's life. In other words, let the protective function of a particular interruption become clear and its importance validated. Siding with interruptions can disarm defensiveness because it avoids a power struggle between the guide and seeker, and supports the seeker's sense that her interruption was, or still is, vital to survival. Keep in mind that siding with interruptions is not a manipulative trick. Rather it is a way to show profound respect for another person.

First, let the interruption speak. As soon as there is evidence of an interruption, it needs to be honored. There is no sense ignoring it. Asking a person to try to do an experiment designed to push the process along when there is a major interruption is like asking a bee to stop buzzing. Instead suggest a new experiment that expresses, and even heightens, the interruption.

Consider Julia, a young mother who never allowed herself to grieve for her husband who died five years before. After he died, she was so busy trying to take care of three little kids and keeping up with her demanding job, that she just put her own life and grief process on hold. She got through those difficult early years pretty well, but five years later she realized that she was feeling dead inside.

Julia's first Gestalt Pastoral Care session was proceeding well as she went back in time and began to contact feelings associated with her profound loss. Soon she found herself sad, devastated, abandoned, teary. Then she stopped cold. She changed the subject; she made a joke; she wondered what good it will really do to dredge all this up. Quite effectively, Julia put the brakes on her healthy homeostatic process.

There was no use at all to encourage her to remember how sad she really was and so on. Because something new was happening, a new experiment was called for: "Julia," I said, "would you be willing to be the part of you that just shut down? Maybe you could start by telling the Julia who wants to grow what you were just saying to me – that no good will come from opening this can of worms."

This experiment was not the only one I could have suggested. Another variation could have been to ask Julia to make a verbal list of ten reasons why it's *not* a good idea to dig up all these old feelings. Or, Julia could have let her interruption talk to the part of her that was just crying for her husband. Her interruption might have reminded her tears that she still has little kids to take care of, and she can't afford to let herself turn to jelly. If I saw that her interruption was being expressed physically, I could have suggested an appropriate experiment. For instance, "Julia, I see you twisting your wrist with your other hand. Would you do that some more and see what your hand is doing to your wrist?" Finally I could have asked Julia to take responsibility for stopping by saying clearly and with awareness that she just didn't want to get into these devastating feelings right now.

Second, encourage expression of the catastrophic expectation. As Julia goes further with letting her interruption have a voice, she will likely discover an underlying, irrational fear of catastrophe. She may find herself saying something like "I *can't* let myself fall apart. I don't know if I'll get myself back together again. Anyway, my Dad always said I should be brave when things get bad. I can't imagine what he would think if he saw me blubbering like a baby." Julia has just expressed two catastrophic fears: that her tears will open floodgates so tremendous that she will lose not only her marbles, but also her father's respect as well.

A third step is to support the healthy impulse that set up the interruption in the first place. As Julia continues it is important not to argue with her. Instead, the pastoral minister reflects the wisdom of what is being expressed: "It sure is true that you have a handful with your kids and your job, even now. I can see why you needed to keep yourself together when Bob died and things were so chaotic. Your good control helped you get through that awful time. And added to that, you were just never taught that it would be O.K. to let go." When a minister is able to support an interruption well *and mean it*, people feel understood and loved. It does, in fact, take a loving heart and a good measure of grace to see people in this way.

It may be that Julia will decide that she truly does not want to open the door to her grief. Perhaps it is just too much for that particular day. If so, it may make sense to end the session, or Julia and her minister might just chat a bit, knowing that Julia has stopped the work. No sense of failure is implied here. Nor is there is any accusation of the terrible sin of resistance. There is, however, a definite acknowledgment that Julia, who has a perfect right to put her healing process on hold, has done so. Julia could even decide that she will let well enough alone and not explore her feelings any more, ever. Whatever she decides needs to be okay with the minister. If the minister is not emotionally or spiritually able to allow this freedom, the *minister* has work to do with *herself.*

Reflecting the healthy origin of resistance and honestly accepting refusals to put growth on hold, does a great deal to help create a safe environment. More than likely if Julia feels genuine freedom to say no, soon she will be ready to say yes.

Finally, teach some ways to have some control over scary or overwhelming feelings. In other words, show her how to shut down. Julia could practice dipping her toe into her grief for a few seconds and then returning to the present. Then she could try going back to her well of grief, and again returning to here and now. Julia may discover as she shuttles back and forth that her grief doesn't have to flatten her each time. She might learn that she can allow her grief to wash over her and then find her way back to the relative calm and safety of the present.

If Julia feels panicky, she could learn to pay attention to her five senses as a way of grounding herself in the present. She can look at colors in a room and name the objects: a red chair, a brown wooden table, gray dust bunnies in the corner. She can rub her arm or face with a cold wet washcloth. She can listen to sounds: a car going by, a dog barking, the refrigerator humming. She can feel her feet on the floor and her breath going in and out. She could take a bite of something with a strong flavor. (One person I know keeps a supply of fireball candy just for this purpose.) She can ask herself what she smells. Sometimes it helps to write down these perceptions, or to say them out loud even if she is alone. Quite often when she becomes aware of her perceptions *in the present moment,* she moves away from the feelings of past suffering and future worries.

Finally, Julia can invite Jesus into her perception that she is simply overwhelmed with intense feelings. One way to do this is to ask Jesus if he will hold her grief until she is ready for it. People who pray this "holding prayer" often see a picture of Jesus tenderly holding a package or perhaps sense him putting something carefully in a box. The effect on the pray-er is an astonished sense that the Lord is treasuring and preserving the very feelings and memories that are so feared. Often there is a sense of peace and order where there was chaos only moments before. This prayer also tends to erase any sense of failure at deciding not to go on; clearly Jesus loves the person in her interruption. Usually the person will be ready quite soon to continue exploring her feelings once she has had this experience.

After siding with the interruption, coach awareness of the organic push toward health. Even though a healing process is interrupted, it is still urgently there. In Julia's case, her tears and feelings associated with Bob's death are still pushing for resolution. She will not be free to love again with abandon until she deals with this major unfinished business. Once she does, she may find that she has much more energy and that other feelings, not just her grief, will have come unstuck. Just as Julia was encouraged to give her interruption a voice, she will also be invited to let her emerging unfinished business speak as well. In fact, when an interruption has truly been heard and honored, the healing agenda often seems to come forward almost automatically. If it doesn't, a minister can suggest an experiment. For example, "Julia, would you be willing to let those tears you were experiencing a few minutes ago talk now? What would they say to the part of you that stopped?" Julia may well find herself making a case for dealing with her grief. It happens just this way quite often. Julia's response was typical:

> I can't hold onto this grief forever. It's dragging me down. I feel depressed a lot of the time. It's hard to get up in the morning. If I want to really be there for the kids, its time I dealt with this stuff. I'm sick of doing things the way Dad would want. What about me?

Now Julia is back on track with her process. She is working on an inner polarity and is deciding for herself how she will live her life. (I will discuss polarities in Chapter Twelve.) She is not fighting with the minister because the Gestalt Pastoral Care minister refused to fight. A power struggle was avoided by siding with the interruption.

Julia's work illustrates the advantage of choosing with awareness when to flow with one's healing process and when to press pause. When one is in charge of his own growth process, he is free to decide how and when he will attend to it. He may, for example, interrupt his tears when he is at his job, knowing that he will make time to cry later. He may decide to wait until he is with a person whom he considers trustworthy enough to companion his journey. He may decide some approaches to healing won't work for him even when an authority recommends them. He may even decide to put his growth on hold for a season. Or he may decide to plunge in deeply, passionately, and vigorously. It is his responsibility and his choice.

Choosing to stop one's process with awareness naturally opens up a new way of taking control. When a person becomes aware that he is not helpless in his resistance but is interrupting himself for good reason, he can then decide with awareness when it is time to stop the interruption. Either way he has taken important steps to discover who he is and what he is getting out of interrupting himself.

174

Interruptions embraced with awareness can be fully as valuable for healing as breaking through long-held resistance.

Inviting Jesus into Interruptions

I have discovered that Jesus very often makes a way for people to allow interruptions to dissolve. Almost always he will encourage someone to go on with his or her work during faith imagination. This encouragement is particularly helpful in someone who is encountering "unchristian" feelings like rage or jealousy. If she asks Jesus if it okay with him if she allows the expression of these unsavory emotions so she can be rid of them, almost always she hears an enthusiastic "yes!" Jesus seems to desire for us to take an honest trip through our inner landscape, and is not the least put off by the messy emotions we will surely encounter there.

For instance, Julia, the woman whose husband died, is afraid that she will be virtually swamped with sorrow. If she tells that to Jesus she is very likely to hear something like "I know. I will be with you, and your tears will not destroy you. Let me have them." Such messages from Jesus seem to give deep permission to allow her inner stream to flow again. They can even overrule her father's old message: "Be brave when setbacks come."

Another way Julia could invite Jesus into her resistance is to ask Jesus if he would go back with her in time to the day Bob died. She could allow herself to re-experience this trauma, but this time with the awareness that the Lord is nearby to comfort her and to receive her tears. His presence might make the memory and the associated feelings infinitely safer. She could also prayerfully ask permission to speak with Bob, who is now with God, especially if there is something unfinished in their relationship. Many grieving people have been able to give and receive forgiveness, speak words of love, and hear words of peace and joy from the one who died, and to finally say goodbye. Often they have a clear sense that God arranged the meeting for everyone's healing, and experience a great relief to discover that in Christ, they are still mysteriously united with the one who died.

The hardest thing of all to give up is your suffering.
Fritz Perls

11

CLEARING THE STREAM

In the last chapter I discussed how we learn to interrupt ourselves so we can survive. We learn this when we are tiny children, and the habits we adopt can follow us all our lives. As we grow to adulthood, our patterns of interruption help insulate us from life's knocks and pains. They are good protection against real dangers and having to grow in risky ways. They keep us safe, maybe even sane. They are a great gift.

As we grow, however, the shell that once protected us becomes a prison, keeping us from growing, stifling our creativity, damping our joy, and diminishing our capacity for love. Being uptight is painful. We begin to fervently wish that we could break out, let go, have some fun – even as we cling to familiar ways. We may long to connect with our passion, our childlikeness, our courage, but we are too afraid. Ordinary feelings such as anger, sorrow and delight can seem out of the question. It can feel utterly outrageous to be just a little outrageous.

Most patterns of interruptions are combinations of many different behaviors, and are highly unique. "How does *this* person dam up his stream?" is the question. How does she distort and interrupt herself? How does he say no to awareness? How does she keep herself in the dark about her own life? How does he prevent himself from living deeply and joyfully?

In this chapter I will discuss four resistance mechanisms[37] and how a Gestalt Pastoral Minister might approach them. It is important to keep in mind that these mechanisms will be blended and molded in the crucible of each personality. It should also be understood that when someone has lively contact with his inner process and then decides *with awareness* to bank his fires for the time being, he is not really interrupting himself in the sense discussed here. Instead, he is simply taking responsibility for his life.

---

[37] See Polster and Polster, *Gestalt Therapy Integrated*, pp. 70-97.

PROJECTION

Projection is the process of disowning whatever is unacceptable in ourselves and attributing the unacceptable material to another person or object. We can project almost anything that is a part of us – traits, feelings, actions, parts of our body, and so on. Projection is a perfect way of getting rid of what we don't like about ourselves, because once the material is projected, it honestly feels like it doesn't belong to us. Then we are free to judge another for the very thing that we dislike in ourselves.

The comedian Lily Tomlin used to do a hilarious riff regarding projection. She played a prissy, self-righteous woman who always had her hand down the front of her dress, nearly fondling her own breasts, while she declared that beastly men have only one thing in mind. It was clear to her audience that she would never admit that she herself was the one obsessed with sex. It was funny because it was so familiar.

Projection is an important part of human maturation. Babies are born feeling that everything happening around them is located in themselves. If they are cold and wet, the entire world is cold and wet. As they mature they learn to differentiate what is "me" and "not me," and that they are no longer the center of the universe.

When our daughter was about 18 months old she would often recite a little litany: "I'm not Mamie. I'm not Barney. I'm not Cindy. I'm not Noah. I'm not Mommy or Daddy." This was our cue to ask, "Well who are you then?" "I'm Shana!" she would bellow, obviously pleased with herself that she was figuring it out.

Very young children who have learned that they are persons in their own skin start locating their "bad" qualities outside themselves, thus protecting their fragile self-image. A stuffed animal or an imaginary playmate are handy projection screens, and may well get blamed for the spilled juice or the broken lamp. In the process of disowning what is unacceptable a child begins to forge a good self-identity.

In adulthood, however, projections are a particularly seductive interruption; they not only make us make us blind to our own foibles and faults, they are also part of the basis for racial, ethnic and gender prejudice, and for homophobia. It is that group, that person, over there that is dirty, sneaky, lazy, weak, ornery, dangerous, sinful, or whatever. Not me, not ever me. Projection is the cause of a great deal of injustice and misery.

Recognizing Projections

The simplest way to identify projections is to listen for what is particularly disliked in another person. For example, a person who absolutely cannot stand arrogance and reacts with vehemence every time there is a whiff of it, may well be full of unacknowledged arrogance. One who has accepted his capacity for arrogance is usually able to recognize arrogance when he sees it in another person, but can react with tolerance and perhaps even compassion.

Particularly important are complaints about spouses. Quite often a mate is chosen as an ideal projection screen; if a husband needs to project his tears he may choose a wife who cries about everything. Opposites attract in this context, and in the bargain we also get to nag at someone who has the very traits we can't stand in ourselves.

When people are projecting there is often a jumping-to-conclusions quality about their statements. Projections distort and exaggerate. For example, there may indeed be anger in the other person, but the projector will perceive much more anger than is really present.

Listen for clues in pronouns. If, for example, someone is projecting her stomach (and its attendant emotional and physical pain) out of her body, she might say, "It hurts," rather than "my stomach hurts" or, even better, "I hurt." Perls put great importance on how pronouns are used. When working with people he often suggested simply changing the pronoun "it" to "I." With a tiny difference in pronoun, a statement becomes much more personally riveting and true. "It's depressing" sounds and feels very different from "I'm depressed."

Observe behavior. Is the person doing the very thing he is accusing another of doing? For example, is he loudly insisting that someone else pipe down? Is he whispering that so-and-so is a terrible gossip?

Remember that just because projection is present does not mean that the problem is located solely in the mind of the projector. Actually there may be a genuine situation to deal with. In other words, a genuinely sneaky person makes an excellent projection screen for one who disowns her own sneakiness.

Watch how a person relates to you as a minister; those in a pastoral role often are used as projection screens. What minister has not encountered someone who, puffing herself up, accuses the minister of doing the very thing for which she, the accuser, is well known: "You're just as bad as all the other ministers we've had. You're too critical and you're lousy at relating to people!" Ministers will also recognize that some people disown their strengths and project them onto the pastor: "I can never figure anything out, but you always know just what to do. You're so wise and holy. I'm so glad you came into my life, etc. etc."

Working With Projections

Healing comes when projections are taken back and re-owned. That is, you admit that you yourself resemble all those people you dislike and envy. In this process you begin to recognize, by golly, that not everyone hates you; it is you who are hate-filled. Instead of so many people being much stronger and more competent than you, you discover your own strength and competence. You begin to see yourself as you are, and in the process, become more honest, softer, less judgmental, and more tolerant of differences.

A temptation in working with projection is just to give candid feedback: "Don't you see that you are the pot calling the kettle black?" The idea behind this sort of statement is that people can accept the truth if they hear it. This confrontational style is popular in some therapy groups.

I believe that this approach does not work very well. It is hard to talk anyone out of a projection without destroying his or her sense of self, and an argument will likely generate a power struggle between the minister and the one doing inner work. Also, the person may cite evidence to justify and even strengthen the projection. Instead of talking about the projection, suggest a re-owning experiment. For example:

Suggest that the person pretend to be the one chosen as a projection screen. "Would you be willing to describe yourself as your wife for a minute? What are you like?...Now switch back and be you." In this experiment the person is now set up to playfully claim the projection, and maybe a real discovery will be made.

Ask the projector to look at other people in a group and begin sentences with "I see"...(fill in the blank) and "I imagine..." Sometimes making a separation between what is actually seen (colors, shapes, physical positions, movements) and what is imagined (projected) can foster the discovery: "I see you looking at me, and I imagine you are critical...I see you with your arms crossed and I imagine you are thinking that I'm just taking up time...I see you in your perfect hairdo and I imagine you think I'm a mess."

Invite the projector to change her pronouns from "it" to "I," and discover how she feels.

Propose a "homework" experiment in which the person makes a list of the traits of someone he dislikes or admires. Then make another list of any way he is even a tiny bit like them.

Re-owning projections usually takes time, even with these Gestalt experiments. It is not easy to give up habits that may have been life-long. *Truly the best way I know is to invite the person to pray using faith imagination.* I might say "Would you invite Jesus here and tell him how everyone is so critical of you? See how he responds to you, will you?" Jesus almost always does something to break the projection; often he simply confronts the person with the truth. Quite often this leads naturally to confession, for projection is at the root of hypocrisy, prejudice, self-deprecation and harsh judgments of others. In projection we are blind to our own faults and focused on the faults of others.

Religious Projections

Perls believed that God is nothing more than a fearful, childish projection of human power and goodness. Belief in God, Perls would say, offers permission to comfortably relinquish responsibility for our lives. Perls insisted that genuine maturation means breaking this projection and having the courage to reclaim the human power that is ours.

He does have a point. There certainly are Christians who blame God for their own foibles saying, "God just made me this way." Others react to social ills by saying, "I'll pray about it, but if God wants things to be different, God will have to change it. God is in charge, not me." They sing that "I am weak and he is strong" while not understanding that Jesus invited his friends to risk modeling their lives on his. These good folks collapse inside, abdicating their own responsibility to move ahead with volition and energy. They are relieved from truly living their lives because, after all, what can they do as mere mortals? Obviously, this is a distortion of the gospel. Clearly there are some who would do well to work on their religious projections.

Perls' absolutist slant on religious belief is also a distortion. But it does serve as a reminder to Christians to embrace the challenge of discovering the difference between giving up and surrender, between interior crumbling and discipline, between putting our light under a bushel or putting it "out there."

INTROJECTION

Perls uses the image of force-feeding infants to describe both introjects and confluence.[38] (Confluence will be discussed later in this chapter.) Children are often persuaded to eat food when they are not hungry; at other times they must cope with hunger because parents won't allow them to eat until dinnertime. Soon they learn to tune out their own signals of hunger and satiety and adjust to what will please their parents. They give up their own internal sense of themselves in order to be loved – a hard bargain indeed.

Forced to accept our parent's wishes, demands, beliefs, hang-ups, we "swallow" them, just like unwanted food. Even against our best interests we disown our inner reality and adopt distorted views of our parents, society, or church. Children absorb such admonitions as:

•Make Mom and Dad proud by being just like them.

•Don't be a pest.

•Do what you're told.

•Always keep quiet. Never cry or make a fuss.

•Behave yourself even if something is wrong.

•Be a nice young lady. Always be a little gentleman.

•Don't be angry, dirty, loud, or demanding.

•Be nice, clean, cooperative, sweet, and just like that good kid down
  the block.

Or they may be taught family mottoes such as:

•It's a dog-eat-dog world.

•Hard work never hurt anyone.

•Never waste time with foolishness.

•Only a sap would get tied down with responsibilities.

---

[38] Perls, *Ego, Hunger and Aggression*, pp. 128-133 and 192-199.

•Live in luxury as much as possible; after all you can't take it with
you.

Heard often enough, children accept these admonitions as rigid rules for life, and an introject is born. Introjects insist that you cannot be the child you are. The belief which usually accompanies an introject is, "My impulses, feelings, needs, talents, desires, interpretation of experiences, and energy are wrong. *I'm no good.*" An undigested childhood introject has great power; it can shape our lives far into adulthood. Introjects sit heavily inside, not digested or even tasted, making us feel sick, weighed down, and hemmed in. This disgust is healthy; it pushes us to question and "digest" (or throw up) what we have swallowed and decide what is true and right for ourselves.

Surely children need to learn to behave in a civilized manner. Kids can't grow up by themselves, without direction or sanction. But even well-meaning parental 'shoulds and oughts' can throttle a child's sense of self. Civilizing a child can mean squashing her budding creativity, her fragile self-identity, and her plain joy in being herself. Most parents don't want to hurt their children, but little children misunderstand easily; damaging introjects are formed even with the best of parents.

When I was a child, I was high-spirited and rambunctious, roaring around the house, bumping into walls and furniture, dancing, swaggering and having a wonderful time. I'm sure I was a handful. My harried parents would sometimes say, "Tilda! Cut it out! Be quiet, for Pete's sake! Get off your high horse!" They were simply asking me to calm down once in a while, but the message I heard was that my noise and passion were truly unacceptable. I heard the 'high horse' message many times, and over the years I swallowed it. I stopped being noisy and assertive and tried to be humble and quiet. As an adult I had to work hard to *reclaim* my high horse, and then integrate it with the quiet center of myself that I had come to appreciate.

My parents were basically healthy and loving, yet I had plenty of introjects to deal with as an adult. Badly wounded parents, full of their own undigested introjects, can send terribly damaging messages that a child cannot digest because they are so toxic. These messages do not have to be verbalized in order to have life-long impact. Based on the way she is treated, a child draws conclusions about herself and the world. For example, if she is ignored when she is upset, she may form an introjected belief that her feelings don't matter, indeed that *she* doesn't matter. If a child is beaten he may conclude that the way to get what you want is to beat others. A child who is smothered and controlled by over-anxious parents may well decide that he is not strong enough or smart enough to do anything alone, or that the world is an incredibly dangerous place.

Some introjects take on the strength of commandments which, if not questioned, can actually shape personality and the course of a life. For example:

- You will follow me in the family business.

- How can you be happy if the rest of us are miserable?

- Your job is to make sure that others feel good!

- You'll always be alone if you don't stop acting so different from everyone.

- Nobody likes a domineering woman or a wimpy man.

Introjects don't always have a negative effect. They can also be gifts of wisdom and faith passed down from older generations to younger ones. Even if undigested at first, the message is there to draw upon and chew over. Not long ago someone said to me, "I never knew what my mother was talking about until I got sick. Then all those things she told me about having faith and never giving up and leaning on the Lord suddenly made sense." This person's crisis of a major illness spurred her to digest her mother's beliefs and make them her own. She was grateful that they were somehow planted in her. Acceptance of her mother's truth was never a condition for her mother's love; thus her introjects were not toxic. When she was ready as an adult, she was able to quickly assimilate what she had learned at her mother's knee because she had little guilt, fear or anger to deal with first.

How to Recognize an Introject

Introjects are characterized by statements of "shoulds and oughts." I ought to work harder...keep my temper...do what my boss wants with a good attitude. Scratch the surface of an "I should" statement and you may find what Perls calls "the fighter," a disgusted inner voice that protests and disagrees with the deadening introject. Some people, upon contacting their fighter, report an almost physical experience; they feel constricted, stuffed, controlled from within, and if the introject is particularly damaging, actual nausea. If an introject sends the message, for example, to have rigid control over sexuality, the fighter will very likely be angrily chafing under this restriction and will be eager to experience sexuality for all it is worth.

The fighter is quite apt to be rebellious and even unreasonable; but important to remember is that the fighter usually carries the seeds of health, and is the voice of life-giving creativity and passion that got disowned when parents wanted a more compliant child. It is the fighter's agitation that urges a person to digest an introject or get rid of it altogether. It is the fighter who has the energy for change and for healthy integration of the two warring sides. Perls uses the terms "topdog" and "underdog"[39] to describe the struggle of an introject and a fighter. The topdog is the voice of the introject: self- righteous, rigid, and moralistic. The underdog is the fighter – often whiny and helpless at first – who carries the seeds of healthy integration. (I will further discuss topdog and underdog in Chapter Twelve.)

Sometimes the topdog/underdog conflict is most clearly expressed in the person's body. Just a little body awareness might reveal, for instance, that one arm and hand are angry with tensed muscles and clenched fist, while the other arm is shyly tucked under a thigh or even "making nice" by caressing the arm of a chair. It is likely that the two arms will have radically different messages when invited to "speak." (I discuss working with body awareness in Chapter Fourteen.)

As introjects are explored, they can usually be identified with the parent or teacher or perhaps church that planted them. If a Gestalt Pastoral Minister asks, "Who taught you that you were worthless? Who treated you that way?" the person usually knows quite well who it was.

As soon as the fighter gets mobilized and begins to challenge the introject, even in a safe office setting, there will be guilt and fear and, later, anger. Reflecting this guilt, fear and anger, a fighter might say something like, "It would simply kill my mother if I talked back to her, even in my imagination! She would never accept me if she knew how I feel. She drives me crazy with her put-downs and nagging, and I'm sick and tired of it!"

Working With Introjects

When I went to Michigan State University immediately after high school, I badly needed help. The tremendous stress brought about by the recent death of my parents and the subsequent upheaval of everything that was familiar and dear was compounded by the demands of a huge university and trying to perform perfectly as a violin major. During my first year, I began seeing a counselor at the student clinic.

---

[39] Perls, *Gestalt Therapy Verbatim*, pp. 38-40.

It wasn't long before I discovered that I was having trouble even identifying, much less owning, what I was feeling. As soon as I felt the stirrings of any emotion, I would immediately cancel out the feeling by jumping to its opposite. Then I would doubt that I really felt either one, because I wasn't "singleminded." Quite simply, I had tied myself in knots.

This dynamic played out in a major way when I finally admitted my anger at someone whose very real generosity to me had been laced with cruel barbs. Whenever I felt a little twinge of anger at this person, I automatically reminded myself how grateful I was for the considerable help I had been given. Minutes later, I was back to an angry re-hashing of grievances which I deflected by telling myself that as a Christian I had to forgive. Why couldn't I let bygones be bygones, especially after all the kindness the person had shown? Back and forth I went, paralyzed, stuck, and not really expressing in depth either side of the conflict.

There didn't seem to be a way to break out of this rigamarole, even when my counselor assured me again and again that it was really okay to be angry. Although the supportive counseling helped me feel less alone, I stayed stuck. Most of my feelings remained bottled up in my tense and achy body. I had done a pretty good job of introjecting a distorted version of Christian forgiveness, and I had plenty of retroflected tension and guilt to prove it. (I'll explain retroflection later in this chapter.)

Years later, this inner paralysis was waiting for me when I went to my very first Gestalt workshop. My new therapist, Dan Sullivan, didn't try to talk me into forgiveness, or acceptance of my anger. Instead, he suggested a Gestalt experiment: "Would you be the part of you that is angry, and talk to the part of you that says you shouldn't be angry?…Then switch sides, and reply…Have a conversation between the two parts of you." He suggested that I sit on one pillow when I was angry, and another when I was telling myself that anger was not the Christian way and that I should be grateful.

What happened next was nothing less than a revelation. I was astonished to discover that I could work with two or more conflicting emotions simultaneously. For the first time ever, one feeling didn't dilute another. Instead, the pillow work enabled me to express each side fully, while the other side "listened." In just a few minutes, the argument intensified and got louder, and finally culminated in my angry side screaming at my "you should" side, "You have been holding me down and shutting me up for years! No more! You've made me hurt! You've made me go numb about everything, not just anger. I'm absolutely sick of you! I have a right to my feelings! I'll forgive when I'm good and ready to give up my anger."

This diatribe silenced the "you should" voice temporarily. Dan then suggested that I speak directly to the person who had hurt me, expressing exactly how I was feeling. He also assured me that my genuinely grateful part could have her say later. Imagining this person on a pillow in front of me, I spoke my undiluted truth, sparing no detail of how I had been hurt. Soon I had to face that I was not just angry, but enraged. To my horrified surprise, I discovered that I was actually capable of hatred. Under my nice Christian persona I had the impulse to beat and tear my tormentor into little pieces.

My "you should" voice returned, taunting me: "You see what happens when you let yourself get angry? You go berserk! Stop this right now, and pull yourself together!" "Shut up!" I snarled back. "I'm gonna get through this! I'm tired of carrying this stuff around. It's way past time to get rid of this crap!"

Then I turned to the pillow representing the person who hurt me. Yelling, kicking, and beating with my fists, I "killed" that person. Although I directed my murderous rage toward an individual, what really died that day was my anger.

Sweaty and exhausted when the storm was over, I felt an amazing lightness and freedom. My body felt looser. I had much more energy, and wonder of wonders, I was not angry anymore. My hatred had drained away, and I was no longer working to keep myself in a box. How very much energy I had wasted trying to throttle myself! And how marvelous to have that energy freed up! I went to a party that night and danced for hours, joyfully reveling in the new me.

My anger at that individual never came back, and within a month or so I expressed my heartfelt thanks to the person, who was back on a pillow in Dan's office. A few more weeks, and I was finally able to really forgive. The remaining feelings for the person were indeed gratitude – and compassion – just as Dan had predicted.

Just three Gestalt sessions had accomplished what I could not do, despite my sincere effort to be a good Christian and years of weekly counseling. Of course, most introjects are not defused as quickly as this one was, but the general contours of my work are pretty typical. I didn't know it then, but it was Dan's understanding of Gestalt work with introjects that informed the experiments he suggested. The introject he saw in me was, of course, the enraged woman fighter versus the introjected nice Christian girl who was denying her anger.

The goal in working with introjects is to allow the person to "chew over," or integrate the material with one's healthy impulses. The idea is to accept the genuine gifts that the introject may carry and reject that which is harmful. For example, an introject that advises, "Always be neat!" might help one get reasonably organized if it is integrated with the fighter's objection that *obsessive* neatness is a burden. Integration comes, not from talking *about* the conflict, but through a here-and-now *conversation between introject and fighter while they are in creative contact.* Occasionally a new integration emerges quickly, as happened for me when I finally expressed rage for the first time. More often it takes a number of sessions in which the person works slowly toward integration.

Although the order is not terribly important, I have found the following steps helpful in working toward the integration of an introject.

First, people need to give expression to the introject itself. Quite often the introject has drowned out the voice of the fighter and the person may be aware only of the introject. The suggestion might be, "Janet, would you be that mean voice inside that keeps telling you to shape up? Be her, and talk to Janet over here on this pillow. Tell her how to shape up, would you?"

The next step is usually letting the fighter talk back: "Now would you be willing to be Janet again and talk back to your mean voice? Tell Mean Voice what it is doing to you, would you?" Remember that the fighter is usually the voice of health, but may need to be tempered by the cautions of the introject. As noted above, the fighter may need to break out of the rigid neatness the introject is prescribing, but it is also important to recognize that the messy anarchy of the fighter is not ideal either.

Let a conversation develop between the introject and the fighter. It is important to encourage the person working to converse with herself in this way rather than just talking about her dilemma. Actual contact between the two sides is crucial if integration is to occur.

Behind the 'shoulds and oughts' is a person (or institution) who planted the introject in the first place. Asking, "Who taught you that?" or "Who made you feel that way?" or "Try saying that to some important people in your life as they parade across this pillow, and see if any of them need to hear it." will often net the name of the person who needs to be addressed. Sometimes the origin of an introject will be clear from a tone of voice when the introject is speaking: "Yikes! I sound just like my father!" Then the fighter can engage the real battle directly – with mother or father or perhaps grandma or a teacher or the church. When the person who planted the introject is identified, the pillow which was the voice of the introject can now become the person who sent the wounding message.

When the fighter is mobilized, there could be a need to express anger which may have been held physically since the introject was planted. This anger may need to come out not only verbally but also physically. A person may need to hit or kick or 'choke' a pillow or smack it with a plastic bat. She may even need to bite a rolled up towel if anger is being held in her jaw. It is important for the Gestalt Pastoral Minister to call attention to any impulses to express anger physically, and to suggest ways for this release to happen safely. For example,

> Minister: *Are you aware you are making a fist? What does your fist want to do?*
>
> Person working: *Hit!*
>
> Minister: *Would you be willing to let grandpa see how angry you are by hitting this pillow with your fist? Want to see what happens if you do?*

If the person is afraid of these "unchristian" feelings, asking Jesus if it is OK almost always results not only in permission, but encouragement; Jesus seems profoundly tolerant both of the ambiguity produced by two different feelings at once, and of the need to express what it is inside even if it isn't pretty. In fact, a good way to work with introjects is through faith imagination. I am constantly amazed at how Jesus empowers even the most fearful person with words of truth and brings liberation after years of suffering. When I first became a Gestaltist, I would expect to work for hours supporting the fighter until enough strength was gained to fight. Now, as I work with prayer, I sce again and again that "deliverance to the captives" happens much more quickly than I could have imagined.

Sometimes Jesus seems to sort everything out even before the person has worked very much. I have often witnessed Jesus simply melting an introject and replacing it with new freedom and a greatly renewed sense of self. Once, in a man's faith imagination prayer, Jesus strode into a room in which he as a child was being told by his parents that he was a really bad boy and that they were fed up with him. The parents challenged him to be like his cousin, "so good and no trouble to his parents." With great purposefulness Jesus scooped the boy up and headed out the door. As he left with the child he exclaimed to the parents, "Stop saying those things to your son! He doesn't have to listen to this." The effect on the man almost immediate relief and release from this wounding introject.

Finally, a wonderful way to work with introjects is through the Liturgy of Lies and Truth described in Chapter Eight. In this individualized liturgy, a supportive ad hoc church can underscore the truth of what has already been discovered in faith imagination prayer, or the little congregation can speak gospel words of love and freedom if the suffering person is having trouble praying for himself.

RETROFLECTION

Retroflection is a process of doing to yourself what you would like to do to another person or to the world. Retroflections often take the form of doing something to yourself physically, such as grinding your teeth instead of impacting something outside of yourself, or slapping your knee in frustration instead of getting angry with someone who is stepping on you. Codependent people retroflect by ignoring themselves and their needs. Instead of ignoring another's incessant and unreasonable demands, anorectics retroflect by maintaining rigid control over their food, while feeling powerless to control any other part of their lives.

Retroflection goes hand in hand with introjection. Introjects are powerful messages, and if the person cannot live up to the standards proclaimed by this inner voice – and most cannot – they take themselves to task:

> The introject: *I should be as organized as my father.*

> The whining of the underdog*: I try and try but I just can't get it together.*

> The retroflected introject: *I am such a jerk!* (slaps his forehead, hard).

The impulse toward retroflection can also be healthy. When it is truly impossible to change the environment, a healthy person does for herself what the environment can't supply. Caressing or stroking one's own body, for example, can be a positive retroflection if there is no one else to caress. Treating oneself with kindness is a sign of health if one is lonely or bereaved. Anne Frank couldn't leave the tiny room in which she was hiding from the Nazis. She had no one to talk to except her family, no peers to help her through her adolescence and no counselor to help her cope with the terrifying events of her short life. Instead, she talked to herself in her diary, becoming her own peer, philosopher, and counselor.

Recognizing Retroflectons

Retroflections are usually quite easy to spot. They are characterized by doing things to oneself. Self-hatred, self-destructive behaviors, rigid self-control, and self-fascination can all be signs of retroflections. A retroflector might find a way to self-sabotage every opportunity for advancement, or might put himself in danger by driving too fast, or push himself to constant overwork. He might be clinically depressed, or even suicidal, for major depression and suicide sometimes consists of anger turned toward oneself.

Retroflections are often quite evident in a person's body. An observer might see rigid posture and tense muscles, and have the impression that the person is holding himself together. Gritted teeth, clenched fists, bitten nails, toes which curl as if to hang onto the floor, constricted breathing and tight voices are all possible ways that retroflection can make itself known. (Reading bodies discussed at length in Chapter Fourteen.)

Working With Retroflections

Working with a retroflection has to do with reversing the direction of its energy; the pastoral guide suggests experiments that symbolically do to the world what is being done to oneself. An example might be to invite someone to say to another what they are saying to themselves:

> Person working: *I really am angry at myself for letting this happen.*

> The pastor's suggestion: *Would you see what happens if you say 'I'm really angry at you' to the man who mugged you?*

A group can be helpful in undoing a retroflection, for the group can deliberately invite the one who is working to use their presence as a foil in reversing the direction of energy. Say that someone reports, "I'm always pushing myself to do more." A good experiment would be to ask the person to push a volunteer from the group gently, but physically, while demanding that the pushee "do more!" (Of course either participant can call a halt to this experiment at any time.) Someone who keeps declaring "I've gotta control myself," might be invited to control a group member who volunteers to be controlled for a few minutes. The person working might also playfully admonish other group members to control themselves.

Because retroflections are so often expressed physically, it is possible to begin work on a purely physical level. *Sometimes just suggesting that a person allow their body to do outwardly what they are holding inwardly is enough to ignite new awareness:* "Would you try using those fists to hit a pillow instead of hitting your knee?" "Are you willing to squeeze this pillow instead of squeezing your elbows close to your sides?"

Working with retroflections can take time, precisely because retroflections may have been held for years in tightly-wound muscles. A person might work for weeks or even months before being ready to allow barriers to fall. What paves the way? Body awareness is paramount, as are small forays into quick trials of reversed energy, followed by a pause to discover that even a little release feels good. Important, too, is coaching on *how* to let go, while reiterating the person's freedom to keep the retroflection. Finally, having a companion who is not afraid when all that retroflected energy gets loose is essential.

When a retroflection is broken and the direction of the energy is reversed outward, there is often a sort of "aha!" about it. "So *that's* what this is all about!" they may say. "I'm beating on myself instead of being mad at that guy." *A person who makes a discovery such as this may then have to deal with the introject which encouraged the retroflection in the first place.*

Christians are prime retroflectors. Church folk often prefer to throttle themselves rather than show how they feel, especially if anger is involved. When it comes down to the question of whether it is really all right to acknowledge the way you feel, *faith imagination prayer can make all the difference.* For example, in a faith imagination prayer Jesus said to a reflector, "It's really time to stop beating yourself up. Your family was terrible and it wasn't your fault." This was a transforming word to the one hearing it.

A Caution

When working physically, it is important to set things up so that no one will get hurt. My office has a rug with a thick pad, soft couches with no metal or wood edges, and lots of pillows of various colors, sizes, and shapes. There are soft cozy throws to wrap up in, and plants and art to gaze at. The four windows look out on trees and fill the room with light. In the corner are several plastic bats. Usually I work sitting on the rug; it's easier for people to drop their polite behavior while on the floor, and to allow their bodies to move in new ways. The rug and the pillows cushion vigorous activity. It is a safe place in which to let go.

When working with retroflectors, however, it is important to remember the tendency toward self-destructive behavior. Most of the time we encourage people to follow their instincts as they work; however if someone begins to hurt himself in any way, I ask him to stop immediately. Only once in my experience did someone not comply right away. Many years ago in a workshop a woman began holding her breath and hitting herself in the forehead quite hard. I asked her to hit the pillow instead of herself; she went right on. I *ordered* her to stop; she just slowed down a little. Not wanting to rob her of responsibility for her own behavior, I gently took hold of her hands and asked her to look at me. The physical contact got her attention at last. "I don't want you hurt yourself in this group," I said. It was as if she hadn't heard me before. She sighed deeply and stopped hitting herself. I suggested she hit the pillow instead, and she did, contacting years-old anger that drained away as she directed it toward the appropriate person instead of at herself.

CONFLUENCE

Confluence is a state in which normal emotional boundaries between individuals are largely absent. Confluent people merge emotionally with others, often with a spouse or other members of their family of origin. This merging can be so complete that it is nearly impossible to tell whose feelings and experiences are whose. For example, a wife whose husband had left her was shocked to hear her mother say, "I can't believe he did this to me!" This same mother made sexually provocative comments to a new man her daughter was interested in. Her daughter's sexuality was in the air, so the mother naturally joined in. This is how it's done in confluent families. (An old joke says that when a confluent person dies, someone else's life flashes before her eyes.)

Confluence means that when a husband does something foolish, his wife gets embarrassed, for she has no resources to separate herself from him emotionally. When a child does something remarkable, the parents are proud, not of the child, but because of the reflection on them. Another familiar example of confluence is found in families of alcoholics or drug users who join the addict in both denial and covering up. Individuals from co-dependent, confluent backgrounds may have trouble knowing what they want, even in small things. For example, many report they can't decide what to order in a restaurant until they find out what everyone else wants. They are pleasers, and spend a lot of energy finding out what other people expect from them. Not being able to please everyone produces tremendous anxiety, and often is the final push to seek help. Others see a professional after experiencing a string of romantic relationships that don't work out. Usually the problem is that confluent people imagine they are in love with anyone who likes them, and if someone pays attention to them, they feel almost compelled to pay attention back.

Confluent families are usually pretty dysfunctional, because emotional differences are not tolerated for long. In addition, a confluent person may well have an inner voice that forbids getting well if the rest of the family stays sick. Change is seen as disloyal or even as betrayal. Not surprisingly, as an individual begins to differentiate herself, guilt and anxiety surface. Marriages based on confluence, although common, are particularly confining. To outsiders, these families may look normal or even ideal, but members of such families can find breaking free an arduous and sometimes scary process. Those who undertake it, however, find it well worth the effort. The reward is nothing less than finding a missing self.

Because confluence so often runs in families it is sometimes possible to trace a particular behavior or symptom through many generations. Occasionally, large configurations of emotions, experiences and memories seem to be passed down from parents to children nearly intact. When confluent patterns have existed for generations it is even more difficult to break away. (I will discuss generational healing in Chapter Fifteen.)

Can confluence be positive? Yes. Day care workers know that babies will "catch" feelings of distress from each other – if one baby cries other babies in the room join in. Experts in human development cite this phenomenon as one of the possible antecedents of adult compassion and empathy. The bond between a baby and a loving parent is also based on positive confluence. So is a healthy marriage not based on enmeshment and merging, but on two *individuals* who are wordlessly alive to each other. So is the mystical union between Christ and a person well-schooled in prayer.

Recognizing Confluence

Confluence reveals itself pretty quickly. Usually it is possible simply to hear it as an individual talks about his efforts to please, to placate, to fit in. He will waffle in decisions, large and small. He may try to find out from someone else how he should feel. If he is asked directly how he feels, he will have great difficulty answering, for he honestly will not know. Instead he may talk about how someone close to him feels.

In addition, confluent people usually feel responsible for the emotional or spiritual well-being of other adults in their family. Their lives may be organized around serving someone else – even when the demands are not reasonable or possible. For example, a woman refuses to get *any* help in caring for her elderly father who wanders off naked, and who no longer recognizes her, because "Dad would hate to have anyone else in the house. I just can't do that to him." This kind of self-effacement in which compassion has run amok, is often confused with Christian love and humility. Erasing one's self in this way is really about not valuing one's own needs and feelings. It is a way to avoid living one's own life.

Working With Confluence

Suggest experiments that will allow conflicts to emerge. A good experiment would be to ask the person to finish the following sentences ten or so times, alternating between "I want..." and "My mother (father, spouse, etc.) wants..." Another excellent experiment for a confluent person to try is starting every sentence with "Now I feel..." Work with confluent persons offers the possibility of emerging from an enmeshed system and discovering one's real identity.

It is important to keep asking the right questions, with a non-judgmental attitude that does not fish for "right" answers: "How do you feel?...What do you want right now?...What is going on in your body at the moment?" With a confluent person, try to stay very neutral while asking what he is experiencing at every moment.

In addition, pay special attention to non-verbal messages in body language and dreams, realms in which the real self is speaking. For example, a person who claims she does not feel anything may be full of physical tension and movements that suggest otherwise. She might punctuate her speech with karate-like chops, or her legs might make kicking motions. She might dream about terrific conflicts. Of course, a Gestalt Pastoral Minister would not simply confront a person with these observations. Instead, she would create experiments that could create a climate for self-discovery.

Once a person has discovered even a little of herself, she will likely experience a lot of fear and anger at having been stifled and smothered. This anger can be the labor that births a new self and cuts the cord from the deadening, confluent family. Some people need to cut the cord quite literally. I keep clothesline and scissors in my closet just so this drama can be acted out.

As always, faith imagination is important. Jesus often gives permission to have "forbidden" feelings. He tells people who they are, and even illuminates for them the desires of their heart. How liberating it is to find that God's will may be discovered in finding our real selves. A person with a secret yearning to soar with freedom and joy may find that God wants that too.

Other Ways to Avoid Contact

Obviously, there are myriad other ways to avoid fearful and painful feelings and to interrupt contact with oneself and others. Most people have several favorite ways to avoid themselves, and everyone has blended their own unique patterns of interruption.

Some people have simply learned to shut down and have become experts of *denial and numbing* themselves. They are remarkably able to feel nothing much at all. Nothing fazes them; very little gets through. Even their bodies are more or less numb and frozen, although they may experience painful tension or ulcers, or the like. Almost always their breathing is so shallow that it is nearly invisible to an observer. Characteristically they insist that nothing is wrong with them. Numbing and denial are a very effective anesthetic, but the side effects are great. Besides a rigid and beleaguered body, often there is an inability to love another, or to feel joy, passion, or excitement.

Others folks are good at *deflection,* a process in which they distract and divert themselves from their inner process. Being funny, sexy, intellectually profound, or blaming others, and changing the subject are all good ways to stop themselves cold when painful feelings emerge. Deflection works very well, and in addition others may find it attractive and charming. Socially, it is a good skill; the problem comes when it is impossible to stop.

Simple experiments that might increase awareness of how a person is stopping her own process through numbing or deflection will sometimes help a person get back on track. For example:

• A person can be invited to tell you all she is *not* feeling. Or what she is not allowed to feel. Or what she won't feel.

- •He could also teach others in a group how to numb themselves as effectively as he does.

- •She could let an achy part of her body make a noise, and listen to herself. She could let the sound get bigger and more intense.

- •He could go to each group member and say one sentence describing how he just deflected his process:

  I was talking about my wife's serious illness, and then I made a joke. I was talking about my wife's serious illness, and I laughed through the whole story. I was talking about my wife's serious illness, and I tried to ignore how afraid I am by saying, "Oh well. That's life."

Once I worked with someone who was a wonderful storyteller. She could make any experience interesting with her intelligent wit, her marvelous ability to turn a phrase, and her sense of timing and irony. She was so good that I found myself looking forward to her sessions; it was like listening to Garrison Keillor talk about Lake Woebegon. Finally I realized that she was an incomparable deflector, and I was being a party to it. When I asked her to stop talking and pay attention to her body instead, she was uneasy and uncomfortable. However, her process got back on track as she gingerly allowed herself to explore, via body awareness, the riches she had been avoiding.

12

POLARITIES: FEELINGS IN CONFLICT

WHAT ARE POLARITIES?

Gestaltists speak of polarities as opposing aspects in a personality, or of splits in the feelings of the moment. Whenever we are aware of one aspect of ourselves, we can also find in ourselves, if we are honest, the polar opposite.[40] Many fresh, green discoveries sprout when one is exploring the very opposite of one's self-identity. For example, a person who is always even-keeled and dependable almost certainly has some flash and capacity for delight in there somewhere. If she acknowledges and appreciates both sides of herself, the way is well prepared for genuine integration to occur. As we play different roles in our lives – parent, employee, sexual partner, best friend, and so on – it is obvious that we are really bundles of polarities which change all the time, day to day, even hour to hour. When we are able to allow different aspects of ourselves to emerge at the times of our own choosing, and without denying the polar opposite, then we have achieved healthy integration – at least for a time. To keep growing we need to be working toward integration all our lives, for most certainly life itself brings new experiences and identities to explore.

The concept of polarities is not really new, although it has gone by many other names and descriptions through the years. Carl Jung called the part of us that we usually deny the "shadow side," a human trait so universal that it is symbolized in myths and fairy tales. If we are honest, most of us can find fairy tale characters inside ourselves: a waiting, helpless beautiful princess and an assertive rescuing prince, or an innocent, naive Red Riding Hood and a wily, controlling, gloating wolf. And what about Chicken Little, Humpty Dumpty, or any of The Seven Dwarfs? Consider, too, the hypocritical Pharisee, the betraying Judas, the brave Esther, the impulsive Peter, the contemplative Mary and the hospitable

---

[40] For another discussion of polarities see Polster and Polster, *Gestalt Therapy Integrated,* pp. 57-69.

but obsessive Martha in each of us? Jung well knew what wonderful riches could be tasted by reclaiming the shadow.

In his letter to the Romans Paul points to a keen sense of two parts of himself in conflict:

> I do not understand my own actions. For I do not do what I want, but I do the very thing I hate… For I delight in the law of God in my inmost self, but I see in my members another law at war with the law of my mind, making me captive to the law of sin that dwells in my members. Wretched man that I am! Who will rescue me from this body of death?...So then with my mind I am a slave to the law of God, but with my flesh I am a slave to the law of sin (Romans 7:15; 22-25).

A Gestalt Pastoral Care minister would love to invite Paul to allow the two sides of this polarity to talk to each other!

Topdog Versus Underdog

Perls taught that the polarity of topdog versus underdog (as he called it) is present in just about everyone.[41] Topdog, says Perls, is self-righteous, responsible, perfectionist, demanding, condemning, nagging, blaming, and usually reflects an introjected parent or other authority. "You're so stupid. Don't you know better than that? Pull yourself together, for Pete's sake!" Topdog is a master of the double bind: "You should take some time off. And, you should be getting straight A's." Topdog insists to the self, "I know what's best for you," and often the topdog actually does have good advice. However, most every communication from the topdog reveals a maddening, condemning "you should" attitude, designed to whip the underdog into shape.

In contrast, underdog's theme song is "I can't." Helpless, self-denigrating, manipulative, a master of passive control, underdog answers the topdog's demands with "I'm sorry," or "I'll try harder" and then sabotages all the best intentions. Underdog usually wins the conflict; the person doesn't actually do what topdog demands, but the price is guilt and anger at oneself.

When underdog begins to fight back directly, the scene shifts dramatically, and it becomes evident that the underdog's position is usually the healthier one.

---

[41] Perls, *Gestalt Therapy Verbatim*, pp. 38-40.

Scratch the surface of the underdog and there will be anger about being pushed around and demeaned. Instead of passive sabotage, there will be a clear refusal to buy into the sneering, condemning voice of topdog, or to meet harsh demands that don't make sense. Instead of a whiny "I can't," there emerges a healthy "I won't!" Further, when this polarity is integrated, we make the lovely discovery that topdog and underdog need each other. Underdog needs topdog to keep life organized and on track, and topdog needs underdog to sort through the shoulds and oughts to ferret out the ones which really do need to be obeyed.

The topdog/underdog split points to the close connection of introjects with the simplest polarities. Most introjects manifest as polarities eventually, but not all polarities are introjects. Furthermore, there is more to polarity work than digesting parental and cultural introjects. Working with polarities also offers a way to embrace parts of oneself that have yet to be recognized and developed. As a person grows, he tends to move from attending to his undigested introjects to discovering wonderful parts of himself that have been latent or germinating. He gradually moves from suffering to expansion, from rigid boundaries to creative interaction, from inner conflict to graceful integration.

Thus, work with polarities doesn't stop with awareness, nor is it limited to work with simple polar opposites. Instead, as growth occurs, the work begins to include all of a person's rich and multifaceted life. Integration and balance are really the goals, but this does not mean that we get homogenized into a bland inner compromise. Integration is not about losing contrasts and intensity; rather, it is about having all of ourselves available. When we are increasingly balanced and integrated, we are free to choose which part of us will sing moment by moment. Gestaltists call the ability to make these choices "creative indifference."

WORKING WITH POLARITIES: INTROJECTS

The basic way Gestaltists work with polarities is to let the sides talk to each other. A simple suggestion might run something like this:

> Would you let the part of you that learned that tears are weak,
> talk to the part of you that is almost crying? And would you let
> those tears that are stuck in your throat talk back?

It is important to have the two sides actually talk *to* each other, rather than just talk *about* each side of the conflict, perhaps sitting on different pillows representing each side. To resolve a polarity, each pole needs to have its say *while in contact with its polar opposite.* There needs to be a dialogue, a meeting, a real conversation in which each side is played out. (Working with introjects is also discussed in Chapter Eleven.)

Say a woman carries the introject that she is not pretty enough. It is fairly certain that somewhere inside her is a healthy protest against this demeaning judgment. Making the separation between "her" and her "judging voice" is one way to uncover the polarity. For example, the Gestalt Pastoral Minister might say,

> Nancy, would you sit on this pillow and be your judging voice?
> Let this other pillow be Nancy, and tell Nancy that she isn't pretty
> enough.

Once that is done, Nancy can be asked to switch pillows and be herself responding to her judging voice.

What happens to you when you hear this judgment? the minister might ask. *Would you be willing to tell your judge?*

The two sides might argue back and forth a number of times before any resolution or integration is reached.

It is important to note that polarity work is not necessarily a negotiation of equals, and often compromise will not be the answer. It may be, as it was with the woman who was not pretty enough, that the judging voice will decrease in strength or even shut up completely. Or a vestige of that voice may be transformed into a caretaking impulse that simply keeps the woman well-groomed. Perhaps a new conversation may emerge which enables her to revel in being a delicious woman, whether fat or thin, young or old, beautiful or interesting-looking. Thus, allowing the polar opposite of an introject to confront the introject's voice is an important step in healing.

Polarity work, especially in the beginning, may not be very genteel. Anxiety may surface as people attempt to step over long-held inner boundaries. Work that has been flowing along may suddenly freeze up as a result of an inner objection to growth. Typically, the two poles may be something like, "I really want to change and I'll do whatever it takes!" versus "I'm scared! I don't wanna go there!" Polarity work may also reveal plenty of anger. The catastrophic expectation may well surface. One side may actually want to destroy the other, particularly if the person is confronting a cruel, demeaning inner voice. When the work is this intense, almost always there is an introject fueling the fire; in the encounter, a person may discover that in confronting a part of herself, she is actually expressing that which needs to be said to the person or institution that planted the introject. An experiment that might open the way for such a discovery is "Would you be willing to repeat to your mother (or father or spouse or church, etc.) what your underdog just said to your topdog? See if any of your words need to be said to someone in your life, would you?"

A woman was confronting a topdog that told her a dozen times a day that she was stupid. As she allowed this heartless topdog voice to speak, she told herself aloud that she was a stupid idiot and would never learn to do things right. I asked her to repeat what she had just said and see if she sounded like anyone in her life. Right away she exclaimed,

> *I sound just like Miss Jones, my fourth-grade teacher! No matter how hard I tried I was still stupid to her. She was so awful to the kids that she was fired, but not until I was out of her class. For a whole year I was scared to go to school.*

With this important discovery, polarity work was dropped, for now she could deal directly with the tyrannical Miss Jones who had lived inside her for so long. Allowing her underdog to angrily confront Miss Jones brought much healing. Soon the woman was able to claim a new, integrated identity based on the awareness that while she could make mistakes, she was a person of considerable intelligence, talents, and gifts.

Polarity work with introjects can be much enhanced if combined with faith imagination prayer. Wonderful things happen when Jesus is invited into the middle of an inner conflict; at the very least the process usually goes faster. Jesus is able to love that part of us that we have rejected, and gives radical permission as we struggle to express scary or "forbidden" feelings. Because Jesus encourages growth from the inside, there is even less need for a minister to push for a particular outcome. With Jesus present, an explorer may well find the courage to challenge a damaging introject – and the person behind it. The woman who confronted Miss Jones was greatly helped by a faith imagination prayer that enabled her to tell Miss Jones that she was *created* smart and gifted. Furthermore Jesus said that she didn't have to live by Miss Jones' cruel barbs any more, a statement that was the capstone of this important work.

From Introjects and Two-sided Polarities to Multifaceted Polarities

The nature of our growth changes as we mature and become more whole. We can expect to make progress. In regard to polarities, we tend to evolve from dealing with simple, two-sided and conflicted polarities to more complex, multi-faceted and nuanced ones. Gestalt Pastoral Care recognizes this progressive development, and the role of spirituality in human growth. I illustrate below some broad contours of this progressive movement.

The Pharisee and the Tax Collector; an Implicit Introject

An introject is implicit when one pole is so identified as *me* that the other scarcely comes to awareness. The result is rigid, exaggerated behavior characterized by judgment and denial. The Pharisee at prayer is a good example:

> God, I thank you that I am not like other people, thieves, rogues, adulterers, or even like this tax collector. I fast twice a week; I give a tenth of all my income (Luke 18:9-14).

In an implicit polarity, the person's ego boundaries become tightly drawn to exclude anything but the chosen persona. Implied in the strong denial is a rigid taboo against admitting to behavior, impulses, or fantasies outside one's self-identity. I once heard a nun insist that she had no sexual impulses *at all*. Another acquaintance claims to be absolutely single-minded about work. His job defines him; it is the only role he knows, and the only thing he will talk about. Both are afraid to discover anything else about themselves. Both spend a lot of energy keeping their façade unsullied and their denial intact.

Nevertheless, the other side is there, unrecognized, covert, present in the very strength of the person's emphatic denial. Underneath each "Pharisee," is inevitably a repentant "tax collector" who needs to pray, "God, be merciful to me, a sinner!" One who has to be a tower of strength at all times, and who never allows a show of weakness, almost certainly has weakness that would show if the façade cracked. Someone who insists on always being gentle is likely capable of strong assertiveness.

People with major implicit polarities are at the very beginning of the journey toward wholeness.

I believe that Dissociative Identity Disorder, formerly called Multiple Personality Disorder, is an extreme version of implicit polarities. When someone suffers from DID there is often no awareness at all between the alternative personalities, or "alters." The splintering of personality is so complete that the person hosts a crowd of inner people of different ages, experiences, memories, abilities, facial expressions and voices. There may well be, for example, one personality who is a competent and solid professional, another who is small, frightened child, and still another who is a flighty teenager. Such splintering usually begins when just one part of an abused child is designated as the bearer of intractable pain and fear. Then the rest of the child can survive without being devastated.

Those suffering from DID are often encouraged to do inner work similar to that of Gestalt. Slowly they allow the various alters to get acquainted and talk to each other. Eventually they learn to cooperate and make room for each other, and perhaps in time, some will decide to integrate.

An Active Polarity: The Rich Young Man

A young man came to Jesus, yearning for something more in his spiritual life besides keeping the commandments. Jesus issued an electrifying invitation:

> If you wish to be perfect, go, sell your possessions, and give the
> money to the poor, and you will have treasure in heaven; then
> come, follow me" (Matthew 19:21).

The young man goes away grieving, because he was very wealthy. Clearly, he is not ready to let go of his money and the status that comes with it. His grief suggests that he is not able to let go of his desire to follow Jesus either. The gospel writer doesn't elaborate on his dilemma, but it is easy to think of him going away to wrestle with yes or no. Jesus must have sensed his turmoil, for he comments that it is easier for a camel to go through the eye of a needle than for a rich person to enter the kingdom of heaven.

The young man's response is a perfect example of an active polarity. In an active polarity, both sides pull on a person, and the person has awareness of both. One side may be dominant for a time, then the other will be in control for a while. Sometimes the pull from each side is about equal, which feels particularly uncomfortable. The story told in the last chapter of my own conflict between expressing rage and being nice is another good example of an active polarity dragging a person from side to side with nearly equal force.

Active polarities are characterized by conflict, physical tension, confusion, and fatigue. It takes a lot of energy to pull constantly on oneself in two directions at once! Some people will simply become numb in order to escape from the constant turmoil and emotional paralysis; others will just feel stuck. Active polarities are often identified in Perls' Gestalt process schema with *the impasse,* sometimes called *the implosion,* a point just before *the explosion* into a new integration.[42]

Progression: Nancy's Work With an Active Polarity

Nancy, a young woman who has a very responsible job in a social agency, had been trying to make a decision for many months. Some days she loved her job, one that put her in a position to give direct help to the needy. She was good at her work, and at one time she had felt a clear vocation to do it. Yet she was thinking of leaving, and the question was tormenting her. Many times she had prepared a letter of resignation, determined to place it on her boss's desk. It never got there, for just as she was about to deliver the letter, she would find fresh enthusiasm for her work and decide to stay. Neither decision held for more than a week or two. When she first began to work on this active polarity, her conflict ran something like this:

> Ms. I Want Out of Here: *I'm sick of this rat race. It would feel great to just chuck it all and quit! It's not lifegiving, not worth the stress, not worth the Mickey Mouse paperwork, not worth the hoops I jump through every day, not worth the sexism I have to put up with.*
>
> Ms. Yeah, But: *You have to work at something. This job is not perfect but you get to do the things that you know are important. You get to help, and the help is very real. Someone else in your job might be more interested in furthering a career than in helping people. You are needed – your gifts of listening and compassion, your heart for the poor. And don't forget, you've been called to this!*
>
> Ms. IWOH: *Calls can change!*

---

[42] Perls posits five "layers of neurosis"; I believe a more descriptive name would be "layers of Gestalt work". As one goes deeper into one's healing process, one may encounter the following layers: 1. Cliches, 2. Roles and games, 3. Impasse, 4. Implosion, 5. explosion. See *Gestalt Therapy Verbatim,* pp. 75-77.

Ms. YB: *Has yours? Or are these complaints another example of how you never finish anything?*

And so on – and on. After the poles had their say, I asked her if she would invite Jesus to be with her in this conflict. She agreed, and immediately she saw herself – actually both of her selves – sitting at a large conference table. She, Nancy, was somehow standing outside of the conflict, and was watching the two parts of herself locked in battle. Jesus was standing close beside her. As she watched and listened, the conviction grew in her that these two could continue to argue forever. Suddenly it was clear to her that they were less interested in resolving the issue than in keeping the fight going. She looked over at Jesus and his nod and smile confirmed for her that she had understood. Then she felt Jesus usher her out of the room and close the door.

Being separated from her "companions" was scary for Nancy. The sudden inner quiet was disconcerting, and she felt herself pulled toward the conference table and the familiar merry-go-round. Jesus, however, looked at her and un-tangled her polarity with just two quiet sentences. "Nancy, you have been ad-dicted to inner conflict for a long time. Now is the time to let it go."

Nancy was stunned at both the clarity of the Lord's words, and her sudden capacity to shut up inside long enough to hear them. The new truth virtually ex-ploded in her consciousness, reframing old memories and bringing new meaning to them. As the dust settled, she was aware of a new polarity emerging, one more hidden and more truthful. When this new polarity was allowed expression, inte-gration came quickly.

One side of her new polarity allowed Nancy to admit for the first time that yes indeed, she needed inner conflict. Whenever she was relatively at peace, she saw that she would quickly manufacture another twisted knot with which to wrestle. Withstanding this inner turmoil told her that she was powerful, deep, and smart enough to embrace ambiguity, and sensitive to all sides of every issue. She could take in everything, and hold it all together. Constant inner chaos was an old famil-iar friend shaping her identity. The other side of the new polarity was an inner voice that seemed empowered by Jesus. Speaking from this position, Nancy was able to say that constant turmoil was exhausting, kidnapping her energy, her peace, and her zest for life. She was tired of it, and *ready to give up the need for conflict.* "Jesus tells me who I am, not my knotty questions," she said. "I don't need to be torn up to exist." As she repeated these last sentences to herself, she burst into tears of relief.

This beautiful integration did not cancel out her tolerance for ambiguity; in fact her new integration was built on ambiguity, which became an asset. She was able to allow the question of her job to be there in a gentle way, recognizing that her job wasn't perfect but that she could enjoy her work there anyway until God seemed to prompt her in another direction. What had been a tormenting question was transformed into openness to the future.

INTEGRATED AND MULTIFACETED POLARITIES: ST. PAUL

When a polarity such as Nancy's is integrated, the individual is fully aware of both sides of himself, and has the choice of going in either direction. There can be a choice, for example, to be assertive or to fade into the background; either could be well and truly okay, depending on the circumstances. An integrated polarity results in freed energy, and sometimes even a new configuration of the two sides that seems like a whole new personality trait. Once I worked with a sober, intellectual, Catholic priest who discovered in himself an impish Dennis-the-Menace little boy. When these poles were integrated, his intellect became witty, playful, and puckish. A bit astonished by the delightfully alive man who seemed to be emerging, members of his community began to call him "the holy terror."

The Apostle Paul writes of his experience of the radical integration of Saul, his old Christian-persecuting self, and the converted Paul. As he tells it, he "died." Yet, Saul's fiery temperament, his scholarly bent, and his religious zeal did not vanish when he was bowled over by the Voice. His old self was not lost, but transformed. Surely he must have worked hard to keep his forceful and multifaceted personality balanced as a servant of the Lord. Tempered by discipline, courage, suffering, and a good measure of grace, a saint was born, a saint who became a down-to-earth preacher, a skilled theologian, a writer, an organizer, and a man who still had to contend at times with his worst impulses. Saint Paul knew well that he was capable of murder, and knew equally well the power of grace. He had few, if any, illusions about himself. We hear evidence of this tremendous change in his ringing affirmation to the Galatians:

> For through the law I died to the law, that I might live to God. I have been crucified with Christ; and it is no longer I who live, but it is Christ who lives in me. And the life I now live in the flesh I live by faith in the Son of God, who loved me and gave himself for me (Galatians 2:19-20).

Multifaceted Polarities

As we grow emotionally and spiritually, like Paul, we may discover fewer polar introjects and more multifaceted polarities. Multifaceted polarities occur when there are several internal voices that are nuanced parts of ourselves with differing points of view. What starts out as a two-sided argument represented by two pillows may develop into a more complex discussion with several pillows representing various interrelated concerns. As we allow the inner voices to speak we discover a rich internal discussion. My colleague, Gestalt Pastoral Care Minister Sara Goold, describes this more complex internal dialogue as a "committee meeting." In a committee meeting there may not be an introjected admonition or childhood taboo on the agenda. Instead, each of the facets may have a vital contribution to be balanced with the others. In fact, committee meetings may not have to deal with conflict or woundedness at all, but may focus instead on spiritual and emotional growth. Thus, committee meetings tend to reveal a flexible inner working task force rather than two adversaries. True multifaceted polarities are a great gift, for they are a place where tension between the parts of a self is creatively maintained. It is a place that invites ongoing discernment and dialogue with the Holy One.

We can find much evidence of multifaceted polarities in the writings of Christian saints. St. Francis of Assisi was always trying to balance his call to solitude with his call to provide leadership to his new brotherhood, and with his call to serve the poor. St. Theresa of Avila knew well that God was doing something very wonderful in her. At the same time she wanted to make sure that she was getting it right. She consulted many "learned men" to help discern if she was making it all up, or perhaps was being fooled by Satan. None of this drama stopped her from moving ahead with what she felt God wanted her to do.

In our own time, someone might discover in himself a budding artist, and he finds a way to make time for his art. Or a new father might discover that a new tender softness was born in him at the birth of his first child. He wants to treasure and make room for this melting loveliness as he adjusts to less sleep and learns the parenting ropes, while still maintaining his job. Another person might simply be reminded again that she must balance her hunger for solitude with the demands of her family and with her desire to return to school one day. Still another might become aware of increasingly strong inner tugs which seems to add up to a new call, along with a need to take seriously her financial obligations, and figure out how she would get the necessary training to enter a new line of work.

Once these inner voices come to awareness, how are they to be honored and nurtured in a busy, complicated life? Gestalt Pastoral Care Ministers work with multifaceted polarities in much the same way as with polar introjects. All the voices are allowed to "speak" individually and fully while in contact with each other in a conversation. Obviously, this conversation does not have to be simply verbal. Instead each side could make a noise or take a posture or make a gesture or allow a dance to dance itself. Or each side could invite Jesus to sit nearby while the committee pays prayerful attention to what the Lord might do.

Usually a new integration doesn't happen overnight. Especially when there is a need for discernment concerning a major decision, it is not wise to hurry the process. Naturally, it may be a bit scary to allow something new to emerge, even tentatively. However, as a new integration is given more room or a new behavior is increasingly present in various experiences, there is more comfort with it, maybe even enjoyment. There is new freedom to go with one side or the other. Sometimes the various sides seem to mix a little, so that, for example, a person who has been known for her steady, even-temperedness might find as she integrates her passion that she is able to be passionately steady, or even steadily passionate. The integration, which claims the gifts of all sides of the polarity, seems to produce what seems like a whole new personality characteristic. What was formerly a conflict becomes a rich continuum of available responses.

The Gifts of Polarities for the Gestalt Pastoral Minister

Working with polarities helps keep a minister honest. Whatever the feeling or experience reported by another person, we know we can find something similar in ourselves. Having awareness of our own polarities is the best way I know to learn to identify with those of others. Polarity work helps us join another's world as we come to believe that nothing human is foreign to us. Staying in touch with our own polarities is a good way to deal with whatever might shock us in another. Furthermore, knowing that all of us are made up of polar feelings, traits, committees in session, and committees that have never met, is an antidote to the outdated professional arrogance that believes that the seeker is sick and needy and the minister is healthy and together. Thankfully, that distorted attitude is dying.

Once I worked with a woman who considered leaving her husband and young children and getting her own apartment for a few months so she could "find herself." I had a toddler and an infant of my own at the time, and I was horrified. "What! Leave your helpless innocent little babies for months at such a formative time? Selfish! Terrible!" So screamed a voice in my head, and I knew I had work to do before she came back.

I knew I passionately loved my kids, and that I would never leave them, but I had to find my polarity to that conviction. I didn't have to search very long. Almost immediately, I recognized in myself an exhausted mother who had to admit that she would absolutely love a good long rest. How wonderful to be kid-free for a while! To sleep through the night! To have no icky messes to clean up! To enjoy an adult meal! To go and come as I pleased! To own a cream-colored couch! It was an extremely powerful fantasy, and admitting it helped me stop judging the woman with whom I was working. I began to understand – from the inside – the stresses on the young woman who had far less support than I. Even though I still did not think it a sound idea to leave her family, I was then able to be compassionate with the impulse underneath it.

Dreams are a way around the head.
Frederick Perls

...the Lord appeared to Solomon in a dream by night;
and God said, "Ask what I should give you."
I Kings 3:6

13

GESTALT PASTORAL CARE DREAMWORK

THE FLIPPING MINISTER

Marie was the pastor of a large, old, and traditional congregation. As the first woman minister in the church's long history of distinguished clergy, she was eager to do a good job. Dedicated and gifted, she worked long hours, visiting parishioners, planning programs, teaching Bible study and confirmation class, preparing sermons, responding to the needs of the many poor people in the neighborhood. She prayed for her church, and truly loved them. Still, most of her parishioners seemed unresponsive and unmoved. Her best efforts just seemed to go nowhere. The congregation, stuck in its own hoary traditions, was mired in fear of spending their considerable money. Furthermore, church members balked at taking any responsibility for activities of the church. They wanted a variety of programs that made their church look successful, but they wanted Marie to do all the work. When she protested, they accused her of not being as good as her male predecessors.

After six years of this, Marie was exhausted and discouraged. Her life was dominated by working long hours, followed by a few hours of sleep so she could work again. She plodded along, trying to be faithful to her vocation, but with little hope that anything would change.

Then one day she reported an absolutely wonderful dream, excerpted here from her journal:

> I am in a book store/gift shop, just browsing, when I am delighted to find a 'flipping minister in a box,' a little wooden toy figure– usually a clown, but in this case a minister – suspended

between two sticks. The idea of the toy is to take the two sticks in your hands, and manipulate the minister who was suspended between two sticks. With just the right pressure and speed, the minister runs back and forth on the sticks, occasionally flipping head over heels. I pick up the sticks, and try to get the minister to flip, but it's more difficult than it looks. As I try, I see that the box is full of confetti which spills all over the place if you do it wrong,

So, I'm trying hard to make the thing work, but I'm frustrated. I can't do it right, no matter what, and confetti is flying all over the store. Then somehow the minister flips, flies off the handles, and soars way up in the sky.

A duck is flying by and catches the flipping minister is its mouth, and flies away. I try to chase the duck, but it's useless. It is gone. The duck keeps flying, and gently puts the minister down in a new place. I see that the duck was flying by at the precise pinnacle of the minister's trajectory, and that the minister is caught before she begins to fall.

As she told this dream, I tried hard to listen seriously but after she said the words "flipping minister" for the second time, I couldn't help it; I burst out laughing. In an instant she was laughing too, and for some moments neither of us could stop. Every time we sobered up a little, we cracked up again as she tried to tell her dream. Actually the whole dream struck us as hilarious – the silly toy, the confetti, the flying duck to the rescue, and especially the flipping minister.

Our laughter seemed to bring new energy to Marie. Her face came alive, her eyes sparkled, and her whole being exuded a new lightness. "Whoo!" she said. "I've *never* had this much fun in a session!"

According to Gestalt theory every image of a dream is a projection of a part of the dreamer; so, in this dream Marie was, of course, the flipping minister, but also the one making the toy go, and the confetti, the gift shop, and so on. As we began to work on the dream it was clear right away how perfect her dream images were. Trying hard to get the minister to flip seemed to capture exactly how she had been trying to make herself "do flips" to challenge her congregation to greater faithfulness. When she playfully became the little minister figure, frantically jumping, rolling and somersaulting along her track of two sticks – in response to pressure – she found herself describing precisely how her personal rat race felt. When she became the confetti she contacted a part of herself that was ready to celebrate that she couldn't get the minister to flip right. It was a revelation to Marie that she had been trying to do flips to please and appease. She saw that her overwork was neither healthy nor faithful. Our own gales of laughter gave a delightful lightness to an issue that had seemed heavy and onerous just the week before.

As the dream continued to yield its secrets, Marie saw that the minister "flying off the handles" was another image of health. Flying off the handle, i.e., getting angry, was a healthy response to the way the church was treating her. And, flying off the handle was the direct prelude to the freedom of "soaring way up in the sky."

Then we came to the duck. As she had done with the other dream images, Marie began to describe herself as the duck. We were still proceeding on the classical Gestalt idea that every image in a dream is a projection of a part of the dreamer. As the duck speaking to Marie, she said:

> Marie, I love it when you soar. I created you to soar. You don't have to do flips to please others; I just want you to please me. Don't be afraid, because I will always catch you and set you down in a new place.

It was immediately clear that the dream duck was not just a projection, but an icon of God's communication with her. Marie was awed that God would speak so clearly in her dream. She spent many weeks assimilating the Holy Duck's message, and discerning what it might mean. What was God saying? Slowly she came to the conclusion that she would continue to be a flipping minister trapped in a confining track as long as she stayed at her church. It was time to shake the dust from her feet. She decided to resign from the church and take a sabbatical, allowing herself time to rest, discern, soar a little, and perhaps reconnect with the "confetti" part of herself.

During her sabbatical, the dream continued to be a reference point; she called it "my catharsis." She carefully and joyfully discerned that the parish ministry was not where her gifts were best used, and for a time she worked as a denominational program staff person, and later, for a secular social agency.

It has now been many years since Marie was a flipping minister, and she reports that the duck dream "still sustains me." She is now the Community Minister for six congregations, a position she loves. "I remember that the duck carried me and then set me down in a new place. I feel that my present job is right where God dropped me." She is still awed at how directly God is concerned with her happiness and growth as a person, and is convinced that God has a great sense of humor. For Marie, ducks are now a holy icon of God's tender and constant love. "In the spring there are two ducks who visit our small swimming pool. They remind me again of how deeply God touched me." Truly she is "soaring way up in the sky."

GESTALT DREAMWORK: FRITZ PERLS' MODEL

Gestalt dreamwork is simple and powerful. It is also an art. People with no experience can learn the basics of Gestalt dreamwork in an afternoon, though it takes much experience to be good at it. Because Gestalt dreamwork is non-ana-lytical, it is not necessary to figure anything out, (in contrast to psychoanalysis) nor is it important to know a lot about myths and symbols, (in contrast to a Jun-gian approach). Gestalt dreamwork seldom encourages a discussion *about* a dream; instead it focuses on *letting a dream itself talk*. Once that is understood, it is relatively easy to work with your own dreams.

Freud taught that dreams were "the royal road to the unconscious." Perls, in his iconoclastic way, would say that dreams are a "way around the head," a wonderful way to discover what is underneath a person's thoughts, theories, and resistance. He used to tell his students that bodies and dreams never lie.

Furthermore, Perls had great trust in people's ability to find the message in their own dreams; for him the real authority in dreamwork was the dreamer. He had a sense of what sleep researchers confirm: that dreams are necessary to emotional health. If he were alive, I could imagine him repeating that dreams have to do with homeostatic regulation. He would mean that dreams bring to awareness whatever needs to be taken care of inside.

Here is a summary of Gestalt dreamwork as Perls taught it,[43] followed by a discussion of the additions made by Gestalt Pastoral Care.

According to Fritz Perls, every object, every person, even every idea in a dream is a projection of the dreamer. Imagine someone dreams that he is in his car driving down the highway, enjoying the scenery and listening to the radio. A rabbit hops in front of the car and just makes it to the shoulder of the road as the car speeds by. This hypothetical dreamer could rightly assume that he is himself in the dream of course, but he is also the car, the driver, the driver's enjoyment, the radio, the road, the scenery, the speed, the terrified rabbit and the shoulder of

---

[43] Perls, *Gestalt Therapy Verbatim*, "Dreamwork Seminar," pp. 93-246

the road. All these dream symbols represent some aspect of himself. This is absolutely basic to Gestalt dreamwork theory.

Simple to understand, but when a dreamwork beginner tells his dreams it is often difficult for him, for example, to imagine that *he* is really his mother in his dream, as well as the chair on which she is sitting and the rug under her feet. Mother, chair and rug are all personal symbols of parts of himself. He will tend to see dream symbols as actual objects or real people. However, if he is willing to experiment with Gestalt dreamwork just a bit he may make some important discoveries – discoveries which can come so rapidly and feel so true, that he will know he has understood in his bones.

In Gestalt dreamwork, the dreamer begins by telling the dream in the present tense, as if it were happening now. For example, "I am in my bedroom looking for my sweater…" There is no discussion of what the dream means, or what the symbols might represent. Instead, the dreamer then playfully *pretends to be* each aspect of the dream, letting each object or person describe itself, and converse with the other objects or persons. For example, here is a condensed version of what happened when the dreamer worked on the bedroom and sweater dream:

> Dreamer as the bedroom: *I am my bedroom, and I'm messy. I have clothes and junk and stuff all over the place. My paint is peeling and I look like I've been neglected.*

> Dreamer as the sweater speaking to the bedroom: *I'm a beautiful sweater, soft and warm. I was a birthday gift, and look what you've done. You lost me! I'm tired of you burying me under all this crap! I'm getting lost in your mess.*

Usually the dreamer hears herself say something surprisingly truthful, or a polarity is revealed and recognized. Very often an "aha" quickly comes to light:

> Dreamer as herself: *I really am a mess, at least I pretend to be, and my warmth and softness, my gifts, get lost all the time."*

Whatever is unhealed or disowned urgently pushes for resolution in dreams. We can trust that dreams will speak the liberating, and sometimes scary, truth that we shy away from during waking hours, and that dreams, with an exquisite sense of timing, will bring up only those things we are ready to use to grow. In this context, a recurring dream is extremely important. It is as if the dream itself is insisting that we pay attention to its message. It is marvelous, really. In our very being God has imprinted the capacity to dream, and thus to perceive that push toward health.

So, if a person is disowning (denying and ignoring) her sexuality, it will surely show up in her dreams, in her own quirky dream code. If she needs to risk launching out on her own, that, too, will somehow work itself into a dream. If she denies, even to herself, that she is afraid, fear will figure in dreams until she is able to come to terms with it. Dream images can even represent parts of the dreamer's body, especially if the dreamer has rejected or ignored them. If her introjected mother is still a big player in her emotional life, her dreams will be full of mothers – in dream code. Remember, although her real mother might appear in a dream, in Gestalt dreamwork we still assume that mother in a dream is either an aspect of the dreamer, or the dreamer's introject of mother. Every dream can be worked on using this formulation, and this is what makes Gestalt dreamwork so easy to grasp. Even dreams that seem to "go beyond" classical Gestalt dreams can also be approached with this in mind.

For example, I once worked with a woman who made a habit of mentally rejecting anything that was good about herself. She claimed to be stupid, dull, ordinary, ugly, chaotic, and terribly screwed up. She focused almost entirely on her problems – while imagining me as a paragon of wisdom, beauty, knowledge and health. She held tightly to the fantasy that I was perfect and she was a perfect mess.

In the end, it was a series of dreams that melted this projection. She didn't dream of chaos, ugliness, stupidity, or of insurmountable problems. No, she dreamed about elegant houses with beautiful curving staircases, finely carved woodwork, and museum-quality furnishings. She dreamed about being in a canoe on a beautifully serene moonlit lake. She dreamed about being a teacher in an adult education class. Clearly her dreams were sending the message that there were some wonderful parts of her that she had disowned, and they were just waiting to be claimed and celebrated.

As she worked on these dreams, I invited her to playfully describe herself as her various dream images. She was reluctant at first, and didn't believe a word of it. "But I'm not an elegant house! If I'm any kind of house, I'm a broken-down fixer-upper!" Similar dreams finally convinced her to open the door a bit to her own inner riches, and finally she was stunned to hear herself saying, "I am an elegant house, a little unused, but well preserved because I hold such rich furnishings. I am graceful – grace filled – and someone has taken a great deal of care to build me well and make me especially beautiful inside." When she was able to let her own words in, her life began to change, starting with the way she felt about herself.

The disowned material can also be conspicuously absent from dreams. "Present" through their obvious absence, those elements clearly missing in a dream are always important. What minister has not dreamed of being in the pulpit ready to preach, only to discover his notes are nowhere to be found? Other common "missing" themes are being naked in public, discovering a house with no windows or doors, or searching in vain for a particular person or object. Perls would often ask dreamers to be what was missing in a dream.

One man who dreamed that he was not able to find "the route out of town," discovered as he worked with the dream that what was missing was "his way." "I've lost my way", he concluded, and as soon as he said it, he knew it was true. It was as if the dream put words to something he had been feeling for a long time.

Some dreams announce or invite immediate growth. These "announcing" dreams seem to come along just when a person is on the verge of making an inner change, or when the new integration is still fragile and needs to be recognized and named. When something has been newly reclaimed, there seems to be a time of adjustment and germination before the material is fully integrated. Often a dream assists in this process.

I had such a dream as a young woman. It was after some important therapy work in which I was finally willing to face life without covering up how much I didn't know. I was really sick of this fakery, and even though it was scary, I was ready to drop my pretensions. Later that same week I recorded the following dream in my journal:

> I am on a beach looking at a pretty stone church, but I can't see it very well because it is covered with a rickety wooden scaffold. It looks like the church was being fixed at one time, but the scaffold has outlived its usefulness. It doesn't look like it would hold anyone up; in fact it looks downright dangerous. I notice that there seems to be nothing wrong with the building underneath the scaffolding.
>
> Then I observe a tornado headed inland from the sea. I am not afraid, but I go into the church for shelter along with everyone else on the beach. The tornado hits, but we are all safe inside, singing hymns and having a fine old time. When the tornado is

over I go outside and see that the scaffolding has been completely torn away, and that the sturdy church is beautiful, and glowing in the reflected light of the setting sun.

This dream gave me a strong visual picture of the change that was taking place in me. I was losing the rickety scaffolding that was no longer necessary, the covering up of ignorance and inexperience. I was being cleaned off, only to discover strength and beauty in myself of which I had no idea. Although Perls would not be pleased, I also had a strong sense of God's action in the dream. What is more "an act of God" than a tornado? This dream was pure gift, and greatly helped reinforce the work I had done the week before in therapy.

Perls taught that a dream is not complete without the dreamer's waking interaction with it. As the dreamer tells the dream both teller and listener pay attention to feelings such as fear, anger, or sadness, to the way the dreamer's body reacts, to changes in the tone of voice or in excitement level, and so on. The need for healing not only appears in the dream, but in the here-and-now experience of re-living it. For instance, when Marie and I worked with her flipping minister dream, our laughter seemed to be a crucial part of the dream's message.

Paying attention which dream image stands out from among the others, which is the scariest, which is the most intriguing, which adds to the dream message and helps unscramble it. Sometimes work on a dream may even involve going back into the dream and finishing it in fantasy – a clear instance of how a dream is completed by being awake to it.

If a person can't remember her dreams, it may mean that the person is avoiding what's inside. Of course, forgetting dreams can have other causes. People who are exhausted, under unusual stress, or those who instantly leap out of bed at the first sound of the alarm clock, may have trouble bringing dreams to awareness. However, one who seldom remembers dreams might do well to ask, "What don't I want to face these days? What am I so afraid of?"

Perls was fond of asking those who didn't remember their dreams to talk to their missing dreams, and let the dreams reply. A woman in one of my classes, chagrined that she could not remember even one dream to bring to class, followed this advice, and her work took the following direction, abbreviated here:

Dreams: *You don't know anything about me. I want you to listen to me for once.*

Student: *How can I listen to you if I can't remember you? Anyway, dreams are silly and frivolous.*

Dreams: *Who told you that you were frivolous?*

Student: *Mother! Oh my gosh! She was in control of everything. I wasn't supposed to have any feelings at all!*

Now, many years later, she looks back on that Gestalt work as opening "a gate to the garden of her inner life." She reports that this "turning point" introduced her to "the real me" and marked the beginning of "finally realizing I was a child of God."

Finally, every dream is rich with many layers of meaning. If the same dream is worked on more than once, we can expect new insights and nuances to appear as we delve deeper. Symbols may broaden or even change their meaning – and both meanings will be right.

A REMINDER

According to Perls, dreams are never to be taken literally, nor are they to be analyzed or explained. Newcomers to dreamwork can easily scare and confuse themselves by thinking that a dream of mayhem and terror might be a movie of something that really happened or a prophecy of impending doom. If someone dies in a dream, let us say, it may be that something unhealthy in the dreamer, such as a pattern of behavior, needs to "die" for the continued growth of the dreamer. If the dreamer is assaulted in a dream, it is an indication that part of the dreamer herself – possibly an introject – is assaulting her.

In addition, despite knowing that Perls was dead set against "aboutism," beginners in Gestalt dreamwork inevitably slip into a discussion *about* the dream symbols or speculate *about* the dream's probable meaning. Perls would insist that such discussions are both confusing and futile.

THE ADDITIONS OF GESTALT PASTORAL CARE: OPENING TO GOD'S PRESENCE IN DREAMS

The above is all according to Fritz Perls. Although not all dreams fit the model proposed by Perls, his model is a wonderful place to start with almost any dream, and most dreams will "speak" if worked on in this way. Gestalt Pastoral Care adds concern for the spiritual dimension.

Just as the Holy Spirit works in our awareness continuum to bring us to wholeness, the Spirit also works in our dreams. Once I heard Morton Kelsey say that when he first began to work on his dreams, what exploded in his awareness was that God was still creating him. God was not only working in history, and through the ministry of the church, but in *him* to shape him into the man he was created to be. This awareness moved him to tears, and set his entire life in a new direction.[44]

Through my work with others, as well as my own dreams, I, too, am convinced that dreams are evidence that God is at work. God really and truly wants us to be whole people, and often uses dreams as a way to communicate. Sometimes God's communication is simply an invitation to grow in a particular direction, to mature, to integrate. Occasionally, God seems to literally inhabit a symbol or entire dream so clearly that the message is impossible to mistake. The Bible records a number of revelatory dreams of this nature. When revelatory dreams occur they are a great gift.

Once I dreamed I was in the kitchen of the house in Saginaw, Michigan, where we lived when I was a teenager. A cat on the back porch was trying to get inside so insistently that I was having trouble shutting the door. Determined that there was no way that cat was getting in the house, I was trying to push the cat out of the way when the cat looked gravely at me and said, "Will you love me with all your heart, soul, mind, and strength?"

I awoke, stunned at the clarity and truth of this message from God. There was no need to work on this dream; its meaning was immediately clear. Indeed I was trying to push God out of my "house," even as God's invitation was insistent – and gentle as a house cat. The words from the cat showed me in an instant what I was doing, and called me to repentance and renewal of commitment.

Another way that God seems to speak with clarity is in the mystery of precognitive (or foretelling) dreams. I think this type of dream is rare, but it does happen. My mother had such a dream while she was a student at the University of Michigan. She dreamed that she met a man on the steps of the college library. In her dream he stumbled and fell; she picked up his books for him and helped him to his feet. Then he asked her to play tennis. She agreed, and woke up. Soon after this dream, it all happened, just as the dream predicted, in every detail. A year later she decided to marry "the man of my dreams," and he became my father. Everyone who knew them said they were wonderfully suited to each other.

---

[44] See Morton Kelsey, *Dreams, A Way to Listen to God.*

Obviously, there is an element of the mysterious and numinous in dreams that Perls doesn't take into account. There is so much we don't know, so much uniqueness in each person, so much capacity for change, so much room for God to work. For example, the Senoi people of Malaysia regard dreams as the organizing focus of their culture. Anthropologists estimate they spend fully a third of their time dealing with dreams. Each morning the young people of the village tell their dreams to an elder who carefully listens, and then counsels the dreamers. Quite often the advice is to return to the same dream the next night, and finish it in a different way. Children are taught, for example, to face down the monsters chasing them in their dreams, and to make friends with them. This they are able to do, not knowing that most Westerners would find such a challenge an impossible assignment.[45]

Gestalt Pastoral Care Dreamwork

Ordinarily we begin with prayer that we hear the dream and the dreamwork with "ears of faith." Then the dreamer begins by telling the dream. The dreamer will probably need to be reminded to speak in the present tense, as if the dream story is occurring now, in the present. This Gestalt technique is not just a matter of semantics; sometimes speaking in the present tense is all that's needed to reveal one of the dream's messages. Imagine, for example, that someone dreams he is cooking in his kitchen. Nothing more than that, and he wakes up. Hear the nuance between, "In my dream I was cooking," and "I'm cooking." The present tense invites an immediacy that allows the dreamer to be present to the dream.

I listen and intuit as well as I can as the dream is being told. *Dreamwork is no different from other Gestalt work in that tone of voice, gestures, bioenergy, posture, physical tension, and so on, are as important as the dream itself.* In the cooking dream, for example, the way the dreamer said "I'm cooking" caught my attention. There was a whiff of intensity about his words, and his body reflected heightened tension at that moment, but I couldn't tell whether he was cooking with anger, excitement, or steamy sexuality, or what. So, I suggested the simplest of experiments: "Would you say that again, and listen to yourself?" "I'm cooking. I'm cooking! I'M COOKING!" he said. "I'M REALLY COOKING!" Then came the "aha": "I'm on a roll with my work. I'm cooking with my new project, but I need to stir the pot a little."

---

[45] See Patricia Garfield, *Creative Dreaming.*

After the dream is told, usually the easiest way to work on the dream is to ask the dreamer to be various parts of the dream. Good places to start are with the object that seems to have the most feeling attached to it, or with a missing element, or with the first object mentioned as the dream was told. For example, in the cooking dream, the dreamer could be the pot talking to the stove, or the cook talking to the food. Another way to begin is to just ask the dreamer what he is most aware of as he recalls the dream. (Remember the process of homeostasis, and how unfinished business surfaces in order of importance.) Actually, one can begin by playing almost any part of a dream, and usually some valuable awareness will come out of it.

In the dream I had about the church being hit by a tornado that tore away the scaffolding, I played the church first:

> I am a strong stone church. I'm not especially fancy, but I'm OK. I've been built right on the beach, and sometimes I'm ignored. People playing on the beach don't want to come to church. But there is a lot going on inside me, and people found shelter in me when the storm hit. They have a good time, and I protect them. I am a place of prayer and worship. I'm warm and welcoming. But I have this scaffolding on me that covers me up. Something about me must need to be fixed.

With the coaching of the minister, a dialogue develops among the various parts of the dream. As each part is played, it is likely that contrasting emotions, and viewpoints will emerge. Sometimes, the polarities and conflicts will be obvious. In my dream, the difference between the church and the scaffolding was clear almost right away, so I let the scaffolding talk to the church.

> Scaffolding to church: *I was put on you a long time ago because your front was crumbling and you needed a lot of repairs. You don't know it, but I've actually been holding you up. As rickety as I seem, I've been really important to you. You needed me to feel OK.*

> Church to scaffolding: *I don't need you any more! A tornado has torn you away, and I'm glowing with the light of the setting sun. With you gone, I can reflect the light, and I see that I'm much more beautiful without you.*

By this point in the work I recognized, of course, that I was talking about the recent work I had done to let go of my arrogant façade. The dream image of rickety scaffolding seemed to perfectly express the role my façade had played in my life. On the other hand, the church image held some surprises for me. I had been largely unaware of my strength or warmth or my ability to nurture and protect others. As the dialogue continued, I dropped the dream images and just spoke as two polarities in myself.

Once a dreamer has some awareness of what the dream is referring to, the dream images can be dropped. Once the code is broken, there is no longer any need to continue to speak in code. Thus I could let the warm, nurturing, sturdy, light-reflecting me converse with the self-important façade I had constructed. Or of course with God, who was still creating me. Often dreamwork leads naturally to work with experiments in just this way. I have found it helpful, however, to return more than once to dream symbols, letting them speak again. Often parts of a dream have something new to say in subsequent explorations. There seem to be multiple layers of messages in dreams that aren't always apparent at the first telling.

Very often there is one dream image that seems to express the work of the Holy Spirit in the dreamer. I have learned to listen for it. For example, as the tornado in my dream, I said:

> I have great power, and I'm coming across the sea to tear away your scaffolding. Don't be afraid. I won't hurt you, but I am going to remove what is holding you back. I want you to discover who you are without that old scaffolding covering you up. I want you to reflect the light.

I was startled by what I heard myself saying. Ordinarily I would think of a tornado as scary, destructive, impersonal violence out of control. In contrast, my dream tornado was powerful, but also gentle, loving and healing. Another dreamer who dreamed about being in a small room, found that God spoke as the door: "I am the door to a new environment, a new life" Still another dreamer recognized God speaking as a mouse:

> *You don't see me. I'm hidden, but I'm always here. You see evidence of me, and you try to get rid of me. You can't get rid of me. I'll always be in your house.*

A third person found God speaking to him in a dream as a bungee cord which helps him bounce back and keeps him from falling too far.

When God speaks so clearly in a dream, drop the dreamwork as such and respond to God's invitation. In the church and tornado dream, it seemed that God's invitation was to become a "place of prayer and protection" and to "reflect the sun" and to "discover who I really was." My response was to tell God that I was willing, but not able to do these things. I asked God to do these things in me, and show me how to cooperate.

Sometimes there seems to be no clarity at all about how God is at work in a dream; there may be no object or person in the dream in which God seems to communicate. There may be much dream conflict, but even after a good bit of dreamwork with plenty of "aha" moments, nothing seems resolved, and the dreamer is at an impasse.[46] For example, a psychotherapist dreamed that she had the assignment of climbing a huge mountain. She knew she had to climb it, but she was overwhelmed by its size and her own fatigue. As she wearily started to climb, she discovered that the mountain was made out of landfill: barely covered garbage and trash. Repulsed, she woke up.

As she worked on the dream, she could get no further than the realization that the dream was exactly accurate. As a therapist she did spend her life "climbing around in other people's garbage," and she was, in fact, exhausted. (In this instance, she had an immediate clear sense that the garbage was not something inherent to her, but represented the garbage she "took in" as she worked with others.) She was stuck with the pile of garbage and her inability to climb it. Neither could she just walk away; in the dream the mountain was "her assignment."

When the conflict or situation becomes clear, even when there seems to be no transcendent symbol in the dream, we can invite Jesus to enter into the dream. He usually changes or finishes the dream in a new way, and faith imagination takes over where the dream left off.

The therapist/dreamer invited Jesus to be with her as she looked at her garbage mountain. He came right away, and in her mind's eye she could see him with her. She explained to him how tired she was, and that she just couldn't climb the mountain.

I know you want me to be a therapist", she said, "but I've had it! I don't have any energy or desire to do anything! I don't want to see anybody! I don't want to listen to any more terrible stories! I'm really, really sick of sex abuse and

---

[46] The impasse is what Perls called the level or "layer" of work that is characterized by deadness, numbness, blankness, great tension, and paralysis. See *Gestalt Therapy Verbatim*, p. 76

neurotic confusion and people bent on keeping themselves in a bind while insisting I get them out of it!"

It felt good to her to be so honest, but wanting to be faithful, she asked Jesus to give her enough energy to climb the mountain. Instead, Jesus took her hand and led her into the woods. There he showed her a beautiful brass bed made up with creamy sheets, feather pillows, and soft blankets. He invited her to sleep as long as she needed, and to climb the mountain later when she felt better. He said he would go up the mountain with her when the time came. She began to cry, and in her tears she realized that she had been so focused on other's needs that she had ignored her own – again. Jesus' loving response to her fatigue gave her permission to take some time off, and to structure more rest time into her schedule.

The above discussion of dreamwork in Gestalt Pastoral Care is the result of a long journey to my present belief that dreams are not only the province of psychotherapy and brain/sleep research, but also an ordinary, nightly "open mike" God uses to communicate with us. We go to sleep; our brain cells fire; pictures and impulses flash; we experience movement even though our muscles are paralyzed – and God is at work in it all. Dreams are holy ground, a private school in which challenges are presented, growth is enabled, healing is given, avenues for prayer opened and God's work is revealed. I hope for the day when ordinary churches can reclaim these riches as they engage in nurturing the faith of its members.

PART FOUR

BEYOND THE BASICS

Part Four is addressed to both pastors and pastoral counselors who are invited to widen their awareness, to pray more boldly, and to be alert to some factors which, if not addressed, can block healing.

When we make our body experience an "it" instead of an "I,"
we make ourselves less than we are.
James Kepner

14

BODY READING: SEEING THE OBVIOUS

THE RULES: DON'T FEEL! DON'T LOOK!

Traditionally, the church has been phobic about bodies.[47] When reading biographies of saints one quickly becomes aware of a dark thread weaving through their otherwise superb lives: that of abusively subduing their bodies. We read how some fasted to such excess that they ruined their health or ate things that would ordinarily inspire disgust. Others allowed themselves very little sleep or forced themselves to sleep on boards. Still others flailed themselves with ropes or "disciplines" and wore hair shirts – or worse – next to their skin. Nearly all fled from contact with the opposite sex.

We moderns are appalled by such frightful excesses. Yet even in our own time Christians have been taught to disregard, or even fear, their own bodies and those of the people around them. Bodies are sensual, the distortion goes, and sensuality leads directly and inevitably to lust. Bodies are first and foremost the arenas for sin, particularly sexual sin. Sex is shameful, scary, and by nature uncontrollable. Many of us who grew up in the church can remember just how these attitudes were conveyed. I recall, for example, as a teenager getting a personal admonition from a fundamentalist preacher that if I didn't stop wearing lipstick and sweaters that fit, I was going straight to hell.

What is the result of this somatophobic attitude hovering in the background of many of us? What is the power of these cultural underpinnings, which most of us would now intellectually reject? I believe it is this: American popular culture, while gripped by a nearly pathological obsession with sex and physical violence, is also divorced from genuine experience of bodies. Ask the average person what he is experiencing in his body at the moment, and quite often he will reply "noth-

---

[47] Some material in this chapter was previously published by the author in an article entitled "Healing Prayer and Lomi Body Work" in *The Journal of Christian Healing*, Fall, 1987.

ing" or "I'm OK." This is accurate, as far as his awareness goes. For him, nothing *is* going on unless he is in physical pain, feeling ill, or sexually aroused. Or ask someone simply to look at the body of another person in a nonsexual way, and he or she may well respond with acute discomfort or embarrassment.

This odd proscription against looking even extends to the medical profession. A nurse in one Gestalt Pastoral Care training group reported that in three years of nursing school she had never once seen a penis. Even more astounding, my Lomi Bodywork[48] teacher, Dr. Robert Hall, said that in medical school he never saw the whole naked body of a living person. Yes, he studied a cadaver, but living bodies were always draped so that only one part at a time was visible. No wonder medical science has been slow to adopt a holistic orientation to healing. The marvel is that it has happened at all.

Body reading is the practice of looking at a body with the intent of seeing or intuiting physical locations for emotional and spiritual pain, and the health that is surely there. In reading a body we ask what combination of life experiences, unhealed pain, growth accomplished, and need for growth this body might be showing us. Body reading is a nearly subversive activity, particularly in the context of the church, and flies in the face of cultural taboos. A class learning to "read" clothed bodies for the first time will quickly encounter this cultural prohibition against gazing at another's body, for in our sexualized culture, looking itself is felt to be sexual. As members of the class stand in shorts or leotards to allow the others to take a good look, it is hard for students to see much at first. They may find themselves comparing the cultural standard of very thin "hard bodies" to every body. Frequently they experience a culturally-conditioned internal boundary that tells them to avert their eyes completely.

PERMISSION TO LOOK

A Gestalt Pastoral Minister must learn to look at clothed bodies and see them as they are. He must work with his own feelings about bodies until he can genuinely love them, knowing that when he looks at a body – *any body* – he is seeing the beauty of creation. In other words, he must give himself permission to look at another lovingly, without judgments, shame or voyeurism. He might begin with his own body, for most of us carry plenty of bodily shame.

---

[48] Lomi Bodywork is a system of direct physical manipulation designed to stretch shortened muscles, and to free "stuck" energy, so that the emotional and spiritual content of the muscles is released.

Many find it helpful to remember how comfortable Jesus was with physicality. He washed dirty feet and allowed a woman to wash his; he put his hands on lepers, held kids on his lap, and at least once he made a poultice of mud and his own spit. He went to parties where he ate and drank with "sinners," and despite religious laws to the contrary, he was not the least put off by the touch of a menstruating woman. Jesus had a body of his own which got tired, hungry, and sweaty, which felt pain and pleasure, and which excreted urine and feces. The incarnation of Jesus in a human body fairly shouts the holiness of human physicality. When one really looks at a body, no matter what its size, shape, or condition, God's handiwork shines out.

When learning to read bodies, inner permission to look takes the student halfway there. When one is free really to look at a body – and experience one's own – suddenly there is much that is obvious. It is not difficult, for example, to identify shallow breathing, jerky motions, caved-in or pushed-out chests, clamped jaws, and tightly-held legs. With a little more practice, it is possible to see evidence of more subtle physical tension and blocked energy.

As we become familiar with body reading we learn to perceive distortions or regularity of physical structure, tension or ease, frozenness or fluidity of motion, extra fat or gauntness or slimness, various colors of the body and of its aura, depth of respiration and the nature of the person's bioenergy. The extraordinary assumption in body reading is that when we look at a person's body, we are looking at spirit and emotions as well. We catch glimpses of personal history, and hints of the person's growing edge.

Obviously, body reading is not like reading a well-written book in which everything is made perfectly clear. Although we can easily learn to notice, for example, that the muscles on the left side of a body are more shortened than on the right, we don't know exactly what this means in the person's existence. We must hold our perceptions lightly until we can test them out, usually with experiments. (Later I will suggest how to use body reading to create experiments.)

Body reading is both an art and a skill, and it can be developed to a high degree. My teachers at the Lomi School in San Francisco, and my friend Rosemary Feitis, a Rolfer and homeopathic physician in New York City, for example, are able to see intricacies and subtleties that I still cannot until they are pointed out to me. Like many professional bodyworkers, their ability to see is sophisticated and nuanced. But even ministers who are rank beginners at body reading will find that rudimentary awareness of bodies pays big dividends in ministry.

The material that follows in this chapter is the merest introduction to body reading. Mostly it invites a simple shift in attention, a new permission to observe the obvious, and a new trust in the importance of what you see.

WHY IS BODY READING IMPORTANT?

Because our bodies profoundly reflect who we are. Because expanding our awareness as far as we can is part of our job. And because bodies present us with a wealth of information if only we have eyes to see. The importance of body reading becomes clearer when you consider the assumptions below:

All expressed feelings are expressed bodily. This is patently obvious, when you think about it. Although we can be aware that our feelings are present, and perhaps we can even talk about them with great insight, we cannot express emotions with our rational mind alone. When we are expressing sadness, for example, our bodies may curl up and sag all over. If we are deeply sad, our breath becomes more labored as sobs are pushed up from our diaphragm. Tears drop from our eyes, and sounds come from our mouth and throat. In expressing anger, perhaps fists punch the air and feet stamp, or an angry yell comes out of our throats. When we have a milder feeling, nostalgia for the past, let us say, our eyes may gaze off into the distance or close altogether, perhaps our breath deepens, our energy slows, and muscles let go as we sink into the memory of a better time. Whatever the emotion being expressed, various sets of physical responses are activated; *there is no way to express a feeling except somatically!* Even our spirituality has physical expression, in altered breathing, for example, or in the subtle loosening of muscle tension as we surrender more deeply to God. A guide attuned to be acutely aware of physical changes can see both the fragile dawn of an emotion, and all too often, its suffocation.

Emotions have a location somewhere in the body. The energy for a particular emotion gathers force and takes shape in a particular physical location. A person who has cultivated awareness of her own body will usually have no trouble telling where in her body a particular feeling is located. If she is angry, for example, she will know that her present anger is located in her stomach, let us say. Other times she may sense that she has heaviness in her chest, or jitteriness in her hands, or anxiety in her shoulders. She may know that she is carrying guilt on her back. A minister well versed in body reading can often sense these locations in another person, sometimes even before the other person is aware of them herself.

When a person denies the expression of emotion, it tends to become embodied in the person's muscles. When a feeling is not expressed, it doesn't go away. Instead, the body mobilizes to store the unexpressed feeling. In order to hold in a feeling, muscles must shorten; a body literally tightens up to contain the feeling in various physical locations.

Here is an exercise to illustrate how embodiment works: Let your clenched fist make punching motions. Be vigorous and energetic! Now, continue to try to punch, but stop yourself before you actually make any motions. In other words, exert the energy both to punch and to stop punching at the same time. What happens to your body? What muscles do you use to stop yourself?

Be on the verge of yelling, but stop yourself before any sound comes out. What muscles do you use to stop yourself?

Try the same exercise with other feelings, such as grief or fear. Let your body begin to make the motions or assume the posture of the feelings, then vigorously stop the flow. What happens to your body? Be sure to shake out your tension before going on!

How does embodiment work in real life? If a man will not allow his tears to surface, for example, his diaphragm must tense up to contain the crying. His chest and back muscles may also tighten. His throat probably constricts, and perhaps his jaw clenches. Maybe his fists tighten along with his shoulders and neck. He may even tighten muscles not directly involved in the release of tears – his buttocks, for example, or his thighs. Thus not-crying produces shortened muscles that the man experiences as physical tension. When this tension continues over a long period, connective tissue grows over the chronically shortened muscles, making the tears contained there more and more inaccessible. At some point, the man may actually yearn for a good cry, but he may well find it difficult, if not impossible, to let go; his tears are literally buried, frozen into muscles held in chronic tension. In time, he will probably not be aware of his tears at all. Gestaltists and bodyworkers speak of "frozen emotions" or "frozen muscles" to describe this embodiment.

Even spiritual attitudes can be embodied. If we say "no" to God's continuing invitation, this spiritual "no" may locate itself somewhere in our bodies. Consider how the Bible speaks, for example, of "hardness of heart" and "stiff-necked people."

In a similar way, entire memories of traumatic events can be stored somatically in rigidly tense, carefully defended muscles. When an event occurs that is too painful to bear, especially in childhood, the child's body mobilizes to contain both the memory and the attendant feelings. This is particularly true when the event is traumatic or is repeated over a period of time, *and* the child has little emotional support. An abused child who has no consistent safe adult will probably need to store a great many of his feelings until he is bigger and stronger. A child whose parent dies might need to do the same.

In this marvelous mechanism, the tightened muscles literally shield the pain from the child's fragile sense of normality, enabling the child to survive. As muscles continue shortening in order to stop the flow of feeling, eventually the event itself may be lost to conscious memory. To a Gestaltist, the memory is not floating about in Freud's unconscious, nor has it gone away. Instead, it has been stored, often nearly intact, awaiting the day when the muscles are ready to release their emotional/spiritual load. If a trauma such as childhood sexual abuse is repeated over time, a number of separate experiences may merge and become efficiently embodied in one physical location as a few paradigmatic memories.

This process of embodying disowned material is physically uncomfortable. Muscles ache, for example, and a stomach is in knots. Neck tension can lead to headaches, and clenched teeth can bring on chronic jaw pain. Physical pain, however, is more acceptable to the person than the contained feelings or memories. The next step is often to disown – and not feel – the part of the body carrying the pain. That is, the person withdraws his awareness and energy from the site; he hates it or ignores it as much as possible. At this point, he is not willing to experience what that part of his body holds. He has successfully "numbed out" part of himself; he really doesn't live there any more. It is in this sense that Gestaltists and bodyworkers speak of a person "having no pelvis" or of "not standing in his feet."[49]

Such a person may be surprised to find that she is not willing to let anyone touch parts of herself that she has disowned. She may not even be willing to invite God to touch her there. These disowned storehouses, or "dumping grounds," are strongly guarded, even as they are consciously ignored.

Each of us constructs one or more somatic dumping grounds in which we tend to put all we cannot handle or express. Necks and shoulders are favored

---

[49] Some bodyworkers feel that the particular location of the disowned site may have some predictive accuracy for physical pathology: e.g., ulcers, tumors, heart disease, and the like.

places for this, but any part of our musculature, and even internal organs, can become storage sites. Some people pinch their buttocks tightly together, for instance; some hold their abdomens tightly, some get tension headaches or back pain, while still others hold onto the ground with their toes. Most of us know quite well where we habitually ache when we are under stress. One woman I know gets sore knees; she now knows that when her knees act up, she has inner work to do.

Thus a body carries the growth and maturation agenda of the one who inhabits it. Furthermore, evidence of this agenda can be quite easily visible to the guide, and accessible to the one working on herself. Whatever is trying to surface will find somatic expression somehow or other. When there is resistance to the process, that too will be expressed physically. Noticeable also is evidence of healthy integration, emotional balance, openness, even faith. It is all right there, perceptible and available. Remember, too, that perceiving what is going on in a person's body is not just the task of the guide; the one coming for help bears at least as much responsibility – as soon as she is trained to be aware of her own body.

PAYING ATTENTION TO BODIES: GETTING STARTED

One of the easiest ways to pay attention to bodies is to listen carefully to what people say about their bodies. Minor physical complaints such as headaches, colds, backaches, and slight nausea are often quite important in emotional and spiritual growth, for they can indicate that something inside the person is struggling to be expressed. Remember, if a person does not directly express what is inside, it is a good bet that the unexpressed material will come to light somatically.

Of course physical complaints can be explained in physical terms. But without denying the causes and cures of illness known to medical science, body reading asks that we see physical, mental, emotional, or spiritual symptoms as expressions of a person's entire being. They invite us to discover, for example, the larger meaning of a little headache, or the emotional/spiritual antecedents and components of a more serious illness.

Another fruitful avenue for paying attention to bodies is to listen for physical metaphors that just might be accurate expressions of the person's reality. The English language is full of juicy phrases that describe emotional/spiritual states in physical terms. Even though the person who uses them may not be aware of what she is saying at the time, quite often these expressions are literally true. Examples are:

•I've got a chip on my shoulder.

•I need elbow room.

•I can't stomach that.

•It makes me sick.

•It's a drag, a pain in the neck, a pain in the butt.

•Get off my back.

•It burns me up.

Also consider *heartbroken, flattened, smitten, lovesick, coldhearted, hotblooded, in a good space, and jumping for joy.*

Observe how the person moves. What postures does he assume? Is his movement stiff, jerky, constrained, or loose and easy? Does he use all of his body when he moves, or is some part habitually left out? Does he put his weight on one side or the other, or is it pretty well distributed? Is he gesturing, scratching, trembling, pacing, twitching, jiggling, twisting, rocking, holding himself, shredding tissues? Does his body seem to match the words he is saying? Is he slumped, or balanced and straight, or rigid? Is there part of his body presenting a "minority report," such as one hand caressing the chair while the rest of him is expressing anger? Simply paying attention to what the person is doing with his body in the present can open wonderful doors for growth.

BODY READING: LOOKING AT STRUCTURE

Learning to read bodies is best done in a group of women and men gathered for that purpose. In the beginning it is much easier if group members wear swimsuits, shorts, or leotards. Once people have had a little experience reading bodies with few concealing clothes, it is possible to see a great deal even when the person is fully clothed. Before attempting to read the body of another, I suggest praying for genuine inner permission to see what is there. Ask for loving, nonjudgmental, and Christ-like eyes that simply see truth. Ask the Holy Spirit to show you what each body is saying to the world. As each person takes a turn, ask the one being observed to stand still, turn, walk, or breathe deeply in silence until everyone has had time to form his or her own impressions. In the sharing afterwards you may discover a striking similarity of perceptions among the participants. Additional practice outside the group is helpful in learning this new skill. When I was first learning to read bodies, I practiced by watching fellow subway riders, or even better, performers in a concert or play. Soon I was able to see quite a bit about another's body as he or she walked into my office.

The following are a few questions to guide your looking:

How deeply is this person breathing? Is she breathing? That is, is her rib cage falling and rising, even in her back, or is her chest relatively still? Is she holding her breath? If asked to breathe deeply, does her abdomen fill and release, or is the movement only in her chest? Does she raise her shoulders in order to take a deep breath? (She shouldn't have to.) Just watching respiration is an easy way to detect possible encircling bands of tension that cut off the flow of breath. Stopping breath or breathing shallowly is a nearly sure-fire way to stop the flow of feeling. Reminding a person to breathe is one of the simplest and most effective tools available to a minister.

Where is evidence of shortened muscles? When muscles tighten they get shorter, so looking for shortened muscles is another simple way to make a good guess where tension is located. Do you see, for example, his raised shoulders, legs turned inward toward each other, arms held close to the body? Are her hands relaxed or clenched a little? Is her stomach being held in? Is his head thrust forward, or tilted to one side? Are her knees locked? Is his pelvis tilted so that his buttocks look like a small, sloping shelf? Is his chest caved in, or perhaps rigidly thrust out like a soldier? And so on.

Is there asymmetry between right and left sides? Do his hands touch his thighs at about same height when his arms fall from his shoulders? Is one hip higher than the other? Are his shoulders the same height? Is the distance from neck to shoulder tip about the same on both sides, or is one side shorter? Cover half his face with a piece of paper so that one eye, half his nose and half his mouth are visible. What expression do you see? Now look at the other half of his face in the same way. Is it different? Quite often inner polarities are expressed somatically by such left/right differences.

Are there parts that don't seem to match the rest of the body in size or shape? Is she a sturdy, strong-looking woman with spindly legs that don't look substantial enough to hold her up? Does he have beefy legs and pelvis under a chest and arms that look like they belong to a much smaller man? Does this adult's hands look like those of a child? Naturally, some of these differences are inherited, or are the result of disease, accidents, or other factors. Frequently, however, they

234

point to inner polarities. For example, once I worked with a woman who had almost no breasts on her small chest. In dramatic contrast, she had very large hips. When she allowed these parts of her body to speak, she discovered that her small upper body and her tiny breasts embodied her girlish fear of becoming a grown woman, and her lush, full hips disclosed a sensual, earthy, sexual woman yearning to be recognized. The ensuing verbal dialogue between her hips and breasts was a turning point that led to a new integration of girl and woman.

Are there color differences or blemishes in the body? Is there a pasty-white face combined with a tanned and healthy-looking torso? Do sturdy pink or tan legs connect to delicate, bluish, "transparent" feet? Does a dark brown chest contrast with much lighter arms or legs? Are there patches of scaly, dry skin, red splotches, or rashes? Are there "angry" boils, "miserable" bruises, or "weeping" sores?

Does this body carry extra weight, or not enough weight? Is this body thin and reedy, or is it stocky and thick? Is the weight distributed evenly or is some part disproportionately large or small? Is the body bony or plump, "weighed down" or is it insubstantial looking? Is it carefully sculpted and toned, or does it simply look natural?

Does this body look healthy and vigorous or does it seem to lack energy? Does it move with ease and grace, or is it awkward and stiff? What is the general "feel" of this body? Does this person strike you as strong and robust, or as puny and weak? Do you imagine that this body belongs to one who is happy or melancholy? Is there something draggy and limp about this body, or is it full of pep?

MORE ADVANCED BODY READING: SENSING ENERGY

When microscopes were first invented, not everyone who looked through the new-fangled contraption could see the "animalcules" swimming in a drop of pond water. Those who were open-minded enough to consider the possibility of the existence of these tiny creatures, saw them and marveled. Those who insisted that nothing could be there, saw nothing.

I find this story fascinating, for it illumines how closely worldview is related to perceptions. We edit out what we believe is not there. A similar relationship can come into play when Westerners are introduced to the idea of sensing energy. For some, it all seems like puffed air and mummery, the realm of quacks and maybe even the occult.

235

Actually, most of us perceive energy all the time, but frequently we toss out these perceptions as not important or valid. I believe that most empathetic, intuitive people are very good at sensing energy, although they may not be aware of what they are doing. If you have ever suddenly become aware of the presence of a person whom you didn't see or hear, you are sensing energy. If you have instinctively moved away from – or trusted – certain strangers on a bus, you may well have been sensing the nature of their energy field. When you sense heaviness or lightness, aliveness or deadness, creepiness or safety, centeredness or scatteredness, murkiness or clarity, or certain "vibes" about a person before they have said a word, you are surely perceiving something about his or her energy. If you have ever found yourself whispering in an empty church, becoming unaccountably anxious in a particular building, or relaxing almost instantly in the presence of someone you were meeting for the first time, you were probably responding to energy.

I believe there is evidence in at least one gospel story that Jesus responded to energy states, both his own and those of others. When surrounded by a large crowd, he startled everyone by asking, "Who touched me?" To his bewildered disciples, who pointed out that there were people pressing in all around him, he replied, "I felt power go out of me." (Bodyworkers would recognize this experience!) Jesus' awareness was acute enough to isolate the particular touch of one woman in the crowd, and to know that an energy exchange had taken place with someone.

Human beings are an energy system; energy circulates a little like blood, infusing and enlivening every part of us. Asian scholars have been working with energy systems for thousands of years, and have made a detailed map of the human energy flow. Energy channels, or "meridians," discovered by ancient physicians are still being studied today, especially by acupuncturists. Many other kinds of bodywork embrace an understanding of energy: for example, Shiatsu, Polarity Therapy, Acupressure, Reflexology, Reiki, Bioenergtics, Rolfing, Lomi, and some forms of massage. Although cultural suspicions remain, growing numbers of people attest to the effectiveness of these body energy therapies.[50]

Those who are skeptical might find the work of Dolores Krieger illuminating.[51] Dr. Krieger is a nurse who observed that patients felt better when certain

---

[50] For an interesting introduction to bioenergy see Barbara Ann Brennan's *Hands of Light: A Guide to Healing Through the Human Energy Field.*
[51] Krieger, *The Therapeutic Touch: How to Use Your Hands to Help or to Heal,* and *Accepting Your Power to Heal: the Personal Practice of Therapeutic Touch.*

nurses touched them. She set up rigorous experiments to study this phenomenon, using increased hemoglobin count as a measure of improved health. She found that when nurses put their hands on patients with intent to heal, the patients' hemoglobin count went up in a statistically significant way. In control groups, this improvement did not take place. In subsequent experiments she found that other health indicators changed under the same circumstances. Krieger concluded after much observation, that changes in the energy of a sick person were at least partly responsible for improved physical health.

Out of this research, she developed a system called Therapeutic Touch, and taught it to thousands of nurses and other interested people. Therapeutic Touch, now in use in countless hospitals around the country, does not always require actual physical touch, but only contact with the patient's energy – with intent to heal. (Krieger was not working with prayer, but surely her research is of interest to those who practice prayer and laying on of hands.) If you ever observe a nurse with hands held a few inches above a patient's body, Therapeutic Touch is probably being employed.

The benefits of energy work with Therapeutic Touch are well documented, and increasingly respected, by the medical establishment. With her capacity for both intuition and her rigorous scientific standards, Krieger has become a bridge between Eastern medicine and the West.

In addition to Krieger's work, the human energy field has been measured and documented with extensive photographs by scientific researchers. First developed in Russia by Seymon Kirlian, "Kirlian" photographs are quite beautiful. Interestingly, photographs of the energy aura around a living body are reminiscent of medieval paintings of saints with holy light around their heads. Undeniably, human energy fields exist.

Is it really possible to perceive another person's energy field? Yes, with a little inner permission, and a setting that helps students honor what they are sensing. In Gestalt Pastoral Care training groups, beginners to body reading are usually surprised at how much agreement there is when they share their first tentative perceptions of energy.

In these groups we play with perceiving energy in various ways. For example, we ask someone to wrap herself from the neck down in a white sheet, and stand in front of a white wall. Gazing just above her head, most can detect a faint glow; others see what looks like heat rising from hot pavement; still others see the hint of colors. When we ask the person in the sheet to imagine, for example, that she is preaching in a large church, most can see an immediate jump in the size of the aura, as she imaginatively puts out more energy.

Another exercise, this one in aural perception, is to ask, "If this person were a motor, what would he sound like?" There is usually general agreement, for example, that some people sound like a busy little Volkswagen bug, others like a deep throbbing turbine, others like a chugging washing machine, still others like a water pump or the steady quiet hum of a new car. Asking the person to imaginatively return to a time of deep joy or sorrow or fear usually results in a distinct change in the "sound."

In the Gestalt Pastoral Care training group I try to recruit some volunteers previously unknown to the class. Looking at them we ask such questions as the following:

- If this person were aching and sore, where in his body might that be happening now?

- Where do you imagine she carries her burdens?

- If you were a member of his family, where would you touch to soothe and nurture him?

- What part of her body has she vacated? Is she present just below her diaphragm? How about her feet? Her thighs? Her pelvis?

- Where do you see evidence of health and growth in this body?

- Where in his body does he seem welcoming, open? What part of him says, "Go away?"

- Where is her energy blocked? Where does it flow easily?

- Where is she most alive? Where is she dead? Numb?

- What one or two words describe this person's energy right now?

Again, when students are given a little time to form their own responses to such odd questions, they are often astonished at how much they are perceiving. Although perceptions are usually not precisely identical among group members – partly because English doesn't have many words to describe energy states – there is usually agreement that they are all looking at the same thing. More often than not, the volunteer confirms the accuracy of their comments too. Of course, the class is also seeing facial expressions, body structure, posture, and the like, and this information feeds into their impressions as well. The idea is not so much to isolate energy perceptions, but to perceive energy along with everything else they are aware of.

How is perceiving energy helpful in body reading? It's like the difference between a little black and white TV and a large color set; suddenly there is just so much more to see. Everything is more vivid, clearer. Sensitivity to energy, along with awareness of bodies in general, helps a minister form an impression of the general "feel" of a person's existence. She can ask herself if the person is hard or open, wary or confident, alive or numb. She can begin to sense – or guess – what is underneath a verbal story. Perceiving energy most certainly helps inform hunches, as well as subsequent prayerful discernment. She can tell with some accuracy where energy is blocked; this is important because energy blocks are often present where one has disowned the spiritual/emotional content of muscles. She can make deliberate changes in her own energy at times; with practice, she can speed up her own energy for energetically "speedy" people, and slow down for "turtles." Alternatively, she can be very centered and steady in her own energy, a response that can be tremendously helpful to someone who is awash in intense feeling. In the presence of a broken person with whom she consistently feels drained, she can pray that her own energy and vitality be protected.

Even the rudimentary awareness that an energy change has occurred in another person can be tremendously helpful. Energy changes usually accompany a shift in feeling, so just noting energy changes allows a minister to stay with another's process even when there are few physical or verbal clues. With just simple awareness of a change, she can ask, "What just happened?" or even, "What just happened in your chest?" or "What did you just release?" When an energy change occurs in the telling of a verbal story, she can suggest that relevant words be repeated with awareness.

Using Body Reading with a Gestalt Pastoral Care *Perspective*

Gestalt Pastoral Care Ministers will work with body awareness differently from those who are in the process of integrating a simple Gestalt perspective. I urge caution for those who have not had training in Gestalt or some form of body-work. Some Gestalt experiments based on body awareness can lead to vivid re-experiencing of early traumatic memories. Intense feelings may flood in as muscles release, frightening both seeker and minister alike. If the minister has not had firsthand experience and training, and if he has not gone to these depths in himself, he shouldn't be facilitating it in others. And as always, no one should push against resistance, whether it be physical, emotional or spiritual. In particular, pushing physically against physical resistance – trying to force muscles to release before they are ready to do so – can feel like an assault. Bodyworkers have been specifically trained to feel physical readiness to let go; to attempt direct muscle manipulation without training can be disastrous. Remember, we depend on resistance to keep people within safe boundaries.

However, I don't mean to scare you away from the riches of body awareness. There are five important ways that most ministers can utilize insights from body reading even before they have been trained to do deep work with bodies:

First, ministers can use body reading to help decide where to put their hands as they pray. They can literally "put their finger on" the location of the spiritual or emotional hurt, just as they would prayerfully put their hands on a broken arm. They can touch a place where there is deadness and pray for life. They ask that emotional and spiritual pain be healed as they touch the actual place where the pain is stored. (Obviously they will not touch inappropriately, and they will ask for explicit permission before touching anywhere.) Prayer and laying on of hands can melt physical tension and expose old, well-guarded pain to the light of God. When this happens, all the minister has to do is keep quiet and stay out of the way of what God is doing.

Secondly, ministers can monitor the breath of the person with whom they are working, and remind the person to breathe when she stops. This sounds simple, but it takes some practice to attend to it. As I have already said, this small bit of bodywork can be enormously helpful. When someone is approaching an insight, memory, or feeling that is a little scary, the usual reaction is to stop or restrain breathing. Without free-flowing breath, the mighty healing stream becomes sluggish. The diaphragm tenses, feelings "disappear," numbness takes over. Ordinarily the person is completely unaware that her breath is stopped or has become shallow. At such times I usually just say softly, "Breathe!" and frequently that is enough.

Willingness to keep breathing fully and gently can make the difference between continuing to hold onto stultifying patterns, and experiencing a bit of new integration. I have observed that emotional, spiritual and muscular release takes place primarily as the person exhales; it is the way we let go. Inhaling seems to be the moment of taking in new life and healing. Inviting a person to breathe out whatever they are ready to get rid of, and to breathe in God's grace, sometimes opens the door for healing.

Third, ministers can use body reading to help inform any prayerful discernment process. Expanding our awareness and intuition seems to open the doors for impressions in prayer. A Gestalt Pastoral Minister once told me that upon seeing a man for the first time, her attention was caught by his rigid, energetically dead shoulders and the tension in his neck. Silently she prayed, "Lord, what's with his shoulders and neck?" Her answer was an image flashing through her brain of a child being dragged along by an adult in a big hurry. The child's small legs couldn't keep up, but the preoccupied adult held his hand tightly and plowed on. She did not know, of course, if her image was literally accurate, symbolic, or completely wrong. However she remembered it, and continued to discern as she worked with the man. She continued to pay attention to his shoulders and neck and her own sense that something important was contained there.

Most ministers can use body reading to help prompt body awareness in another person. Questions prompted by the minister's own awareness can invite another person to learn to pay attention to his own process. She can suggest that certain things that catch her attention be repeated with awareness. Such questions as the following are easy, simple, and basic to Gestalt work:

- Would you move your arm that way again, and pay attention to how you feel?

- What's going on in your stomach right now?

- Did you hear your tone of voice just now? What did it sound like to you?

- What happened for you just now as you breathed out? Would you breathe out like that again and see what you feel?

Perls' great discovery was that simple awareness of what is occurring in the present results in healing. Remember that unfinished business constantly pushes to be finished. Although we can easily resist letting unfinished business come to awareness, our censors don't work very well when it comes to our bodies. Remember Perls' maxim: "Bodies never lie!"

As suggested in Chapter Nine, ministers can teach simple body awareness by suggesting that the person be a part of her body and describe herself. This is a very simple and safe experiment which allows a body to "talk," and can be good preparation for healing prayer.

During a healing service, a woman asked for prayer for her chronically aching shoulders. Knowing there was not much time during the service for a long discussion, the minister nevertheless asked her, "Be your shoulders for a minute, would you? Let them speak as if they had a voice of their own." The woman replied,

> *OK.* I *hurt and* I'm *tense. I feel squashed, like I am carrying something heavy. I'm tired of carrying so much. I'm not breathing very much either. Even my breathing is squashed. I'm just squashed all over!*

With this small bit of body awareness, she had gotten much closer to her unfinished business. The prayer group gathered around her had much more understanding of how to pray for her. With her increased body awareness they could pray for much more than sore shoulders. Without needing to know specifics, they prayed for God to work in whatever situation was squashing her, whatever was heavy in her life, whatever was making her tense and tired and squeezing the breath out of her.

USING BODY READING AS A GESTALT PASTORAL CARE *MINISTER*

If a minister has had Gestalt or Bioenergetic training, she can create body experiments that carry the possibility of deeper work. A good body reader will have a great deal more material to use when designing experiments than one who does not have this skill. For example, some polarities are not as evident verbally as they are somatically. From information gleaned from body reading, she can suggest that feet talk to thighs, or a left side converse with the right, possibly moving into polarity work or work with introjects. Conversation between body parts, (rather than just allowing one part to describe itself), will often open a door to in-depth work: "Would you see what happens if your head and your feet talk to each other?"

Somatically focused non-verbal experiments also hold the capacity for wonderful discoveries. The person working could be invited to allow a part of his body to make a sound: "Let a sound come from the pain in your stomach, would you?" He could also be asked to let a part of his body take over and suggest exaggerated postures and motions: "Let all of you be your stomach, would you? Let your whole body respond to the knots in your stomach. See what position you might take, or if there is some movement that might suggest itself." In doing these experiments, of course, he is learning to pay acute attention to what is going on in his body. One person who was leaning on his left elbow was invited to let the left-leaning side of his body speak to his right side. He found himself saying, "I want to lean. It's comfortable, and I'm tired of always sitting up straight." His right side replied, "Sit up, you dummy! Don't be so sloppy and weak!" This tiny snippet of work based on body awareness almost immediately opened the door to a polarity between his introjected father, whose verbal abuse was embodied on his right side, and his left side, which carried his own healthy protest.

A person who is gesturing widely with his left hand while his right hand is hidden in a pocket may well discover an emotional or spiritual polarity if one hand talks to the other. He might say as his left hand, "I know what I'm talking about. I'm confident and able to get my points across. Why don't you, right hand, come out of hiding?" The right hand might reply, "I like to stay hidden where I won't make a mistake. Remember how Dad used to get mad when I sounded off?" Thus the way is opened for a possibly fruitful conversation with his introjected father. A similar discovery may emerge if a man's thin, spindly legs are allowed to speak with his muscular arms. He may discover that his legs "carry" an inner small child, while his arms express the strong adult he has become. How fascinating to imagine Jackie Kennedy letting her hesitant, breathy, girlish speaking voice communicate with Jacqueline, the beautiful woman with tightly-drawn muscles and a carefully controlled image of sophistication.

Back when I was seriously studying the violin, I heard a story about a professional violinist who did life-changing work with a polarity expressing itself physically. "Sasha" was suddenly having trouble controlling his bow arm, and it got increasingly achy as he played. Medical doctors could find no evidence of physical pathology in his right arm, and referred him to a psychotherapist with training in body awareness. The therapist asked Sasha to stand and play so he could observe Sasha's body; a gorgeous Bach sonata poured into the office. The therapist noticed right away that the musician's weight was predominately on his left leg, which was firm and grounded. In contrast, his right leg shuffled about and even left the floor a few times. Sasha was not aware of his legs, for he put all his attention into playing the violin with his upper body. When the therapist asked Sasha to allow his legs to converse, the subsequent result was revelatory. The grounded leg said, "I love to hold up Sasha when he plays. I can tell that he is really good, and he brings a lot of pleasure to many people. He has tremendous skill and talent, and is firmly grounded in his musicianship." The right leg replied, "Yeah, he's good, but at what cost? He never gets to see his family because he's on tour all the time. He has to compete hard with all the other really good musicians out there, and the pressure is terrific. One day he's going to lay a big egg.[52] He'll have a memory lapse while he's giving a recital. I want him to go home and take some time off!"

As the leg conversation proceeded it became clear to Sasha that he had "given too much weight" to his profession, and that he must heed the voice of his right leg as soon as he could finish the commitments already made. He promised both legs some time off soon. Then the therapist suggested another experiment: "Would you play the same sonata again and see if there's a difference in your bow arm? And would you do it while giving attention to keeping your weight distributed on both legs?" As Sasha played this time, he delightedly reported that his bow arm was less tense and painful, and that he was not working as hard to control it. As he finished his tour, he continued to remind his legs that he was going to take time off very soon, and he consciously kept his weight well distributed. The problem in his bow arm gradually disappeared.

Recovering Memories

Can frozen memories and feelings be recovered? Yes. Just as frozen food can be eaten after it is thawed, frozen feelings and memories can be thawed out again, and re-experienced. To the one working, it actually feels as if the frozen material was preserved intact, sometimes for years, decades. She may find herself crying tears she didn't shed as a child, and she might feel and sound very young. She may experience despair and terror of abandonment as she re-lives being left alone as a toddler. She may re-experience physical or sexual abuse. Working with these frozen dumping grounds is like an archeological dig, with the distinct possibility of finding treasures.

Thawing can take place easily and naturally when the person is ready for it to happen. An example of easy thawing concerned Bill, who was a habitual foot tapper. His jiggling foot almost shouted for attention; it didn't take a lot of body reading skill to notice it. Most people, if they commented at all, asked Bill to please stop as they were being driven crazy with his constant tappety tap tap tap.

In his very first session, Bill's Gestalt Pastoral Minister did not ask him to stop tapping; instead he invited Bill to let his tapping become more pronounced, and to make a little more noise with it. Although Bill was convinced that his tapping didn't mean anything – it was "just a habit"– he was intrigued with his guide's suggestion. Within a minute or two Bill was not merely tapping; he was

---

[52] Laying an egg: a musician's way of saying, "making noticeable mistakes during a performance."

stamping his foot, hard. And harder! His guide invited him to stand up and make sounds with his stamping, and Bill stomped around the room, growling like a giant. It felt good, energizing!

When his minister asked if there were now words that Bill's feet wanted to say, he knew immediately what they were. Before he had time to think, Bill found himself stomping and yelling, "No! I won't! I won't! I won't do it! I won't do it ever again, you bastard!" Stunned and now furious, he stopped, letting his words sink in. What was he saying? His minister suggested stomping out the same words a few times more, checking out if they were really his. Even though he hadn't a clue what they meant, Bill continued, knowing in his bones that somehow the words were right. "Is there someone in your life who needs to hear these words?" the minister asked. Bill couldn't think of anyone. So Bill was invited to experiment with saying his words to important people in his life and see if he made any connections. She explained that he could bring anyone he wanted here in fantasy, trying his words – and his stamping – on each one.

Bill consented, and began with his father. Not right at all. His mother, even less. His siblings, not really. Each uncle, aunt, no. Then the crucial connection was made: "Oh my God. It's Mr. Olsen, my high school English teacher. He's the bastard!" As Bill stamped and yelled his words to Mr. Olsen, the energy release was immediately obvious to both of them; they were now pretty certain they were on track. Stamping and yelling, Bill confronted Mr. Olsen. He literally "put his foot down," and the story emerged. The teacher had paid special attention to him, encouraging his writing, inviting him to dinner on occasion. The boy had loved it, and was more than willing when Mr. Olsen asked him for a favor. Bill was to deliver a little package across town. Later there were more deliveries and the boy's growing uneasiness that something was really wrong. The word "drugs" whispered around the edges of his consciousness, but he told no one. Finally he simply avoided Mr. Olsen until graduation. Every time he came home from college, he was afraid that Mr. Olsen might come after him. He never spoke to Mr. Olsen again, but the betrayal, the secret denial, the shame, the fear, and most of all the anger, stayed with him, embodied in his tapping feet.

Confronting Mr. Olsen at last was wonderfully freeing for Bill. The stomping, growling giant, the no-saying adult, had been ready to burst forth when he came for help. The liberated energy was apparent right away in increased vigor and in a new sense of himself as a strong man who would not be bamboozled again.

Embodied memories such as this one are like time capsules that can be opened through increased awareness and experiments. Even though Mr. Olsen was not really forgotten, he had receded into fuzzy memory until Bill's own body paved the way.

When a person learns to be aware of his own body and knows some ways to let it speak, often he can do this work by himself. However, when the embodied event has truly been lost to memory, when the feelings are terribly frightening, a trained coach is usually needed. When muscles holding a repressed memory are finally released, the result is often a "body memory," a vivid, somatic *re-living* of the emotions and physical sensations of the original experience. As formerly rigid boundaries fall, it is important to have an unafraid companion who knows that the world is not ending as a result. Faith imagination can help a great deal as well.

I have often been with individuals experiencing body memories of sexual and ritual abuse, terrible accidents, deliberate torture, or cataclysmic disasters.[53] These valiant survivors were not destroyed by allowing these memories to surface. Although the process was arduous, the usual end result was increased freedom, more energy, and deep healing. Further, if they were willing to work with faith imagination as a body memory surfaced, they didn't have to return to the horror all alone; this time Jesus went with them, giving comfort, support, protection, and healing. They also learned ways to stop the body memory if they didn't want to go on; having a bit of control was healing in itself. Many of them found that one way to stop a body memory is simply to change physical positions, and with some coaching, to become acutely aware of the present. Another is to ask The Holy One to seal up the memory somehow – to shut the door, bury it, crate it, or hold it – until the pray-er is ready to go on.

Gestalt Pastoral Care Ministers trust that when a body memory emerges, the person is now ready to metabolize whatever comes to the surface, and that the Holy Spirit is in charge of the process. Again, they never push through resistance; they simply make a way for it to melt if the time is ripe. Thawing out repressed memories, expressing ancient emotions, and letting frozen muscles have their say, not only allows for improved emotional and spiritual health; this process enables the muscles to physically relax and lengthen. Quite often a layer or two of achiness and tension simply disappears, and in its place is a new freedom of move-

[53] Released energy that held such terrible memories can temporarily "pollute" a room. The energetic residue after an intense session can make an office seem "heavy" or "murky" and sometimes so palpably toxic that a minister might actually feel a bit nauseated. Opening the windows and praying that God will cleanse the room usually solves the problem. Taking a shower and changing into clean clothes can help too.

ment. Although people are often exhausted right after releasing long-held feelings, frequently they also speak of "not hurting anymore," of having "more room" inside, or of "feeling lighter." Best of all, they have renewed faith that even unimaginable terrors are healable. I certainly experience this myself as I sit with these brave survivors. I often remember Paul's words:

> But we have this treasure in clay jars, so that it may be made clear that this extraordinary power belongs to God and does not come from us. We are afflicted in every way, but not crushed; perplexed, but not driven to despair; persecuted, but not forsaken; struck down, but not destroyed; always carrying in the body the death of Jesus so that the life of Jesus may also be made visible in our bodies.
>
> *II Corinthians 4:7-10*

Nothing has a stronger influence psychologically...
on their children than the unlived life of the parents.
Carl Jung

15

GENERATIONAL HEALING

KAREN AND JOAN

Many years ago I worked with two women who had remarkably similar family backgrounds. Not related or known to each other, both women had grandparents who were survivors of German concentration camps. Both sets of grandparents met in prison as young teenagers, and were married soon after liberation. Both young couples vowed to put their awful memories behind them and never again speak of the terrible past. Leaving their Jewish identity in Europe, they came to America, raised their families, and kept their vows of silence. In both families, their children grew up with seemingly few problems.

Fast forward now to the generation of the couples' grandchildren, the women who were working with me. Although Karen had a decent job, she lived in a hovel which she kept nearly dark all the time. She allowed herself very little to eat, and she wore raggedy clothes. She was sexually promiscuous because she was convinced that if she didn't favor her boss, her landlord, and whomever else, she "would never survive." Always, Karen was afraid that something terrible was about to happen.

The second woman, Joan, lived in clammy, unreasoning terror all the time. As we explored her life, we could find nothing that could account for such unrelenting, oceanic fear. Joan was a competent professional, but she struggled through her tortured days on desperate prayer and grit.

Only gradually did it dawn on me that both women were experiencing life as if they themselves were imprisoned in a concentration camp. Although both knew that their grandparents had been prisoners of the Nazis, they had not heard any family prison stories; in each family a curtain had been tightly drawn. It was as if emotionally and spiritually they were living a horror of which they had no direct experience. Both Karen and Joan were now devout Christians, but underneath their faith ran hopeless despair and a belief that even God had abandoned them.

I didn't know what to make of all this. If indeed Karen and Joan were somehow living their grandparents' trauma, how could I help them address the issue? If their feelings didn't even belong to them, what could be done? Both were on medication, but it only dulled the pain a little. So we talked. We did Gestalt work. We remembered together that the grandparents' experience had been horrifying. We prayed, but nothing much seemed to change for either one.

Then one day I suggested an experiment to Joan. It seemed to me that since she was already identifying with her grandparents so much, maybe with exaggeration some new awareness might come. I asked her if she would be willing to go to the Jewish Museum in Manhattan. As she looked at each art treasure or religious artifact, I suggested that she say to herself, "That's me," or "That's mine."

Joan was intrigued with the idea and went the following week. At her next session she reported feeling a good bit better. Allowing herself to claim her grandparent's rich cultural and religious heritage opened her heart to more than just their horrifying prison years. Although Joan didn't understand it, it seemed to her that her long-dead grandparents had somehow been waiting for her to do this very thing. I didn't understand it either, but was glad something was helping. We would never have thought to pray that her grandparents actually be healed, however. Protestants don't do such things! In subsequent weeks Joan's terror receded, but did not ever really go away.

If it helped Joan, it might help Karen, I thought, so I suggested to Karen that she, too, take a trip to the Jewish Museum. Before I had even explained what I was proposing, Karen exploded in uncharacteristic fury. "How could you even think of such a thing?" she screamed. "I'm not Jewish! I'm a Christian! I will never, never, go look at that stuff!" And she didn't. Despite my repeated reassurance that it was just fine if she didn't want to explore her Jewish roots, Karen left Gestalt Pastoral Care soon after, still angry at me, and still holding tightly to her grandparent's misery and taboos.

KENNETH MCALL, M.D.

Years later I was introduced to the work of Dr. Kenneth McAll, a British psychiatrist who pioneered in the field of generational healing.[54] McAll must have known that experiences and feelings not resolved in one generation can pop up nearly intact in succeeding ones. Family Systems therapists have long concerned themselves with parents, grandparents, and other relatives who have direct influence on the person sitting in the therapist's office. McAll seems, however, to have been led into generational healing prayer mainly through his own prayer experiences as he prayed for the sick.

McAll discovered that generational influence can carry through even when the relatives lived so long ago that even their names are lost to memory. Distorted emotional and spiritual responses and worldview may be all that is left of an ancient trauma in living family members, but those responses and worldview can have enormous power. It was as if ancestral traumas could become "genetic," passing down like blonde hair and blue eyes, through the generations to certain family members.

McAll also found that neither psychotherapy nor medical science were much help when the problem seemed rooted in generations of the hoary past. McAll's response was to draw up a family tree using whatever facts were known, and then to pray. He began teaming up with an Anglican priest, and together they celebrated Eucharists for the healing of whole families, including both the dead and the living.

They prayed for the healing of the original trauma, and that this healing would flow down through the generations to the living members of the family. They learned to add prayers of committal, normally used at funerals, for any who might never have been laid to rest, including babies who died before birth. They led living family members to confess harm done by the family, sometimes generations ago, and found that repentance, even generations later, can free the family to embrace the family's gifts. (An example of generational confession and forgiveness could be found in a family that kept slaves.) They also discovered that by liturgical declaration, they could break the negative connection between the generations, and that they could replace family "curses" with blessings. They were prompted as well to give thanks for the gifts that a particular family had to offer, and learned to pray that these family gifts would find a welcoming home in

---

[54] McAll, *Healing the Family Tree.*

250

living family members. During these Eucharists, McAll would often receive visual images of grateful people clad in old-fashioned garments responding to the prayers on their behalf and then joyfully being taken to God.

Family members attending McAll's generational Eucharists were often deeply moved. Those whose acute suffering prompted the services in the first place were often healed dramatically of long-standing physical and mental illnesses. Even if the suffering person who was the focus of the Eucharist was not present and had no knowledge that the service was taking place, he or she might experience sudden healing at the time of the service. Schizophrenia, heart disease, anorexia, and depression are just a few of the maladies that yielded to this special way of praying. Over the years McAll collected a large file documenting these healings.

When I first heard about generational healing I experienced my now-familiar pattern of fearfully rejecting ideas that I didn't know what to do with. "Praying for the dead! What's next, space aliens?" protested my Protestant brain. But I had been introduced to Kenneth McAll's work by Douglas and Frances Schoeninger, friends and colleagues I greatly respect. The two of them are among the leading teachers of generational healing in the United States.[55] It was their integrity and Christian commitment that nudged me to give serious consideration to generational healing.

As I pondered and prayed about it, I felt a little dialogue take place inside:

Is there anyone, living or dead, who is beyond the reach of God's love?

No.

Can those who die somehow continue to grow in grace? Can you allow for the possibility of healing after death even if you don't understand just how it happens?

Yeah, I guess so.

Is God big enough to work in ways that shatter your boundaries and theology and worldview?

Of course.

And is time of any consequence to God? Can God go back in time and heal a trauma that occurred years before? Can God re-do the effects of a terrible childhood?

---

[55] See Douglas and Frances Schoeninger, *Tending Family Roots: Papers on Generational Healing.*

Sure, I've seen this happen many times, but just not involving previous generations.

It's a short step, isn't it? Why not try generational healing prayer with someone and see what happens?

Finally, I asked God to bring people to me who had a clear need for generational healing if I was to explore this kind of prayer. I didn't have long to wait.

LARRY CUTS THE CORD

Larry came to a Gestalt Pastoral Care workshop wanting to deal with his mother who dominated every moment of his life. Larry was 30 and still lived at home. Although his mom was in reasonable health, Larry felt compelled to call her several times a day, and would hurry home after work to see to her supper. Evenings and weekends were spent with her too. Despite Larry's solicitousness, mom was always full of complaints, and somehow her misery was always Larry's fault. Whenever he even spoke of getting his own place, his mother would mention her numerous physical problems, her depression, her undying love for him, and how she had thought, up until now, that she could always count on her son to be there for her. She would cry, and her tears were like a rope pulling Larry back in. Larry always quickly dropped the idea of moving out.

At the workshop, Larry was thoroughly fed up with her and with himself. He knew he had to separate from her, but seemed unable to do so. When I inquired where his father was in all this, Larry dropped a bombshell: Larry's father, now dead, had been trapped by *his* mother, and Larry's family had lived with grandma until she died at age 90. His father's father had followed the same pattern with Larry's great grandmother. Before that, he didn't know. Here it was! At least three generations of sons and mothers living out a sort of destiny together that left everyone stunted, guilty, and angry.

I proposed to Larry that the workshop group pray for the healing of his family, with a particular focus on this unhealthy son and mother pattern. Larry thought it was a great idea. We had Eucharist and prayed that God would heal whatever happened way back in this family to start this unhealthy pattern. Although Larry had no idea what could have occurred so far back, all of us trusted that the circumstances were known to God, and that God could indeed heal whatever was needed. We prayed for all the sons and mothers in Larry's family, naming as many of them as Larry could remember, asking that they be set free from inherited patterns of unhealthy dependency and control. In the name of Jesus Christ we declared that the pipeline which was a conduit for these things was severed and that Larry and the rest of the family connect to Christ instead. In addition, we ordered any generational spirits fueling these patterns to leave in the name of Jesus. Then we laid hands on Larry and prayed that he be set free.

As we prayed, Larry said he felt much lighter, but he knew he wasn't finished. Going inside, he saw an image of himself still connected to his mother by a very old and strong umbilical cord. Trying to be helpful, the group prayed that Jesus cut the cord, but it didn't seem to happen. After a pause, Larry said, "I see I have to cut the cord myself. This is for me to do, and I've needed to do it for a long time." Sensing he needed to physicalize this inner shift, I got out some clothesline and a pair of scissors. Larry tied the rope around his waist; then he tied the other end to a large stack of pillows representing his mother.

As the group prayed for him, Larry snipped the cord. It seemed such a little thing, just a snick of the scissors, but what big changes it brought! Larry began to laugh and laugh, hearty, grown-man laughter from his belly. Laughter that was contagious and freeing. Guffaws and chortles, chuckles and great roars that swept away the constrictions and cobwebs he had lived with for so long. He danced around the room holding his end of the severed clothesline, shouting, "Look at this! Just look at this!"

Within six weeks Larry was happily ensconced in his own apartment, and only phoning his mother every few days. And wonder of wonders, his mother got a life too. With Larry out of the house, she began volunteering at the local animal shelter and discovered that the dogs and cats needed her. She loved it, and gradually her complaints and passive control diminished. She too had been set free from generational patterns that had held the family in bondage for years.

Praying for Larry was pretty convincing for me. It really did seem that the prayers of the little ad hoc church had indeed been used to set Larry and his mom free. As if that were not enough, soon there was another situation that fairly called out for generational prayer.

THE TOXIC GRANDPA

A few months later at another Gestalt Pastoral Care workshop a woman I will call Jenny began by telling us that her problem was "a little weird." Since it concerned her whole family, she wasn't sure that it was even appropriate to bring to our workshop. She didn't have much hope that anything could change, but she thought it would feel good to talk about it.

Ever since she could remember, Jenny said, her grandpa had controlled her extended family with an iron fist. None of her aunts and uncles would think of making a move without getting his advice and permission. Grandpa was a master of name-calling and put-downs. He seemed to know everyone's weakness and just how to manipulate everyone to keep all family interactions revolving around him. Jenny remembers having to spend every Sunday at his house as a child, along with her parents, aunts, uncles, and cousins. No one ever stood up to Grandpa; she watched as the adults fearfully pussy-footed about to keep his wrath from exploding. Jenny learned to do the same. She remembered the rides home each Sunday evening, full of silent pain as Jenny and her parents silently nursed their wounds.

This pattern continued even when Grandpa had to move to a nursing home after his stroke. From his bed and wheelchair this man of 86 terrorized the staff and his family, who continued the Sunday visits. A few months before he died, Grandpa escalated his spiteful bitterness. Again and again he let fly with his ultimate threat: "After I die, I will personally see to it that none of you are ever happy for the rest of your lives!" Sure enough, the twenty-six people in his extended family were awash in spite, revenge, and just plain misery soon after Grandpa died.

Jenny told us that she herself had been depressed and edgy ever since Grandpa died the year before. She was certain her own depression and the present malaise of her family were somehow connected to him, but she didn't know what to do about it. "What can I do?" she asked. "It's like we are cursed!"

Her assessment seemed right to me. It *was* as if Grandpa had cursed the entire family. I knew that such a family curse does have power, and may range from an unconscious prediction, as when a child is told, "You'll never amount to anything," to deliberately calling down misfortune on another person. I also knew that the power of a curse could be broken in the name of Jesus Christ, and replaced with a blessing. But Jenny was describing an entire family system, enmeshed, colluding, and long-standing. Clearly it was not only Grandpa who had kept the pattern going. Everyone in the family played his or her part in the drama.

As Jenny told her story, I prayed silently. What experiment or action could I suggest? The idea of generational healing surfaced strongly, but I wondered if breaking Grandpa's curse could really have any effect on this profoundly disturbed family. A liturgical action seemed like a puny response if Jenny needed to express her barely controlled rage at Grandpa, or at her parents for not putting a stop to his abuse. At that moment, moving from concern for an individual to concern for her entire crazy family – twenty-five of whom were not present – seemed like a big, and maybe foolish, step. But finally, because my hunch about generational healing prayer was so strong, I proposed it.

Both Jenny and the workshop group were willing. In the context of Eucharist the little ad hoc church prayed that whatever had happened to grandpa or his ancestors to fill him with such venom would be healed. In the name of Jesus Christ we ordered any spirits that had used Grandpa to inflict suffering on the family to leave the entire family tree, and we asked that the pipeline of negativity from Grandpa to the rest of the family be severed. In the name of Jesus we also declared that Grandpa's lifetime of curses were no longer in effect, naming each one as Jenny remembered them. For example, "In the name of Jesus Christ we in this church proclaim that it is not true that this family is doomed to unhappiness forever. Here and now we break this curse by the power of Jesus Christ." Then we prayed for every one of the twenty-six people by name, concluding each prayer with "By the power of Jesus Christ we declare that any curses against –(name)– are no longer in effect. We claim –(name)– as a child of God whose heritage is abundant life." We prayed for Grandpa too, that in God's mercy he could find peace. As we finished we laid our hands on Jenny and prayed that she, along with her whole family, be healed of the effects of Grandpa's abuse.

Jenny was tired at the end of the service, and thought she felt a little better. About a month later she called me. She reported that since the service she had felt free of depression. She also said that the rest of her family seemed to be changing, and the atmosphere at family gatherings had a lightness that was new to everyone. They weren't tearing each other down; in fact one uncle had even asked and received forgiveness from his brother. Another aunt and uncle were beginning a new adventure. They had always wanted to see the country by automobile, an idea that Grandpa had torpedoed as silly and irresponsible. Now they were filled with excitement as they made their plans. Jenny's parents just seemed more relaxed, as if a burden had been lifted. Jenny, awed and grateful, said she was continuing to pray for her family.

WHAT DID I MAKE OF ALL THIS?

Grandpa's death in itself could have accounted for the new freedom in Jenny's family, and Larry's own symbolic cord-cutting in front of witnesses could have simply been a powerful expression of the change that had been gathering force for some time. As with most prayer for healing, there is no way to say with certainty that our prayers made a difference, although both Jenny and Larry strongly felt they did. I was convinced enough, however, to continue to pray for generational healing when it seemed appropriate. As I did so, I was awed by the power of God as people were set free from generational patterns.

Some of these healings were admittedly dramatic and concerned terribly important issues, such as the woman who suffered from anorexia and was healed after prayer for her ancestors who had nearly starved. Just as often generational healing prayer concerned ordinary issues of growth and maturity. For example, a woman was helped to claim her considerable gifts for ministry after we prayed for her long-dead ancestor who was ostracized for being a woman with gifts for ministry. The living woman had already worked with this very issue, and generational healing prayer seemed to be yet another step in her journey.

I, too, benefited from generational healing prayer. I have a photo of my grandmother Matilda and her four sisters, taken around 1900. The young women are done up in ruffled, lacy dresses and huge fantastic hats full of feather plumes and flowers. All seem happy and confident that they are attractive – except for my grandmother. She looks uncomfortable, as if she is trying to hide from the camera. Her body is tense, her smile frozen. As I look at her I imagine that she doesn't feel pretty, just ridiculous in her fashionable frills. (Her daughter, my aunt, confirmed that Matilda *never* felt she was pretty.) When I saw this picture for the first time as an adult, I immediately recognized my grandmother's feelings; from childhood, I have felt them myself, especially in front of a camera. I believe that praying for Matilda made a difference as I gently worked toward claiming my own face.

PAULINE CLAIMS HER GRANDMOTHER'S HAT

Other prayer for generational healing focuses on claiming and cherishing the good gifts handed down through one's family. Consider the story of Pauline, a member of a Gestalt Pastoral Care training group, who began her work with generational healing prayer by saying that three members of her immediate family had died from heart attacks in their mid-fifties. Since Pauline is also in her mid-fifties, she confessed an irrational fear that she, too, would die within the next year or so. Although she was not ordinarily one to let her feelings run wild, she had a hard time even imagining the future, for she felt as if she would not live to have one.

We first did some Gestalt work in which she spoke to each of the three heart attack victims as if they were present on a pillow in front of her. After expressing her fears, her father "spoke" back to her with loving words of encouragement to take care of herself a little better. The second relative had little to say. It was talking with her grandmother that brought the most healing. With tears of gratitude, Pauline told her grandmother that she was her hero, and that she, Pauline, always wanted to be just like her. Her grandmother had been an artist who wasn't bound by the conventional limitations of being a woman. She was convinced she could do whatever she set out to do, and lived her life with creative dash. She literally taught Pauline to color outside the lines by replacing Pauline's "wimpy little coloring books" with huge pads of newsprint and paints.

At one point, Pauline said to her grandmother, "If you had lived longer, you would have been one of those ladies with the purple hats."[56] Someone from the group piped up, "And you just got that purple hat, Pauline!" Indeed Pauline had recently bought a magnificent handmade purple hat from a local fiber artist. As Pauline mused over her new hat, it seemed that the purple hat was her icon of living abundantly in future decades, and the purple hat gave focus to our prayers for her. In the name of Christ we declared that the age at which her family members died was severed from her grandmother's many gifts, and that Pauline was set free from a deterministic fate based on age. We asked that Pauline receive her grandmother's many gifts in even greater measure, and that she "wear grandmother's purple hat" for as long a life as God would give. While we were praying, someone remembered a passage from the Bible, and read it to Pauline:

> I am reminded of your sincere faith, a faith that lived first in your grandmother Lois and your mother Eunice and now, I am sure, lives in you. For this reason I remind you to rekindle the gift of God that is within you through the laying on of my hands; for God did not give us a spirit of cowardice, but rather a spirit of power and of love and of self-discipline. (II Timothy 1:5-6).

---

[56] She was referring both to The Red Hat Society, and to the popular poem by Jenny Joseph that begins, "When I am an old woman I shall wear purple/with a red hat which doesn't go and doesn't suit me."

Finally, we prayed that Pauline would be both motivated and empowered to adopt the much-needed changes in diet and exercise of which her father spoke.

COMBINING GENERATIONAL HEALING PRAYER WITH GESTALT PASTORAL CARE

Perhaps it is obvious by now that healing prayer of all kinds goes along with, but is not a substitute for, our own work and effort to grow. In preparation for generational healing prayer, Gestalt experiments which invite conversation between the pray-er and various family members not only seems to clear the air somewhat, but also to reveal the contours of the problem and perhaps to give shape to the prayer itself. In regard to generational healing prayer, the one who wants to pray for her family may be the only one in the family who is taking personal growth seriously. She may also be the family caretaker, the one who has taken on the job of making sure everyone else is happy, emotionally healthy, and spiritually fit. This impossible task must be surrendered to God. An active care-taker can actually block the healing of a family, for a caretaker not only *takes care,* but also *takes responsibility from* those who need to be responsible for them-selves. Such a surrender can be accomplished, for example, by assembling the family in fantasy to announce her resignation from this caretaking job, and then by giving each person over into God's care. Such surrender is a wonderful prepa-ration for generational healing prayer.

WHEN TO PRAY FOR GENERATIONAL HEALING

I have learned to consider generational healing prayer when certain condi-tions present themselves.

First, when the problem persists over time despite the person's desire to change, her solid inner work, and her willingness and seeming readiness to let go, it may be an indication that there is need for generational prayer. (It might also be wise to discern if deliverance, discussed in the next chapter, is needed as well.)

Secondly, when the problem seems to be rooted outside of the person's own life experience, I begin to suspect generational problems. Once I worked with a woman who was plagued by nagging anxiety. We did a great deal of prayerful Gestalt work, but the only thing in her experience that seemed to relate to anxiety was a memory of being lost on a playground for less than ten minutes. The child

258

was scared, but believed that her mommy would eventually find her. This memory didn't seem harrowing enough to account for her life-long fear, and nothing changed after she worked on it. I reflected that she might have a deeply buried memory that hadn't yet surfaced. Or that she might be holding on to her anxiety so as not to be responsible for her life. Or that she had a chemical imbalance and needed medication. Or that she needed deliverance. Or that some other factor might be at work. Nothing seemed to shine out as we discerned, however, except for generational healing prayer. So in the spirit of experimentation, the two of us prayed for the healing of anxiety in her family tree, and right away her anxiety was greatly reduced. As always, discernment was of primary importance.

When there is a sense of having the same feelings or experiences as a parent or other relative, or a pattern of behavior that runs through the family, that is a clue that the problem may be partly generational. When someone says, "I've *always* felt this way," this is also a clue. In some families, divorce or suicide or various addictions seem to be almost expected. In others, there might be a pattern of failures to keep commitments, or perhaps a gift for artistry or medicine, or the will to persevere through hardship. Whether negative or positive, familial patterns might well inspire generational prayer.

The presence of pessimistic or cynical family mottoes is another clue that there may be need for generational healing prayer. A family motto is a summary of how that family responds to the world. A few such mottoes are:

•*You've made your bed; now you have to lie in it.*

•*If you don't take care of yourself, no one else will.*

•*Don't get attached to anything. You might lose it.*

•*If you're laughing now, you'll be crying before bedtime.*

And, one of the most poignant:

•*There is no such thing as second place. If you're not first, you're nothing.*

Confluent families are often candidates for generational healing prayer. (I discuss confluence in Chapter Eleven.) In confluent families there is very little tolerance for separation between family members. Emotions, opinions, and choices are shaped so as not to be different from the others. These families might recognize themselves in the tee shirt inscription, "If Mama ain't happy, ain't nobody happy."

Confluent families often have at least one parenting child, a son or daughter whose life assignment is to make everything okay for one or both parents. These children may find they will do almost anything to "keep Mama happy," effectively shielding Mama from having to be responsible for herself. Larry, whose story was told above, was such a parenting child. Sometimes parenting children seem to arrange their lives so that they are dealing with the very issue the parent needs to work out. Thus, if there is a father who is afraid of intimacy, there may be a daughter who won't allow herself to commit to any man. Although she may go to therapy to deal with the problem, she may have a sense that she is doing her father's work for him. Healing begins when a parenting child recognizes that he or she is trying to be a savior, and resigns from that impossible job. Such resignations seem all the more powerful if declared and witnessed by an ad hoc church. Committing Mama or Daddy to the care of the Lord is the second part of the healing prayer, and the third is to pray that God will cut any unhealthy ties between the parenting child and the rest of the family.

When a person is part of a racial, cultural, or ethnic group that has suffered a history of oppression, there is often a need for generational healing prayer. African Americans, Native Americans, Jews, Irish, and Armenians might fall into this category. *Or, when one is part of a group that historically was the oppressor, there is also often a need for generational healing.* Families who owned slaves, for example, or "old money" families who almost surely stepped on others in their scramble to the economic top, or families who settled on land snatched from Native Americans – i.e. most Americans – might benefit from a prayer of confession prayed by living family members as a part of generational healing prayer.

Families that suffered trauma and hardship and didn't process their reactions might also need healing prayer. It has only been in recent times that people have had the tools and the inclination to deal with their feelings. Psychotherapy is relatively new. Self-help groups, crisis counseling, and addiction services are even newer. Not so long ago when people suffered they just plodded on. They coped, they survived – or they didn't – and by and large they didn't talk about their problems. Reading old sermons gives the impression that the church stressed surrender to God's will and looking toward heaven, rather than a joyful, life-long healing journey. Perhaps the need for generational healing could be present in most of us.

Finally, when careful discernment, or even a strong hunch, indicates the need for generational healing, of course it is time to suggest it. Remember we don't need to be absolutely certain that a problem is rooted in generational pain to pray for generational healing. We can pray with a sense of experimentation: "Let's pray for your family and see what God will do." Neither is it necessary to discern exactly what might have happened to a family far back in time. When looking at patterns in a family tree, we may ask, "Lord, when did this all begin? Whom do we need to pray for?" If an image or other impression is given, well and good; below I tell about an African-American woman who received a vivid image of her great-great-grandmother. Most of the time, it seems more important to rest in the faith that God knows the family's story, so there is no need to grasp for details. This is particularly important to persons who were adopted. Although they may need to search for their birth families for other reasons, for the purpose of healing prayer, they don't need to. In fact, prayer for generational healing sometimes calls for giving up historical fascination and the need to know.

JOSIE MEETS HER GREAT-GREAT-GRANDMOTHER

Josie's story is one more testimony to the beautiful way God heals through generational healing prayer. In this story an ancestor is both the source of the problem and a powerful instrument of healing and reconciliation. This prayer experience occurred before the pray-er knew anything about generational healing prayer.

Josie is an African-American woman pastor. Competent, smart, and dedicated, she entered the ministry at midlife after a varied and rich secular career. She came to see me because from time to time she was finding herself cranky, irritated, and just plain angry with her parishioners. Sometimes it was all she could do to keep from lashing out in rage. Of course her church wasn't perfect, and some folks were perfectly maddening, but Josie recognized that her strong reactions were way out of proportion to the normal crabbiness of church life.

She did some Gestalt anger work, exploring the depths and contours of her rage to see if her anger was just displaced from somewhere else. Although she had no trouble expressing anger, her anger work went nowhere. It was as if the anger she expressed poured down a drain, at about the same rate that more anger poured in.

Josie suggested discernment prayer. We asked together, "Lord, please show us how to get at the root of Josie's anger." As we waited in silence, Josie began to see a vivid image that both astonished and moved her. She saw an old African slave waiting her turn on the auction block. Jesus was standing there with her. As Josie went nearer, somehow she knew with certainty that this was her mother's grandmother. I was about to suggest that Josie climb up on the auction block and talk to the old woman, but Josie was already on her way. Josie began to weep in helpless anger and frustration at the suffering of the old woman, saying how indescribably terrible, how evil, how profoundly unjust that she should be bought and sold like an animal. "I will *never* stop being angry about slavery!" Josie declared to her. Then she stopped, amazed at what she had just said.

Then the old slave spoke:

> Honey, you're having trouble, being so angry you don't know what to do. I was angry too, but no more. I ain't going to let anger mess me up ever again. I'm happy now with Jesus, and he's helped me forgive everybody I've needed to forgive. You don't need to stay unhappy and angry just because I was unhappy and angry. I want you to go on now and be happy. Stay close to Jesus. He'll show you the way. It's all right to be happy. Now child, I give you my blessing.

Josie and I were stunned at the power and of her great-great-grandmother's words. A slave bringing freedom. An uneducated woman of great wisdom and profound spiritual depth. Helpless, but a consummate healer. In shackles, but a person of powerful authority. How very like the kingdom of God.

The light shines in the darkness,
and the darkness did not overcome it.
John 1:5

16

DELIVERANCE

CAROL

Carol is a fine pastoral counselor well known for her wisdom and gentleness, a respected retreat leader, and a greatly sought-after spiritual companion. She is also a passionate amateur competitive runner. Running is a vital part of her spirituality, helping her to stay energetic and clear so she can do her work. Understandably, she was dismayed when she developed an injury in her knee, and her increasing pain made running more and more impossible. She put off going to the doctor, hoping that it would get better, but the pain only got worse. It was then that she ran smack into an old phobia about doctors and began to work hard on it.

One day during this time she came in quite upset. She had finally been to the doctor, and found out she needed surgery – routine – but surgery nonetheless. She had been working with her fear of doctors for some time, and her fear had been greatly reduced. In fact, the partial healing of her fear had allowed her to consult with this doctor in the first place. This day, however, she was fearful, angry, depressed, cynical, teary, and had a terrible headache to boot. She wailed:

> I don't know what kind of sick game God is playing with me. I
> pray and pray and finally get up the courage to go to the doctor,
> and what do I get? Another cute little lesson to deal with! Now
> I've got to go through surgery – with no guarantee that anything
> will come of it. Don't say one word about how God is maybe
> going to heal me through surgery! And what if I die on the oper-
> ating table? Just great! Why does God always make everything
> so hard for me? I surrender everything, and what do I get? A big
> nothing! It seems like God loves everyone but me, because ev-
> erything I really want and care about is hard for me. God doesn't
> help me one bit! Oh, yeah, but God uses me to help other people.

> Why can't I just be like everybody else? Sometimes I think I
> should just give up and kill myself.

Throughout this tirade I had the odd feeling that these angry words were not really connected to her. Yes, she was being completely honest, reporting exactly the misery she felt, but somehow her words just felt a little off. They certainly weren't characteristic of the Carol I had come to know so well.

At the same time I had the distinct impression that the Holy Spirit was gently and peacefully present. As I prayed silently, it seemed clear that I was not to try to suggest ways to explore "the mess," as Carol called it, because that would only serve to distract us and derail her process of healing. Instead, we were to *cut away* the mess by the authority of Jesus Christ. As I continued to discern silently, I seemed to hear that indeed Carol's present feelings had to do with an attack from the Evil One, who had used her fear of doctors and her great desire to continue running to knock her off center.

I asked Carol if this discernment made any sense to her, but she was too tangled in her emotions to know right then. She did, however, give me permission to test it out. So I spoke:

> In the name of Jesus Christ and by his authority, I bind the Spirits of Bitterness, Cynicism, Despair, Fear, and Suicide, and any other spirits not of God. I order you to be silent, and you are forbidden to communicate with Carol in any way. I bind you away from her body, mind, emotions, and spirit. I bind you away from her fear of doctors and her love of running. You may not do anything except leave, when I tell you to do so, in the name of Jesus.

Immediately Carol felt a shift. Suddenly she did not feel assaulted by runaway emotions, nor did she feel as "noisy" inside. The discernment seemed confirmed by this reaction, along with Carol's sense that we were on the right track.

The next step was simply to order the spirits away:

> In the name of Jesus Christ I order away from Carol Spirits of Bitterness, Cynicism, Despair, Fear and Suicide and any other spirits not of God. You must leave her immediately, with no stalling or hiding. You must leave silently with no uproar or drama or manifestation of any kind. You must leave completely, leaving no parts of yourself behind. You must detach from her now and leave as she breathes out. You must go straight to Jesus with-

out detours or delays. You must not harm anyone or anything as you go. I order this in the name of Jesus Christ who has defeated you by his resurrection.

After a few moments of heavy breathing, Carol looked up with shining eyes and said, "I can't tell you how different I feel. None of that stuff is going on any more. I feel lighter, much lighter, and very grateful to God. They're really gone!" Ten days later she still felt fine, her life back on track.

Was she cured of all her problems? Of course not. She was still anxious around doctors, but now she could once again let herself hold onto the promise that God would always be with her – especially in her upcoming surgery.

MY RESISTANCE

When I first got involved in prayer for healing, I read voraciously about it. I found some excellent books, most notably Francis MacNutt's *Healing.* I discovered that nearly every book on healing prayer, including MacNutt's, seemed to have at least one chapter on deliverance, the process in which a person is freed from evil spirits.[57] This was not a happy discovery for me; references to casting out demons seemed fraught with fanaticism and nuttiness. I was afraid that people would think I was weird, and what could be weirder than this?

As I thought more about it, I was able to clarify my objections a bit. *First, it seemed to me that the notion of demons – discrete evil entities bent on destruction – revealed a worldview belonging to the first century, but certainly not to our time.* After all, first-century people didn't know about epilepsy or mental illnesses like Tourette's Syndrome[58] and Dissociative Identity Disorder (formerly called multiple personality disorder). No wonder they called symptoms associated with these and other disorders demonic. I was sure that twentieth-century people have no need to speak of demons, except as metaphor for the impersonal evil force that opposes God. Obviously, we claim much more scientific, theological and psychological sophistication than existed in the early church, and to adopt a first-century theology about demons was like believing the world was flat. So I thought then.

Secondly, I was wary of any practice which might attempt to get rid of what Jung called the "shadow." Instead of banishing that which we don't like or fear

---

[57] Francis MacNutt, *Deliverance from Evil Spirits: A Practical Manual.* See also Matthew and Dennis Linn's *Deliverance Prayer* for a collection of articles from various sources.

[58] Some Tourette's Syndrome behavior is remarkably similar to some descriptions of demonic possession: facial distortion, uncontrollable cursing, barking, snake-like hissing, and spitting.

about ourselves, we need to explore and integrate this material. Abdicating our own repentance and discipline while asking God to take away a bad habit is irresponsible. Furthermore, it is impossible to do away with what is simply natural and human; trying to do so is the cause of much anguish. I had heard of church groups spending hours praying with a sufferer to get rid of spirits of sexuality or anger or the "demon of nicotine." Those stories sounded just plain abusive to me.

Third, deliverance seemed like a much-too-easy answer that bypassed the hard work associated with real growth. Taking care of major problems with a few words or a little ritual clashed with all my training as a pastor and a Gestaltist.

Fourth, I asked myself what might happen to a person, perhaps with a shaky self-concept, when told that he has a demon? And what about the possibility of misdiagnosis? I had worked with badly wounded refugees from fanatic Christian groups who sought emotional control over their adherents. The possibility of doing damage to vulnerable, suffering people seemed very real.

Finally, I thought I could detect hints of spiritual distortion and rigidity in the people most eager to talk about deliverance. It seemed to me that some were clearly fascinated with demons and associated phenomena. Some seemed to actually organize their perception of reality around the notion of demons; everything seemed to be associated with evil in some way. Others seemed to enjoy taking authority, and liked feeling powerful. I did note that Francis MacNutt named and avoided these land mines, but I was still completely turned off to the idea. Later I concluded that MacNutt was absolutely right in saying that the ministry of deliverance is more subject to distortion that any other aspect of healing ministry. Power trips and fascination with evil are just two of the possible traps. The whole area seemed to suggest dabbling in magic, simplistic formulas, and self-aggrandizement.

I remember telling God my terms back then: I was reluctantly willing to be a minister of healing, but I would *never* get involved with the ministry of deliverance. Two years after serving notice in this regard I found myself with my back to the wall in the presence of evil, and the only way out seemed to be deliverance prayer.

NANCY

One day a woman I will call Nancy had a brief seizure in my office. Moments later she was lying on the floor, disoriented and confused. Knowing Nancy had a seizure disorder for which she was taking medication, I was concerned, but not alarmed. Trying to help her re-orient herself, I leaned over her, and asked her to tell me her name. Obviously I expected to hear her say "Nancy," but that didn't happen. Instead, out of her body came a deep, scornful, male voice that said, "My name is Dunemis, and I'm going to kill *her*, and I'm going to kill *you*!" Then as Nancy's eyes snapped open, Dunemis began to mumble and curse under his breath. Looking at her I was both scared and repulsed; this was not the Nancy whom I knew and liked, but something infinitely sinister and bent on destruction. Instinctively, I knew that whatever was calling itself Dunemis was not a personality alter (a dissociated part of her personality), nor was it something to integrate or accommodate. This was *evil*. Although I had been a Gestaltist for many years, and had heard more than a few people with multiple personalities speak with alternative voices, I had never before experienced such stomach-turning disgust and fear with anyone. This was utterly different.

I urged Nancy to return, but to no avail. She was gone, and in her place was this Dunemis lying on my office floor, muttering curses and threats. What does one do in such an instance? I considered calling an ambulance, certain that she would be admitted to a psychiatric ward immediately. It would have been so easy, and it was probably even the "right" thing to do. However, Nancy was a new single mother. Her baby boy was six weeks old, and Nancy loved him with all her heart. Because Nancy had a long history of mental illness, and because she had no family, I knew that if she was admitted to a psychiatric hospital again, the baby would be placed in foster care. It might be a year before Nancy got him back. *If* she ever got him back. I didn't want that to occur unless it was absolutely necessary.

Furthermore, I couldn't escape the realization that what was happening was very similar to the descriptions I had read of evil spirits. Despite my intense reaction to Dunemis I still was far from ready to admit that evil spirits really existed, but what if they did? It had surely seemed like something evil had threatened me. I asked myself if I was just being gullible, influenced by what I had read. Was I somehow fascinated with tales of evil, just like in the movies? Could my disgust have sprung from some unintegrated part of myself? Was Nancy in a psychotic state again? If, however, my initial reaction was right and Nancy indeed needed deliverance, there was no chance she would get it in the hospital.

I asked my husband George to come into my office to help me decide what to do. Together we decided to keep Nancy overnight at our house and take care of her baby in our bedroom. We would not let Nancy touch him. Meanwhile I would call some ministers experienced in healing prayer who had been telling me that sooner or later I was going to have to deal with deliverance. I would refer Nancy to someone who knew about deliverance first-hand. Let someone else evaluate the situation and do what was needed. Maybe I would watch or assist in some way, but that was all.

In growing dismay I found that none of the people I called that evening were available. One was out of the country, one had pneumonia, another was leading a week-long retreat, and so on. Meanwhile, George, intrigued with the word "dunemis," had looked it up, and confirmed that it was the Greek word for "powers," as in, "principalities and powers." Learning that dunemis is the root word for "dynamite" did nothing whatever to reassure us. However, it did prod us to consider again that maybe we were indeed dealing with more than just Nancy.

Finally, with a good deal of trepidation we decided to go ahead with a deliverance service ourselves. We would suspend judgment, follow the directions in *Healing* by Francis MacNutt, and see what happened.[59] If Nancy were no different afterwards, we would have to take her to the hospital. (George joked that if she *was* different, maybe *we* would have to be admitted!) It seemed crazy, but under the circumstances, with nothing to lose, we were willing to give it a try. A third person joined us; she was a good pray-er, but as inexperienced as we were with deliverance prayer. We swore each other to secrecy; we would never tell anyone about this!

The three of us had Eucharist together, and asked that we be protected and empowered to help Nancy. Although Nancy's body was there, Dunemis was still in control, muttering profanities as we prayed. After Eucharist, we ordered Dunemis to leave in the name of Jesus Christ. Thoroughly startling us, Dunemis spoke back, telling us that he was not leaving because the three of us were rookies and we didn't know what we were doing. (Nancy had not been in the room during our previous discussions in which we admitted this very fact.) Somehow we found the sense to reply that Jesus Christ was not a rookie, and that he was the one ordering Dunemis to leave.

For the next two hours we continued to insist in the name of Jesus that Dunemis leave, and Dunemis continued to refuse, but we could see that he was getting progressively weaker. During this bizarre conversation, he told us that he hated the name "Jesus" and demanded that we not say it again. At one point, he bragged, "I loved to cause her seizures." Eventually, his voice became whiny as

[59] See Chapter 15, p. 167-184.

he pitifully begged for more time. At last Nancy's body arched, she screamed, and Dunemis was gone.

The three of us were stunned into silence. Nancy blinked as if waking, looked around at the three of us, and asked, "Hey, what's going on? Are we having a meeting?" Other than being quite exhausted, she seemed just fine.

In the next few months other spirits surfaced in Nancy, and subsequently they were expelled. Since that first night many years ago, Nancy has never had another seizure or psychotic episode. Her mental health has continued to improve. Currently she is supporting herself and has raised her son, who is in college and about to be married, as a committed and loving parent.

The three of us who helped Nancy were changed too. During the deliverance itself we had been swept into an unfamiliar world where our usual assumptions about reality were set aside. Afterwards we had to make room in our worldview for what had happened so powerfully with Nancy. George begin to ponder and pray about how the church might address evil within institutions; some years later he wrote a book about it called *Claiming All Things for God: Prayer, Discernment and Ritual for Social Change.*[60] As for myself, I tried to be open to the idea of deliverance, but still adamantly resisted being involved in such a ministry. Despite the fact that the three of us had told no one about what had happened with Nancy, in the next few months a number of people who said they wanted deliverance contacted me. One of these people was John, a seminary student.

JOHN

John came for his weekly session with a disturbing dream. In the dream he is coming downstairs in his house to find a group of nasty-looking "thugs" in his living room. "Who are you, and what are you doing in my house?" he demands. "Lucifer!" they snarl, "and we are here to destroy you, and you can't stop us. It's just a matter of time before we kill you." John woke up terrified.

Gestalt dreamwork revealed that the thugs were completely bent on destroying John's faith and wrecking the relationship with a woman he loved. John and I discerned carefully over a period of several weeks, asking if we should order the thugs away in the name of Jesus. I wanted to be really certain that the thugs were not simply an unintegrated part of John. As I mused over John's dream, I realized

---

[60] George McClain, *Claiming All Things for God: Prayer, Discernment, and Ritual for Social Change.*

that I had no trouble believing that God often seems to be revealed in dream symbols for a person of faith, so why not evidence of evil as well? I also had the clear sense that despite their threatening appearance, ordering the dream thugs away would not be difficult.

With a minimum of fuss, and in the context of a regular session, John and I demanded that the thugs leave him in the name of Jesus. Immediately they obeyed, and John and I both knew it. The result in John was not dramatic, but by the next week he was sure that he was more able to experience his feelings. Before, his emotions had been wispy, muted, and often inaccessible. After, he was feeling joy, tears, passion, and anger, with surprising intensity. His faith was greatly strengthened, and he felt that he had come alive in a new way. His woman friend loved the changes in him, and their relationship deepened.

In the next year or so there were a few others for whom careful discernment suggested that deliverance was appropriate. A six year old girl was healed of anxieties and compulsions when I told "the bad guys" (the child's words) to go away in the name of Jesus. The bad guys had been telling her scary things about her family which she would have had no way of knowing otherwise, and using words which she repeated to her father, asking what they meant. A woman who invariably got a migraine every time she took Communion was set free. Another person felt her long-standing depression lighten, and then over a period of months, disappear.

New Conclusions

When I emerged from the turmoil of having both theology and worldview shattered by these experiences, I found my faith greatly strengthened. I was awed and astonished at discovering that the name of Jesus was so powerful. As I found myself proclaiming that Jesus had indeed overcome the forces of evil, the crucifixion and resurrection took on new meaning for me. I was still squirmy and embarrassed about the first century language – the hierarchy of demons with names and job descriptions – but because no other language seemed to fit my experience as well, I decided to use it. Not surprisingly, I had come to some new conclusions.[61]

---

[61] I am deeply indebted to Francis MacNutt for his sane and wise teaching during this time. See his *Deliverance from Evil Spirits: A Practical Manual.*

Sometimes, but certainly not always, demonic oppression is involved with sin or with emotional, spiritual, familial, physical, or social brokenness. Ordinary sin is not the same as evil, nor is it always fueled by evil. Humans can make disastrous choices, and be desperately greedy, wrong-headed and cruel. We can get addicted to harmful substances. We can be the victim of another's sin, and then harbor hatred, revenge, and violence in return. We can do these things quite well, all by ourselves. We do not have to "have a demon." However, occasionally evil oppresses an individual or an institution. When that happens, free choice can be difficult, because evil exercises some measure of control.

When there is demonic oppression, it is always interrelated with "nondemonic" brokenness. Somehow the nature of the oppression will be directly related to the person's life, specifically hooked into his or her vulnerabilities. Evil can take advantage of unhealed wounds, or can find a way in when a person insists on sinful actions or attitudes, but neither vulnerability nor sin automatically points to the presence of evil. In other words, it is never just demons causing a problem. If, for example, someone is oppressed by a spirit of terror, it is nearly certain that sometime in his life he was terrified. If a spirit of spite is present, it is a good guess that the person has held onto toxic anger. (An exception to this rule is found in cases of generational brokenness, explained in Chapter Fifteen.)

Deliverance ministry is a companion to, but does not replace, psychotherapy, healing prayer, medical help, and spiritual companioning. In particular, the need for deliverance seems to surface in the context of the healing ministry, just as MacNutt and others have written. The time I spend focusing on deliverance is very small, probably less than one percent of the time I spend at work. However, evil spirits can block healing in every area, and sometimes nothing can be accomplished until the need for deliverance is addressed.

Demons act in somewhat predictable ways. They behave as if they are intelligent beings with "assignments" to cause specific reactions. These assignments are sometimes described by their names, such as Hatred, Despair, or Greed. They seem to be organized hierarchically, with stronger demons in charge. For example, Despair might be the organizing focus in one person, with, say, Depression, Fear and Numbness as secondary influences. They cooperate with each other and will act in concert. Although they must obey when ordered in the name of Jesus, they are legalistic, and will actively search for loopholes. If a demon is told to leave, it might not go because it was not told to leave *immediately.* When addressing spirits, I have learned to speak as broadly as I can: For example, " In the name of

Jesus Christ, you must leave *completely, immediately*, and go *directly* to Jesus. You may not stop or influence *anyone* or *anything* on your way."

Demons are evil and committed to destruction. Their mission is to destroy all that's holy and all that's truly human. They prey on weakness, and innocence. They lie.

Most importantly, they recognize the authority of Jesus. They know they have been defeated by his death and resurrection, and that they must ultimately obey a command given in his name. When a faithful Christian orders them away in the name of Jesus, they have no choice but to obey – with certain important exceptions. Sometimes, there is a sort of "invitation to stay" in a suffering person – who may be completely unaware of such vulnerability. Identifying and eliminating these invitations will be discussed later in this chapter.

The gospels attest that Jesus certainly cast out demons as an important part of his healing ministry, and that he expected his disciples to do the same. In fact he was quite angry when the disciples were not able to cast out a spirit from an afflicted boy: "You faithless and perverse generation, how much longer must I be with you? Bring him here to me" (Matthew 17:17).

Jesus has given his followers permission to take authority over evil spirits in his name. When we do this after careful discernment and preparation, the spirits flee – even in the twenty-first century! Again and again I have seen people set free by this simple action. It is never more apparent that Jesus is among us and is still victorious over the forces of evil than in deliverance.

When the temple curtain was torn in half at the crucifixion and when the stone was rolled away from Jesus' tomb at his resurrection, there was a cosmic shift that tilted the balance of good and evil. Evil and death were overcome; the principalities and powers were ultimately beaten. Each time we pray, "…and deliver us from evil," each time we celebrate Eucharist, we affirm again that Christ was – and is – victorious.

Deliverance is like cutting away a tangle of underbrush; once it is done, the way is cleared for new growth. Deliverance is not magic, but it can free up blocks and enable growth to continue. Although many people feel better immediately after deliverance, some do not. Nearly always there is hard inner work to do to assimilate the changes deliverance can bring.

Finally, more experience with deliverance over the next few years showed me that deliverance doesn't have to be a noisy show of shouting ministers and eerie phenomena. Although sometimes a minister discerns that it is necessary to set aside special time for a deliverance service with intercessors to pray in a concentrated way for an afflicted person, deliverance can also happen very quietly and in just a few minutes. It can be a simple matter between a minister and sufferer, who decide together that they need to proceed in this direction. No matter which setting is deemed appropriate, I now believe it is not necessary or even advisable to allow a spirit to speak at all. Instead of asking an evil spirit for its name, I ask the Holy Spirit instead. Furthermore, I order the spirit to not create any drama or uproar, nor show itself in any way. It may leave only on the afflicted person's breath, as he or she exhales. Thus, to an observer looking in a window, a deliverance session might look pretty much like an ordinary spiritual direction session, with some prayer and deep breathing toward the end.

Admittedly, it is a little more difficult to tell when a spirit has left when the service is deliberately quiet and non-dramatic. I do it in this deliberately low-key way for several reasons. Very early on, I found that allowing evil spirits to speak was exhausting. They lie, stall, and prey on the vulnerabilities of both the sufferer and the minister. They can put on such an interesting show that those present become confused, distracted or afraid. Why subject myself and others to that, when it is quite easy to get the spirits to shut up? Why get involved in a battle when the battle has already been won? (The battle with Dunemis described earlier in this chapter tired George and me out for weeks afterward. Nancy, the "host" of Dunemis, was even more fatigued.) In addition, if there is no outward battle, there is no "war hero" except for God. If the minister's ego could become inflated by her apparent power as she takes authority, or if others might put her on a pedestal, these temptations are minimized dramatically.

Most importantly, phenomena associated with evil spirits are fascinating and titillating. Movies and books about demons attest to widespread public interest in "the dark side." It is astonishing how easily our attention can get derailed in a deliverance session in which the spirits manifest themselves; and feeding this fascination can give the spirits more power. I believe that our focus needs to be on the suffering person and on God's mercy, love, and mighty power to bring deliverance to a captive. Truly, we need not be interested in any antics of evil spirits.

DELIVERANCE AND EXORCISM

Before going further in a discussion of deliverance, it is important to discuss its relation to exorcism. There is a difference between simple deliverance and exorcism, and the difference is one of degree. Evil spirits seem to have widely varying strengths; in most people bothered by evil spirits, they are actually fairly weak and easily dispelled. Occasionally the spirits are a little stronger, and seem to require commands from a specially-gathered group in the context of Eucharist. When the person in need of help has will, choice, and desire for God's grace, and can work toward his own wholeness, it is a matter for *deliverance*. The vast majority of cases fall into this category.

Extremely rarely, someone is so controlled by evil that we say he or she is *possessed;* there is so little of the person in control that he or she can no longer choose wholeness. I have had no experience of this, thank goodness. When there is genuine possession, the remedy is *exorcism*.[62]

Roman Catholics and Episcopalians need permission from a bishop for exorcism, but not for deliverance. Most Roman Catholic dioceses have an official exorcist who is an expert in these things. Mainstream Protestant denominations don't deal with evil spirits in any official way, but that doesn't mean Protestants aren't involved in deliverance. Ministers who are confronted with a need for deliverance seem to find out through the grapevine whom to contact. My impression is that more and more Protestant clergy are comfortable, informed and experienced in these matters. However, if I thought that there was need for full exorcism, I would most certainly find someone more experienced and qualified than I.

Ministers with no experience with deliverance would be well advised to do some reading on this subject and find an experienced mentor before getting involved. Despite my own precipitous plunge into deliverance, I believe it is best to learn about deliverance by first observing or assisting someone who is mature, balanced, and experienced in this ministry.

HOW DO EVIL SPIRITS ENTER? WHY DO THEY STAY?

Woundedness

What creates an opening for evil spirits to bother a person? Most often the presence of evil spirits is not a result of some inadequacy or sin. Usually they are there because evil has taken advantage of woundedness. For example, people who have been abused as children may have a vulnerability to such spirits as

---

[62] Once again I am indebted to Francis MacNutt who clearly makes this important distinction. See *Healing*, p. 167.

Fear, Rage, Despair, or Depression. Someone told all his life that he is stupid and ugly can be a target for the spirits of Self-hatred or Discouragement. Survivors of disasters may find that their terrifying experience has created a space for spirits of Terror and Mistrust. Obviously this does not mean that evil spirits are inevitable even with major traumas, just that the traumas create an opening through which they may slip.

Repeated Sin

If a sin is repeated many times, the way may be opened for a spirit to enter. For example, one whose lifestyle includes pornography and one-night stands may well find that a spirit of Lust has come in. Another who insists for years that "I will never forgive her" and harbors thoughts of retaliation may be vulnerable to a spirit of Spite or Revenge. A third person who spends money, time and energy to increase his status while disregarding the needs of others, may be opening the door to a spirit of Arrogance. Once a spirit is fueling a particular sin, it is much harder to stop the behavior. Before these sin-induced spirits will leave, there needs to be repentance, confession, recognition of dependence on God, and a decision to trust God to enable a new way of living.

Attack on Christian Growth

When a person grows in prayer, when a loving and grounded ministry is developing well, when there are dedicated Christians increasingly exercising their gifts and graces, evil may try to erode what is good. Sometimes it seems that people are attacked for no other reason than that they are maturing so beautifully in the spiritual life. Truly, there is a force that directly opposes God, and tries to undermine God's work.

A dying man worked through his fears and anger, finding deep peace about his approaching death. He had strong faith that God was very close, and would soon take him to a new life of unimagined wonder and joy. He spoke freely of this to his family, as well as telling them how much he loved them. By all standards he was immersed in grace, and ready to die. Friends who visited him were deeply moved by his faith and holiness.

Several weeks before his death, he became unaccountably fearful, cynical and angry. His minister, who discerned that these new feelings were nothing but an attack, decided that he would rather not talk about evil spirits to his dying parishioner. Silently she told the spirits to go away in the name of Christ. Almost immediately the dying man said that he felt something shift inside, although he didn't know why. Over the next few days, the man's peace and faith returned, and remained with him until he died several weeks later.

Occult Involvement

Involvement with the occult throws open the door for spirits to enter. By the occult I mean such things as Ouija boards, tealeaf reading, palmistry, astrology, tarot cards, horoscopes, spells, and charms. These practices seek spiritual control, spiritual power, or spiritual knowledge apart from God. Often occult practices are part of the picture when there is need for deliverance. In my experience, it has always been necessary to repent and renounce occult involvement before evil spirits will leave.

A Caution Regarding Addictions

Although addictions may often look and feel as if they are caused by something alien, the presence of a spirit is not the same as an addiction. Addictions do not leave on command. Most addictions are simply *human* bondage to a harmful substance or activity; the way to healing is through honesty, hard work and surrender. In some instances, however, an addiction and a spirit can be tangled together, and both may be operating to fuel addictive behavior. Ordering away the spirit that is involved in an addiction can boost healing, but of course is not a magic cure. Thus, getting rid of a spirit of Lust, for example, might make it more possible to work hard in a Twelve Step program for sexual addiction.

But here is the problem: those in the grip of an addiction are often hoping for an easy answer. A characteristic of addicts is the propensity toward blaming, and who better to blame than the devil? If, after extremely careful discernment, your decision is to go ahead with deliverance, the afflicted one needs to be clearly informed that deliverance may help, but is in no way a panacea. Before beginning, extract a promise that the person will immediately enter a Twelve Step program. Even with this emphatic caveat that a spirit may be only *part of* the problem, and a heartfelt promise to follow up, many addicts may still hope that a deliverance service might just be magic this one time. For this reason I always proceed with much caution with addictions – if I proceed at all.

RITUAL ABUSE

Ritual abuse is perpetrated by secretive groups determinedly committed to evil and the destruction of human beings. They are contemptuous of all that's holy. Fanatically grasping for power and money, they will let nothing stand in their way. Sometimes associated with Satanists, ritual abuse preys on innocence and weakness; many of the victims are animals and young children. Survivors who grew up geographically far apart from each other report stories which are remarkably consistent and utterly horrific.

They speak of groups of hooded people gathered in a circle, making a mockery of the Eucharist. They tell stories of torture: of being hung naked upside down, of being buried alive in coffins, of being shut up in the dark with snakes or rats, of having symbols cut into their skin as they lay bound on an altar. Some remember having been "married" to Satan in a public sexual ritual. Many have witnessed – and been forced to participate in – animal and human sacrifice. Once they have participated, they are told that now they belong to Satan forever.

Victims who survive to adulthood have a very good chance of being diagnosed with Dissociative Identity Disorder or DID, (formerly called Multiple Personality Disorder or MPD)[63] for such brutally cruel treatment causes people to shatter into pieces. Survivors find a way to stay sane by letting "alters" (dissociative parts of a personality) bear and remember the suffering. Quite often among these alters is one that carries a profound sense of God's presence. This can be true even where there has been no exposure to religion before the alter was formed.

A more complete description of ritual abuse is far beyond the scope of this book. There are now many good educational and treatment resources for survivors of ritual abuse, and public awareness about it is growing.[64] No one knows exactly how widespread ritual abuse is, but many police departments know of the existence of ritual abuse in their area. There are now psychotherapists who specialize in ritual abuse. Pastors would do well to educate themselves, so that they will not be incredulous when they first hear about it from a survivor.[65]

---

[63] A good book on Dissociative Identity Disorder (DID) is James Friesen's *Uncovering the Mystery of MPD*.

[64] Two good resources are Emilie P. Rose, *Reaching for the Light: A Guide for Ritual Abuse Survivors and Their Therapists* and Margaret Smith, *Ritual Abuse: What it is, Why it Happens, How to Help*.

[65] A good beginning resource is *Ritual Abuse*, a pamphlet published by The United Methodist Task Force on Ritual Abuse, P.O. Box 2094, New York, New York 10025.

Although pastors will find it prudent to refer survivors of ritual abuse to a therapist who has experience with it, there are certain aspects of healing from ritual abuse that must be dealt with spiritually. Perpetrators of ritual abuse deliberately attack the spirituality of their victims, in addition to what they do emotionally and physically. Thus, it will often make sense for a pastor and a ritual abuse therapist to work as a team.

It is very common to find in ritual abuse survivors a need for deliverance ministry, that is, for someone to take spiritual authority in the name of Christ. The terrible trauma itself opens the way for spirits to come in, but in addition some cult groups deliberately send an evil spirit into their victims through special rituals, just as Christians might ask that angels protect a loved one. The spirits they call forth may be sent into one or more alters, or might even masquerade as an alter. To complicate matters further, some genuine alters can look and sound as if they are utterly evil. Before proceeding with deliverance, it is extremely important to do careful discernment, preferably with someone who has had some experience in this area and is familiar with DID. Dr. James Friesen, who has experience with deliverance of sufferers of DID, warns:

> It can be easy to misdiagnose dissociations. When a different alter takes executive control of the body, the process is often accompanied by a change of posture – a twitch, a blink, or a blackout, for example. It is understandable that some people could misinterpret the postural change as an evil spirit taking control. Whenever such a dissociation is treated as possession, I would call that religious abuse…Alters cannot be erased, and they cannot be cast out.[66]

Ritual abuse cults also subject their victims to various brainwashing rituals and programming techniques. Marriage to Satan is one such ritual. In addition, victims may be programmed to return to the cult upon reaching a certain age, or even to kill themselves on a particular date. They may have been made to believe that if they reveal cult secrets, they will become psychotic.

These brainwashing programs are powerful, but they can be undone by taking authority over them in the name of Jesus Christ. I know that ritual abuse can be healed through hard work, prayer and the power of God. Imagine, for instance, a small group of Christians gathering with a survivor friend to pray together and to declare liturgically that any marriage to Satan is null and void. Together they

---

[66] Friesen, *Uncovering the Mystery of MPD*, p.107.

affirm that the survivor belongs to Christ, and that her true heritage is peace and joy. They remember together that nothing can separate us from the love of Christ. Or imagine another little "church" declaring in the name of Jesus Christ that cult programming for suicide or psychosis is broken. Instead, they affirm the truth of freedom in Christ.

HOW DO YOU KNOW WHEN DELIVERANCE IS NEEDED?

Obviously, it's not a good idea to address evil spirits if they aren't there. Thinking that deliverance is needed might produce anxiety and turmoil in some; others might be only too glad to be handed a quick solution for their problems. Ministers, too, can imagine that deliverance is an easy answer when other healing work is actually called for. Careful discernment is crucial. Francis MacNutt, in his wise and down-to-earth way, counsels caution, prayerful discernment, healthy skepticism, and the patience to let a course of action emerge over time.[67] He teaches that no one symptom is absolutely determinative, and he waits for a prayerful conviction that deliverance is the next step. Sometimes he is pretty sure almost right away, for discernment of spirits is a spiritual gift given by the Holy Spirit. Other times discernment takes place over time, and might include fasting or asking the collective wisdom of a healing prayer group.

I, too, have found that discernment for deliverance can either take time or happen relatively quickly. Even when I am fairly certain, I wait a bit, asking that the Holy Spirit confirm the direction or correct me if I have it wrong. After all, even if deliverance is needed, this might not be the right time, or I might not be the right person to be involved. Perhaps this is an instance in which I need to recruit a group of mature Christians to have Eucharist and pray for deliverance together. Permission from the Holy Spirit to go ahead is important.

What follows is a list of some of the indicators that deliverance may be needed. None of these factors is certain proof that evil spirits are present, but each is a sign that should prompt attention and discernment.

Although the person has done a great deal of good emotional and spiritual inner work, there is no evidence of change. Being stuck in one's growth process is not unusual, and there are a great many reasons why this might be occurring. However, when someone is stuck for a long time it is prudent to ask the Holy Spirit if evil spirits are involved.

---

[67] Francis MacNutt, *Healing,* Chapter 15, "Deliverance and Exorcism" pp. 167-184

Something keeps the person from prayer, worship, and/or Eucharist, even though she desires it. She may hear a cynical, sneering voice inside which denounces all that is holy. She may habitually feel a struggle when she goes to church, or find that she is unaccountably sleepy or nauseated. Be aware, of course, that it could be that she is simply experiencing an unintegrated part of herself.

His behavior is driven, compulsive, or beyond his control, even though he has worked on it through therapy, prayer, discipline, or Twelve Step programs. Compulsions and even simple habits are powerful and naturally difficult to break. Even harder are addictions; the Twelve Steps teach us that we are powerless over them, but that God can pull us through if we surrender. Obviously it doesn't help to escape into the ultimate excuse: "the devil made me do it." Again, prayerful discernment is vital.

A person seems to have a very small repertoire of responses to varied situations. For example, a person who stays angry or sad or suicidal regardless of what is going on, may have evil spirits prompting these reactions. Or maybe not.

She will tell you that something inside her is not her. She may report, for example, hearing a voice that tells her to hurt herself, while she herself is appalled at the idea. Or she may sense an evil presence about her that she knows is not herself. Again, denial, dissociation, and projection are always to be considered, but possibly she may be right.

He may have a history of occult involvement. Even when kids are just fooling around with Ouija boards, for example, a door for evil can open. When the involvement is more deliberate, the risk is great indeed. Occult involvement is a red flag when discerning the presence of evil.

The person may speak with another voice or their eyes may suddenly look very different. Dissociative Identity Disorder and other factors can cause similar phenomena, of course.

The minister may experience feelings of disgust, revulsion, or nausea. Ministers of healing who are good discerners of spirits often have a physical or "gut" reaction to the presence of spirits. Of course, none of us are infallible in this regard.

The suspected spirits are bound and the person feels an immediate shift. When I strongly discern that evil spirits are present, I ask the person if I may pray in a special way to test out a hunch. After explaining what I am about to do in as non-threatening way as possible, I then bind the spirits in the name of Jesus Christ.

Binding spirits is a way to temporarily "tie them up" and stop them from whatever they are doing, but it does not get rid of them. Binding is based on the faith that they *must* obey if ordered in the name of Jesus Christ.

If binding the spirits produces an immediate change in the person's experience, I give this a lot of weight. The person may have been trying in various ways for years to effect such a change, so if it happens after I say a few words, I take this as strongly diagnostic that evil spirits are present. Again, evil spirits are legalistic, so it is important when binding to try to cover all the bases. Binding is a direct command to the spirits, and might go something like this:

> In *the name of Jesus Christ, and by the power of his resurrection, I bind you spirits of _____ and _____ and any other evil spirits in _____(person's name.) Even if you have a name I haven't mentioned, you are still bound by the power and authority of Jesus Christ who has defeated you. I bind you away from _____(person's name). I bind you away from her body, her mind, her spirit, her emotions, her relationships, her memories, her family, and anything that has to do with her in any way in the name of Christ. You must be silent; you may not talk or communicate in any way. You may not manifest yourself in any manner, nor may you hide from this order in the name of Jesus. You may not act together in any way, nor may you act separately. In the name of Jesus Christ you are rendered powerless, and can do nothing except leave when I tell you to do so.*

GOING AHEAD: PREPARATION FOR DELIVERANCE

Suppose you are convinced that deliverance is necessary, and that you and the person agree to go ahead. What then? I share below how I proceed, not because it is the only way, but because it makes the most sense to me.

First, there is probably more discernment to do. Together the person who will receive deliverance and I prayerfully make a list of the spirits that are present. We also try to understand which one is primary, and which are lesser in importance. For example, we might come up with Despair as primary, with Hopelessness, Depression, and Helplessness as secondary influences. We ask the Holy Spirit if there is anything else we need to know. We get as clear as we can about how this all started and just how evil spirits are involved in the person's need for healing. Further, we ask if these spirits might be generational, or if they could be the result of occult involvement.

An important bit of preparation is to clarify whether or not there is second-ary gain in the one hosting the spirits. Secondary gain is the unhealthy benefit derived from suffering. Thus, for example, the person might realize that as long as she hangs onto despair, helplessness, hopelessness, and depression as a way of life, she will not have to get a job, create her art, help someone else, grow up, or claim a new identity as a child of God. She will not have to challenge herself in these important ways because, after all, she is too messed up. She truly suffers, but at least she is protected from risking failure. She never needs to test her limits or find out what she can really accomplish. Being set free is scary, as much as she may desire it. Secondary gain seems to give the spirits permission to stay, despite an order to leave.

The remedy is to confess these things, asking God to give her the genuine protection she needs, and to help her face life with passion and integrity. Thus she commits to trusting God, instead of evil spirits, to be her companion and guide. Even with evil spirits still present, she chooses life, not death.

Perhaps there is even further spiritual preparation needed. Is there a need for deeper confession? for forgiving another person? for re-commitment to God, or a renewal of baptism? for renouncing the occult? If these things are not taken care of ahead of time, it may be that the process of deliverance will stop. When a spirit won't go, it is time to ask again if there is some such obstacle.

This preparation can often be accomplished fairly quickly, perhaps in the context of one session. *When it is clear that there is permission to go on, it is a simple matter to pray for protection, bind once more, and then order the spirits (usually one at a time) to leave.* It is important to repeat explicitly with each order that it is given in the name of Jesus Christ. I would *never* want to encounter an evil spirit, even a weak one, on my own! I have already discussed in detail how this ordering takes place: they must leave immediately, completely, quietly and without any drama or uproar or manifestation of any kind, as the person breathes out. I continue to repeat the order quietly, or just pray silently or sing a hymn until we have the sense that it is gone. It is a joyful and holy thing to watch as the spirits submit to the authority of Jesus, and to feel the person's relief as the bond-age is broken. When all the spirits have left, the last step is to lay on hands and pray that the emptiness formerly occupied by evil spirits will now be filled with God's gifts and graces.

When it seems necessary to call a group together, the process is essentially the same. (I would love to always pray for deliverance in a group, but difficulties of coordinating schedules do not make it practical.) The group meets when they will have ample time to complete what they start, knowing that the process might take more than one session. In the context of Eucharist, they continue the discernment begun by the minister and seeker. Together they confess any way they have allowed evil to creep into their own lives, anything that might keep them from praying with power to set their friend free. Although one person is in charge, they all work through the service, each one free to add a prayer, a hymn, or an insight as the service goes along. After Eucharist, grounded in the presence of Christ, one person orders the spirits to leave in the name of Jesus, while others pray. Together they lay on hands and pray for healing.

After the deliverance is over, the group continues to be a special support group that the person receiving deliverance can call upon during the days of adjustment. Perhaps they will be the only ones who understand what the person went through, and that alone is a great gift. In addition, of course, they will continue to pray for the person.

FOLLOW UP PRESCRIPTIONS

When a deliverance session ends, I say something like this:

> It will be important in the next few days to take it easy, as if you had surgery. Rest a lot, eat healthy food, exercise gently, and let yourself adjust to a new reality. Sometimes there is a period of adjustment, so give yourself time to let it happen. Go to Communion every day if you can, and let God fill you. Spend time in prayer, just sitting with God. You might be tempted to think a lot about demons, but it's a mistake to get fascinated with them. When these thoughts come, don't struggle with them. Just peacefully turn your focus to Jesus and his power.

> I also suggest that you not try to figure out how this experience fits in with your present worldview. Save that for a little later. And, I strongly recommend that you don't talk about it with anyone for a while unless you are sure he or she will not need an explanation. Don't get in the position of having to defend this

experience right away. Give yourself a little time to settle into it first.

I believe that something really left you as we prayed. Some people feel better immediately. If not, you will probably feel different when the dust settles. But I remind you that deliverance is not magic. You may still have habits of thought and behavior that need to be dealt with. Usually people find it much easier to change their habits once the spirit fueling them is gone. Sometimes deliverance just paves the way for more good inner work. I'm sure we'll have plenty of work ahead of us, but I believe it'll be easier than before. And, if we should find that the deliverance is not complete, don't worry, we'll finish it.

I'd like you to call in a few days and tell me how you're doing. And we need to see each other soon to continue our work together.

SUSAN'S LETTER

Deliverance can make all the difference for one who needs it. Many have found that suddenly it is possible to work on old constricting patterns. Inner work is easier; the work seems to progress instead of stagnate. Emotional reactions and patterns of behavior that have exerted control for a lifetime lose their power. Cynical, self-destructive, or despairing inner voices fade away. Faith is renewed, and joy finds a home.

Susan, very successful businesswoman who holds an advanced degree in theology, would agree. After her deliverance, Susan knew right away that something marvelous had happened to her during the service. She also had a healthy sense that deliverance was just a step in a much longer journey, and that God would continue to heal her. She beautifully expressed it in a letter:

> When I remember exactly how it used to be with me, even barely over a month ago, I am amazed at how things have changed. Sometimes the present peace seems unreal, and often the history of depression seems unbelievable, too. And I know in some ways I feel unformed, like a blank piece of paper, without the depression and its companions. I am eager for the process of redefinition, and at the same time my mind feels like it has been liber-

ated. Ideas for sermons, solutions to problems large and small, questions that would take a book to explore seem to present themselves unexpectedly. My heart, too, seems at its best, and I know today has been one of those honeymoon days when life is graced every step of the way...I pray for the faith and grace necessary for the work ahead...I am very thankful.

I believe we are moving into a new era
for living lives which integrate the spiritual
and the social, the active and the contemplative.
George McClain

17

BEYOND INDIVIDUALS: THE HEALING OF INSTITUTIONS

When I introduce the idea of institutional healing as a part of Gestalt Pastoral Care, two particular questions invariably surface. Why mix social issues, some ask, with work with individuals and families? Why take on the wider issues of troubled institutions, as important as they are, when there are already special action groups that organize for social change? These questioners, who generally agree with a holistic approach, would recommend drawing a boundary *somewhere,* and not letting counseling relationships drift off into concern for everything-that-could-possibly-impact a person. Traditional wisdom and practice asserts that counseling is just not the appropriate venue for social change.

I believe, however, that brokenness and grace do not stop at the door of a counseling room, and that there are compelling reasons to include concern for the social networks that surround those who come for healing.[68]

First and most obvious is the fact that a distorted social context has the power to profoundly affect its victims. Just as a dysfunctional family casts a net of crippling beliefs, traumatic experiences, and binding expectations, so can institutions and cultural attitudes and structures. Racism, sexism, classism, homophobia and struggles for power can suck energy, bury gifts, destroy dreams, and crush joy. Social sins can create terrible personal pain and hardship, as well as destroy families, neighborhoods, churches and schools. A power-mad institution gone awry, such as a church that protects itself from "those people" while ignoring the desperate needs just outside the door, can cause much suffering.

---

[68] I am indebted to my husband for his book, *Claiming All Things for God: Prayer, Discernment, and Ritual for Social Change,* for many of the insights regarding institutional healing.

Second, while individual victims of distorted institutions and prejudice need healing, it is also obvious that the perpetrators do too. Confronting deliberate offenders through political pressure and non-violent protest can be tremendously healing, not only for the victims, but also for the deliberate victimizers. The fabric of society is impacted as well when unwitting offenders have their consciousness raised. I've become painfully aware of this lately in my prison Gestalt Pastoral Care class. Again and again the mostly African-American and Hispanic men remind me that we still live in a deeply racist culture – and I, with my white skin and my middle class upbringing, am part of it. Those of us born to privilege may have colluded with racism all our lives, even if we are Christians committed to equality. Despite our best intentions, we may be blind to suffering we have not been forced to experience personally. Growth can be an eye-opening experience!

Third, some Christians confuse cultural norms with the gospel. For instance, there are people who have been consumed with retaliation since the attacks of September 11, making an idol of patriotism and military strength. Others buy into a relentless pursuit of the American dream, spending money on ever larger houses and cars, and increasingly expensive vacations. Most Americans consume way more than our share of the world's resources. Surely for people of faith, grappling with these uncomfortable issues is equally as important as dealing with psychological concerns, especially since spiritual companioning is a component of Gestalt Pastoral Care. Genuine wholeness includes a commitment to "do justice, and to love kindness, and to walk humbly with your God," (Micah 6:8) and helping others work out what this means in their lives is a worthy role for pastoral caregivers.

Fourth, people have a need to act for their own well-being. Gestalt Pastoral Care ministers repeatedly ask, "What are you aware of right now? What do you need to do? What action is being called forth to open you to wholeness?" Quite often, as we have seen, these questions shape experiments in a session of personal exploration.

Occasionally, however, it is clear that some actions must take place in the wider world. When asked what she needed to do for her healing, one woman involved in regular Gestalt Pastoral Care demanded and got a raise previously denied her because of sexism. Then she organized other women in her office to insist on justice for themselves as well. A gay man marched for the first time in the Gay Pride Parade. A Native American who had rejected his heritage felt led to celebrate his roots by learning to drum and dance for the first time. A member of a church with a history of divisiveness and rancor organized a weekly group to pray specifically for the healing of that troubled fellowship. All of these people were encouraged by a Gestalt Pastoral Care Minister to allow their own growth journeys to shape their actions.

Finally, to be whole, Christians need to act on behalf of others. It is not enough to be interested in our own growth; genuine wholeness means being at work on God's agenda to bring shalom to the world. Where there is injustice or suffering, where structures and institutions smother life, where there is racism, sexism, heterosexism, super nationalism, or cultural bias, Christians are called to respond – even if they are not directly affected. It is clear that Jesus' command to love is both personal and social.

Of course this does not mean that every time we see a need we are to jump in; we could not possibly respond with passionate energy and major time commitment to every critical concern. But it does mean that somehow the call to love neighbors will surface in a particular way for each of us – and this might well mean working for social change. When we are well along in our healing, we have more energy for loving and more personal clarity available to make a difference in the world. As recipients of God's unconditional love, our natural response is a desire to share it, and sharing becomes part of our awareness continuum. Joining in God's work for shalom is both an intrinsic component of healing and a fundamental sign that healing has occurred.

INTRODUCING CONCERN FOR THE WORLD

A Gestalt Pastoral Minister would not declare, "You should get involved in something beyond yourself, you know." Instead he trusts that concern for social justice will somehow appear in the awareness continuum of the one with whom he is working. It might not emerge full-blown with a declaration such as, "I think I need to do something for kids who can't read." Concern for social issues might emerge latent in the pain someone feels when he himself, or someone he knows, is crushed by a social structure. Then the easiest and simplest way to bring concern for social context into Gestalt Pastoral Care is to ask questions such as:

•OK. Such and such is affecting your life and making you miserable. You've done a lot of work to deal with it emotionally and spiritually. Would you be willing to go inside and discover if there is anything you are moved to do now to change things a little?

•How about doing some faith imagination to ask what is God's invitation to you right now?

•Are there some others you are drawn to join with in order to address this struggle of yours?

Such questions are not meant to imply that a person who has been wounded by social cruelty can make magical changes so that the problem goes away. But surely he can be encouraged to work toward social and institutional changes as part of his healing. Joining an advocacy group or organizing a new one is perhaps the easiest way to accomplish this. Much healing occurs as people discover that there is indeed something they can do to make changes.

DIRECT ACTION

An obvious way for a pastoral minister to encourage social change is to support various forms of direct action, in which pressure is brought to bear on an institution to persuade or compel it to change.

Consider Emma's story. She had worked hard to overcome many years of sexual abuse by her father. She had already received a great deal of healing when she was assigned to a special project at her job with a charitable organization. This project made it necessary for her to confer daily with the organization's president. The man was well respected, even revered, and known nationally as a pioneer of compassionate social programs.

This man began to make verbal sexual advances to Emma, which quickly developed into grabbing her and stealing kisses. Emma hated it, and tried to avoid him, but it was impossible. To make matters really sticky, he was a friend of her family; he and her father went back many years. She felt that nobody would believe her if she reported him, and she was terribly afraid of his considerable power. He could make it impossible for her ever to work in her field again, and she discovered to her horror that he had done just that to another young woman. She also knew that if she blew the whistle she would probably lose what little contact with her family she had left. Emma's hard-won, still-fragile emotional health vanished. Again she felt as she did as a child: helpless, victimized, enraged, and guilty for not being courageous enough.

Then one day another woman employee cautiously asked Emma if there had been "any problems" with this man. It seems that there was a group of a dozen or so women from around the country who were meeting to talk about their experiences with him, and to decide how to respond. Some of these women had been raped. After talking about it with her Gestalt Pastoral Care minister, Emma flew to the secret meeting with hope mingled with fear.

Together the women decided that this man, despite his many gifts, must be stopped before other women were victimized. They prepared their case and presented their findings to the organization's national board of directors. Emma prayerfully struggled for several weeks with whether or not to add her signature to the report, and in the end decided she must. Presented with the evidence, the board was horrified. At the women's suggestion, the man was allowed to resign if he would consent to an intense program of rehabilitation. If not, he would face court action. He resigned immediately.

The effect on Emma was profound. She said:

> I feel like I've finally claimed my body and become a real adult.
> I know I won't stand for any more sexual exploitation, ever again.
> I'm not helpless any more, and I'm not willing to keep silent
> when something is wrong. I have the sense that we not only helped
> some of the younger women coming along in the organization,
> but we also helped this man get the help he desperately needs.
> And our little group was the catalyst for [my organization] to
> formulate for the first time clear policies for dealing with sexual
> abuse.

CHRISTIAN RESOURCES FOR HEALING INSTITUTIONS

Emma's Gestalt Pastoral Care Minister had nothing to do with the women's plans; his role was simply to remind Emma to stay with her own inner process. Emma and the other women knew perfectly well how to get things done.

Regarding specifically Christian resources for healing institutions, however, a minister might need to make suggestions, just as he might propose Gestalt experiments; many Christians may not know that *spiritual* intervention with an institution is even possible. Four examples of such Christian intervention are blessing spaces, specially planned liturgical and prophetic actions, healing prayer for institutional wounds, and social exorcism. Sometimes all four might be appropriate when praying for a particular institution.

Blessing Spaces

Most of us have had the experience of going into a church or monastery and immediately feeling the aura of peace and holiness radiating there. A building that has long been used for fervent prayer and where love dwells simply feels different. It is as if the prayer lingers in the atmosphere, making the space alive with the spirit of Christ.

Similarly, buildings or even outdoor spaces can retain the disturbed energy that results from contentiousness, hatred, fear, power struggles, possessiveness, or violence. Sometimes buildings carry a palpable sense of sickening heaviness, murkiness, foreboding darkness, or cold, and this can be felt as one walks though the door. Not too surprisingly, this toxic energy infects the people who come into the space, making them tense, anxious, perhaps a bit nauseous. In a toxic space, even people of good will may feel tempted to act in ways that keep unhealthy patterns alive. They may feel guilty, incompetent, out of control, frustrated, and angry. Although they may work hard to change things, it is like attempting to thrive in a building with a gas leak.

Buildings infected with toxic energy can be cleansed through blessing. Church buildings are particularly good candidates for prayerful blessing, and often the effect is obvious even when those who use the building are not aware that a blessing has taken place. As one pastor said about her newly blessed church, "There has been a tremendous, indescribable change here."

Brian had worked for a year in a church infamous for its pervasive rancor among the members. This church growled and gnawed at pastors until each one quit, most within a year. There were so many factions, so much spite and plain nastiness that Brian, effective and well loved in his former churches, felt completely stymied. Almost immediately after beginning with this church, he felt depressed, angry, and separated from God. The building, in particular, seemed to embody this malaise. Just walking through the door would bring him physical tension and an energy sapping, sickening feeling of general dis-ease. Feeling that the church was literally squeezing the life out of him, Brian was profoundly discouraged, and he longed to follow his predecessors in getting out of there as soon as possible.

Open to the possibility that he was part of the problem, however, he did some personal exploring. The first step was to express in my office a great deal of healthy anger at the obstinate church. He was also honest enough to admit that he harbored some anger that was not so healthy. He knew he had a streak of needing to seem successful, and was aware that bringing this church around would be quite a shiny medal in his collection. Those stubborn folks were keeping him from being a hotshot! Recognizing his old familiar folly was the prelude to laughing at himself a bit as he surrendered –again – his need to emerge an ecclesiastical superhero. He prayerfully recognized – also again – that his ministry was not really his, but God's. He was helpless. Neither his best preaching nor his considerable pastoral skills worked with these people. He had done all he could. If God wanted this troubled church to be viable, God would need to act.

Such emotional and spiritual homework is a crucial prelude to bringing spiritual resources to bear on an institution or its buildings. Brian was intrigued with the idea of blessing the building and re-claiming it for Jesus Christ. Given his strong reactions to the building itself, it seemed like a good place to begin. He and a colleague met in the building when no one else would be around. They prayed over some water, asking that it be a vehicle of blessing and healing. Then they went to every room, closet and cupboard in the church, sprinkling the water about and claiming each space for the reign of God. They also ordered any spirits not of God to immediately leave both the building and the folks who use it. In each room they prayed for programs or worship regularly taking place in that area, and asked that each room be filled with the Holy Spirit. Some spaces seemed to invite them to remain in prayer longer than others, or to pray for specific church members. They paid attention to these impressions, letting their prayers be shaped by whatever hunches came to them.

After the two-hour prayer session, the pair felt quite tired, but the pastor had the distinct sense that the building was "cleaner, lighter, and less depressing." Almost right away he himself felt better in the building, and by the next week it seemed to him that there was noticeably less sniping. One person commented that she felt that the church "might make it yet." He resolved to pray briefly for the church each time he went into the building, and over a few weeks it was clear that matters were improving. Although there was still a great deal of work to be done, he now felt he could begin. He saw that his own growth was directly related to the healing of the church and the building itself. He was greatly moved as he discovered for himself the power of God to make a difference in a seemingly hopeless situation.

Liturgical and Prophetic Actions

Certain creative actions speak the truth powerfully, publicly, dramatically and liturgically to call an institution to fulfill its God-given purpose. These carefully planned actions seek to make fresh claim to the gospel in ways that challenge dearly held prejudices. They capture public imagination in a way that both touches pain and ignites new possibilities. They hold the possibility of healing body, mind, spirit, and of course, social milieu. Some familiar examples are:

- Holding a prayer vigil in front of a police station with a long history of brutality and racism, and praying for specific officers by name.

- Fasting as a group to draw attention to the plight of the hungry.

- Organizing a group to spend the night outdoors while singing and praying for affordable housing.

- Walking in a Good Friday Stations of the Cross liturgy that takes participants to various sites of corporate sin, such as industrial polluters, arms manufacturers, and the office of a slumlord.

- Ringing the church bell each time someone reports an act of extraordinary kindness in the community.

Liturgical and prophetic actions have the potential to be a catalyst for social change. At the same time they can present those directly involved with a way of inner growth and discovery. Consider Ben, a small-town school board member. Increasingly frustrated with the feeling of hopelessness and apathy in his poverty-stricken district, Ben bought a few cans of paint and began painting one of the poorest schools in his spare time. For weeks he toiled alone, praying quietly as he painted. A few parents straggled by and joined him, and later persuaded more neighbors to join the effort. Soon a local merchant donated more paint and two good ladders. The small school looked a hundred times better when they finished, and the town was impressed with what a ragtag group could accomplish. Their quiet example led to a reorganization of the board several years later, and a new vigorous commitment to improve their schools. Ben, the man who started it all, had a new sense of personal empowerment and excitement that his little action, which grew out of his own spiritual journey, had made such a difference.

Healing Prayer for Institutional Wounds

An institution can carry wounds similar to those of an individual. Institutions, like people, can suffer traumas, fail to adjust to painful transitions, grieve a loss, be abusive and abused, cover up scandals, and be dysfunctional. Institutions can even have addictions. (One church became so hooked on Dungeons and Dragons that it allowed nothing to interfere with the scheduled games.) An institution can have injuries that are lost to memory but still wield great power to shape its present ethos, style, self-identity, and vision of the future.

Decades ago two dying churches were given an ultimatum from the denomination: either merge or be closed. The churches suddenly felt that their destiny was no longer in their hands. Reluctantly, sorrowfully, angrily, they decided to merge. With this decision came a sense of profound loss. Many folks had been baptized in these churches as babies, were confirmed and married there, and had wept there at funerals for dear ones. Many had memories of good times and good friends, and of booming Sunday schools and glorious choirs from the old days. For both churches it was wrenching to imagine that nothing would ever be the same again. Anger at the denomination was futile; the ultimatum was a done deal. Instead, the two congregations got angry at each other, and the many meetings in preparation for the dreaded day of merger were full of squabbles and turf wars. Neither their grief nor their anger was handled very well by the pastoral leadership, and these painful feelings remained long after the merger. Thirty years later the merger was seldom talked about, but the wounds were still there, covert, unrecognized, debilitating, influential, and bewildering to the current leadership.

Just as a "forgotten" childhood trauma can have great power over an adult, the effect of an institutional wound lives on, even if it is no longer remembered by most of the present members. Because of the tremendous power of institutional wounds, it is important to research what might have happened to the institution to bring it to the present state of chaos. Particularly important are traumas, mergers or mass defections, "lost memories," and similar upheavals in its life. Talking to older members is helpful, but sometimes such institutional wounds can only be discovered by going back through the historic records of the institution.

What kind of spiritual intervention is called for when an institution has been deeply wounded? What's needed is not very different from praying for wounded individuals. Tell the story of how the institution was injured, allow people to react and express their feelings, and then pray individually and in special gatherings for healing. Bless and cleanse the buildings and rededicate the institution to the fulfillment of its mission. Such prayer has seemed to make a difference, not only in the life of the institution, but also in its individual members.

Social Exorcism

When the institution seems particularly stymied and blocked from fulfilling its own good purpose, it may be that *evil* is partly responsible. My husband, George McClain, has coined the term *social exorcism* for the process of liturgically addressing the evil infecting institutions.[69]

If evil is suspected, it is vital to engage in careful discernment and research before making any liturgical response. If evil is present it almost certainly will have found a foothold among institutional wounds. An important question for discernment is just *how* evil is using the institution's woundedness to paralyze and distort. For example, if a church experienced a disastrous fire way back in its history, its members might then be preoccupied, for example, with preserving the present buildings at all costs, keeping carpets, kitchens, equipment, and whole buildings locked up and unused.

Another important part of the preparation for social exorcism is to discover how the dysfunction of the institution interacts with the personal wounds and needs of the pastor and lay leadership. Is there a desire among the leaders, for example, to be powerful, or to be the best? Do they need to protect their turf? Are some leaders shaping the life of the congregation to resemble the dysfunctional families in which they grew up? It is also helpful to list the particular conduits for the current strife and paralysis. (There seem to be at least one or two of these folks in every church! They are the ones who are experts in stirring up gossip, creating factions, and effectively blocking the church from its mission.) Naming these names is not to judge the people involved, but to pray for their healing and for their roles in the institution.

Once these questions are answered, at least provisionally, it is time to identify, through prayerful discernment, the negative spirits that seem to be at work. Most evil spirits are identified by their "job" or function. For example, a group gathered to pray for an institution might list Conflict, Possessiveness, Inertia and Fear.

---

[69] George McClain, *Claiming All Things for God: Prayer, Discernment and Ritual for Social Change.*

Finally, the prayer group stays attentive to the particular gifts of the institution, and especially to any symbols of new life that emerge out of their corporate prayer and research. The group lets these symbols shape their prayer for the institution. One small group meeting to pray for a troubled church was struck as they walked into the building by a magnificent stained glass window of a powerful angel. Acute awareness of this dazzling angel shaped their prayer that the angel bring the church a renewal of "good tidings of great joy." Another group discovered to their surprise that a well- known hymn writer had been one of their church's founders. As the group sang some of her hymns and prayed that her powerful gospel vision would come to pass in the congregation, they had a profound sense of Christ pouring light into this church. Accordingly, during the subsequent service of social exorcism they prayed that the light of Christ would again permeate the church. Thus research and discernment provide the specific content to a service of social exorcism.

Most often social exorcism is done in the context of Eucharist. I believe this not only keeps a prayer group on track, but also opens the group to God's presence and power. It helps keep the focus on God instead of on evil. Further, God uses Eucharist to be present to us in a special way. For these reasons, it is helpful to follow a liturgical form even when other spiritual interventions are added, such as blessing a space.[70]

INSTITUTIONAL HEALING: THREE STORIES

The Mean Church

An experienced and skillful pastor was sent to a church that had just fired his predecessor for sexual misconduct. He knew that much healing would be necessary, but he was not prepared for the seething resentments, rivalries, and rifts that seemed to be boiling in just about everyone. Even though he had a sense that individually these were good people, when they were together they were nearly incapable of being civil to one another.

In an effort to understand what was going on, the pastor phoned as many previous pastors as he could track down. In conversations with them he was startled to note that each one of them, without prompting, used the identical phrase to characterize the church. Each declared that the church had "a spirit of meanness."

---

[70] See Norberg and Webber, *Stretch Out Your Hand: Exploring Healing Prayer,* pp. 111-113 for "A Service of Social Exorcism."

He also uncovered a tragedy in the church's history. Many years ago a teenager had been killed in an accident while on a church outing. Instinctively the pastor sensed that the church had never really recovered from this terrible event. He also sensed that the fading memory of the teenager's death, along with the previous pastor's sexual abuse, was somehow at the root of the church's current "spirit of Meanness."

The pastor gathered a few trusted colleagues to further discern what was wrong, and then to pray for healing. After silently listening to the Holy Spirit, the little group confirmed their friend's hunches. Accordingly, at a service of Eucharist and social exorcism, they cast out the spirit of Meanness in the name of Jesus Christ, and prayed that the church would be filled with love instead. They prayed at length for the healing of the effects of both the long-ago tragedy and the betrayal by the previous pastor. They also prayed that the current pastor would be healed and empowered to guide the church in the difficult times ahead. They ended the afternoon by blessing the building and claiming it for God's own purposes.

The pastor reported that right away there was a subtle difference in the way people treated each other. In the next few months the atmosphere gradually lightened. The pastor continued praying, and a few months later the church was noticeably changed. There was less strife, the rival factions were much less strident, and there was a new willingness to reconcile long-standing feuds. Some folks were actually working peacefully together. Most importantly, there was increased interest in the worship and educational programs. The pastor was changed too. His trust in God had deepened, and, for the first time in over a year, he was finding enjoyment and fulfillment in his ministry.

An Unjust Justice System

Roberta, age 22, was sexually abused by her father as a child for eight years. As she struggled to heal, she made the difficult decision that she must bring legal charges against him for incest and rape. As hard as it was to imagine her father in prison, she felt strongly that he must be stopped from preying on other youngsters.

Roberta's mother agreed, and together they went to the police. What they encountered there was astonishing. They discovered that in their isolated county incest was viewed as something that "just happens." The two were blatantly discouraged by the police from even bringing their complaint. Increasingly, it became clear to them that police, lawyers, and even judges, skirted around the law when it came to sexual crimes against women and children. Cronyism was rampant; men took care of their own. Even an attorney they considered hiring to represent them felt that incest not a serious matter. Roberta was not surprised to learn that in her county no one in recent memory had been convicted of incest.

Even so, the mother and daughter team persisted until they found an attorney who could really represent them, and bravely went ahead. They also called for prayers from their church that justice might be done. When told about the widespread corruption in the county legal system, a few of the church folk, along with two staff members, held a social exorcism. They discerned that there was indeed evil infecting the legal system and preventing it from enforcing the law. They ordered the evil away in the name of Christ. Realizing that they were praying not just for the court case involving their friend, but for far-reaching reform, they prayed that the county courts and police would be filled with a new desire to enforce the law with justice and mercy. Some of the prayer team decided to attend the trial and continue to pray silently in the courtroom.

The trial was short. The jury did not take long to pronounce the verdict: guilty on all counts. Roberta left the courtroom feeling, as one friend commented, "believed, relieved, and radiant."

The prayer team knew that they could not say with certainty that their prayers were what made the difference. Social systems are complex and fluid; who knows how to weigh various factors contributing to a particular outcome? But the team shared a conviction that they had been called to pray the way they did, that they certainly had been empowered, and that God had somehow used their prayers for healing.

A Spiritual Intervention in Java

The following story of institutional healing involved students thousands of miles apart, a creative liturgical process, a compelling prophetic action, prayers for specific people and for institutional wounds, the blessing of a space, a great sermon, a social exorcism and a good measure of grace. It was a moving, exhausting and exhilarating experience for the participants.

For years the Javanese Mennonite Church in Indonesia had been suffering from such strife and division that two competing general assemblies had elected two rival synod boards, each asserting its claim to be the legitimate leadership of the church. Their offices were in two different locations, each using the same letterhead and logo, prompting widespread confusion among church members. Efforts to end the bitter rivalry had ended in failure. Personal resentments, power moves, and betrayals flew between the leaders of the warring factions. At the same time some folks on both sides were concluding that this sorry state of affairs really could not be allowed to continue.

Dr. Lawrence Yoder, professor of Missiology at Eastern Mennonite Seminary in Virginia, had been a long-time friend, observer, and advisor to the Javanese Mennonite Church. As the crisis in Java was moving toward a climax, I happened to be teaching a class with Lawrence on institutional healing. Lawrence proposed that we pray for the healing of the Javanese Mennonite Church. He had already traveled to Java four times to try to help the Javanese Mennonites find a solution to this schism. The very next day he would be making his fifth trip to Java to attend a special "reconciling General Assembly" in which the delegates from all the churches of both factions would try to elect a single new synod board. Everyone in the class agreed that we should structure the class around this important meeting.

We spent most of a day in the process. After Lawrence gave us some background on the issues in the Javanese church and a crash course on Javanese culture, we entered into the kind of prayer that is full of silence and listening, prayer that is intensely focused and deep, prayer that speaks aloud only a few pregnant words. We prayed that any wounds from the past would be healed as we lifted up various pieces of the church's history. We named the people Lawrence told us were hurting the most. We prayed for both factions, and we confessed how we ourselves had acted in similar ways. We asked God to bless the space in which the group would meet the next day in Java, and to fill it with the presence of the Holy Spirit. We identified several evil spirits at work; among them were Spite, Divisiveness, and Possessiveness. We told these spirits to go away in the name of Jesus Christ. We asked that the Javanese church be filled with gifts of the Spirit. We claimed the members of the Javanese Mennonite Church as our sisters and brothers. We reminded them, and ourselves, to be faithful to the gospel.

The long prayer session ended with Eucharist celebrated with a large loaf of bread, far too much bread for our small group of twelve. Lawrence would take the rest of the consecrated bread to Java to be shared – if things went well – with our brothers and sisters at a Eucharist they might celebrate at the end of their assembly. Just knowing that we might be joined in Eucharist powerfully connected us to these Christians we had never met. Surprising all of us, for that day at least, the problems of the Javanese Mennonite Church had become ours. One student commented later that as a result of our prayer a snippet of an epistle just lit up for her: "…so we, who are many, are one body in Christ, and individually we are members one of another" (Romans 12:5).

Meanwhile on the other side of the world, other seminarians and their teacher, Professor Karmito, were also praying and laying plans. The Indonesian students devised a special worship service for the meeting in which each person would be given two sheets of paper. On one sheet each would write things they wished to be rid of. On the other they would write things they hoped for and were committing themselves to. Everyone would then come forward and discard the first paper in a wastebasket and pin the other onto a tree brought inside as a symbol of the Javanese "tree of life."

On the day of the meeting in Java, Lawrence again blessed the space in which the meeting would take place. As the group gathered, Lawrence could sense both tension and a dawning sense of possibility in the crowd. Maybe, just maybe, there would be a way through this muddle. Perhaps many were tired of the struggle and eager for healing. Or maybe not, but when it came time for the students' ritual with the two pieces of paper, there was enthusiastic participation on both sides.

The opening speaker was Professor Karmito, who mesmerized the group with a familiar and compelling image. He spoke of how a single stalk of the broombrush plant is useless for sweeping, but as everyone knows, a bundle of broombrush stems makes a wonderful broom. (Each day, Javanese households use such a broom to sweep their yards clean.) Just so with us. When we are bound together, the Holy Spirit can sweep away all that has been contaminating the church. The meaning was not lost on the group, and as Lawrence said, "It was pretty powerful."

Then came a spellbinding prophetic action. Accompanied by quiet music, a lone student with a broombush broom began deliberately and prayerfully sweeping the large hall. Eyes were riveted on her as she swept and swept without a word or a glance, becoming an unlikely vehicle for the Holy Spirit who was reminding, prodding, pricking consciences, inviting. As tears flowed, many hearts were cleansed and long-time adversaries spontaneously embraced. Finally they shared the bread we sent from Virginia during their Communion service. Many were profoundly moved that our class in America would spend hours in intercession for their church.

The meeting proceeded beautifully, better than anyone expected, and Lawrence, who had begun his peacemaking work with the Javanese Mennonites reluctantly, was surprised and profoundly thankful for the final result. The two competing boards voted to disband to make way for the election and installation of one new board. For the first time in eleven years they held a General Assembly together, and now there was reason for genuine hope that the historic schism would be healed at last. The new mood of the church was that winning is not the answer; reconciliation is.

Did our prayers and spiritual intervention really make a difference? Of course it is impossible to say with certainty, but it surely seemed that we had played a significant part in this institutional healing. Many other people were at prayer as well, and obviously the Holy Spirit was at work. Just as obvious was the fact that there was still a lot of work ahead to make the agreement for unity real in the hearts of the people.

Although a door was opened for an *institution* in Java, I also like to think of the many *individuals* who would grow through this experience. Our group in Virginia was deeply moved. Lawrence was awed and elated. It's not hard to imagine the relief, and perhaps anxiety, of those Javanese Christians. Ahead of them was a process of reconciliation that would require much of each person. Pitfalls would be encountered, resentments would need to be talked out, forgiveness would need to be offered and accepted. Also ahead was the possibility of friendships made and renewed, and new opportunities for ministry and celebration.

The individual I most like to imagine is the Prophetic Sweeper. I wonder what happened to her as the result of being, for a small moment, a magnificent icon of the Holy One among us.[71]

---

[71] The account of the meeting in Java is based on conversation and emails with Dr. Lawrence Yoder, Eastern Mennonite Seminary, Harrisonburg, Virginia.

A FINAL WORD

Chapter Eighteen answers the question, "How can I do the intense work of Gestalt Pastoral Care and keep healthy and spiritually grounded myself?" I discuss some of the exquisitely seductive spiritual and emotional issues which may confront a minister who has been practicing Gestalt Pastoral Care for a while. I share ways to avoid these traps while staying open to God's healing work.

It is not unusual for those in the healing ministry to have direct experience of God's power. Being present when another person opens to grace is awesome and beautiful, *and* such experiences hold the distinct possibility for distortion. I discuss some typical reactions to God's power: trying to possess it and running away from it. Or both. This chapter invites pastors to discover the strength of being personally powerless while saying yes to God's desire to heal.

The heart that breaks open
can contain the whole universe.
Joanna Macy, Despair and the Nuclear Age

18

TAKING OFF OUR SHOES: THE SPRIRITUAL COMPANION'S SPIRITUALITY

When you meet with someone for healing prayer you are entering holy ground, and you must "take off your shoes." That is, as best you can, wrap yourself in a contemplative mantle and leave behind your baggage, including your rules about how things have to go, your rigid systems of healing (even if it's Gestalt Pastoral Care) your need for power, your judgments, and your own need for healing. Unless you have exceedingly clear discernment in a particular instance, you must leave behind any specific expectations about how God will work. Front and center is the conviction that while God is not capricious, God is unpredictable. You can expect to be surprised by the wonderfully intricate, unique, and grace-filled ways that God works with each individual. A large part of your job is simply getting out of the way.

The things you can bring to such an encounter may seem mighty few. You can offer your willingness to be used by God, your Yes. As best you can, you must bring with you your humble awareness that you are also in need of God's mercy and healing. Important, too, are whatever gifts and skills you have, for almost surely God will use them somehow. You must bring your respect and affection for the other person, and your willingness to allow her spaciousness and freedom. Furthermore, you bring your trust that if you are open, you will be empowered with the compassion, hope, faith, love, discernment, and authority you need to be of help.

You should also bring the knowledge that you may not be the right one to help or that this may not be the right time. The person may not be ready, and God may have other plans. Most of all, you bring a clear and simple knowledge that you are not in charge. It is not your work, but God's.

It is uncomfortable to go into a charged situation like a healing encounter knowing that you are not in control. The need to create security is natural. Even though you want to be a faithful servant, you would love to nail things down just a little. Because of this impulse, you may become familiar with certain temptations as you do this work. In fact, the more "successful" your ministry, the more beguiling are the traps. I share what I have learned about these traps, from rueful, embarrassed experience, and address this chapter to myself as well as to other readers who might learn from my mistakes. I have been tempted by all of these pitfalls, and fallen for most. In one way or another, they all have to do with attraction to, or fear of, power.

SPIRITUAL TRAPS: ATTRACTION TO POWER

When you do the work of Gestalt Pastoral Care, powerful things happen to people. It is easy to allow distortions to creep in, distortions that can edge you out of a contemplative attitude. Murky responses to power can spell both spiritual disaster for you, and destruction for the people with whom you work.

Needing to be Needed

Deeply wounded people often look for a guru to be powerful in their lives. They want to lean on someone who will cushion life's blows and tell them what to do, so that they are spared their own difficult, and possibly painful, journey. It is a great temptation to accommodate these unhealthy desires; it is disturbingly easy to create a coterie of dependent, adoring people. You can do this by attacking resistance, by supplying answers to questions that only God can really answer, by taking over in faith imagination, and by concealing your own faults and weakness. Although you may be unaware of it, you may actually have an investment in people staying sick so that they continue to need you. When you do this, you have robbed people not only of their healing, but also of their freedom. You have set yourself up as a false savior and have sinned in your arrogant idolatry.

One of the first signs that you have given in to the temptation of needing to be needed, is that you feel consistently drained after work, with fatigue that goes far beyond normal tiredness. When I begin to feel this, I know it is time to ask myself in what way am I coveting power.

Instead of creating dependency on yourself, you must become less and less important in a person's process. You learn to say with John the Baptist, "He [Jesus] must increase, but I must decrease" (John 3:36). You move aside so that the person is connected to God instead of you. Always you must seek to rest contemplatively in the knowledge that it is God, not you, who says, "See, I am making all things new!" (Revelation 21:5).

Being Impressed with Your Own Gifts

Another temptation is to secretly nurture a belief in your own gifts, instead of faith in God. It is all too seductive to get focused on your fantastic gifts and skills, and the distinct possibility of looking spectacular. Instead of making way for God's liberating work in another, you may start to imagine that you will be the hotshot healer who will succeed where all others have failed. You forget that "apart from me you can do nothing" (John 15:5). If you fall for this trap, you need people to get better – so you can look good. Comments like "When I first saw you work, I thought you were a magician!" can feed your pride and foster this distortion. Others may not see the direction you are taking inside, but surely the poison of pride and possessiveness will eat at you. "I am really, really good at this!" is the treasure you begin to hoard. But your secret, of course, will likely become visible somewhere along the line.

Having an honest appreciation of your gifts is quite different. It is not wrong to gratefully recognize that God has indeed gifted you for ministry. You pray to be gifted and empowered; when it happens, you will be aware of it. But your gifts are not really your possessions, nor are they given because you have earned them. Instead, you hold them very loosely, to be used for the benefit of those God wants to help through you. You must always remember that you can't change anyone, no matter how terrific your skills. It is God who transforms. In this regard, people in Alcoholics Anonymous remind each other, "There are just two things you need to know about God. There is one, and you're not it!" When you really believe this in your bones, you can, as a good contemplative must, set people free to decide if they want to change or not. Change is entirely up to the one who is working, because you have given up your agenda for the outcome.

Overwork

The temptation to overwork can arise out of a good, caring motive: to serve God's people with generosity and love. Most folks in the caring professions *care.* However, *wanting* to help can quickly become *having* to help. If this temptation gains a foothold, it can become difficult, if not impossible, to set limits or simply to say no. Seeing a need can become confused with hearing a call.

There are many forces that fuel a temptation to overwork; most reveal your own need for healing. For example, working long hours may seem to prove that you are holy and important. Meeting the expectations of others may come from a desire to get others to like you, or at least to keep them from criticizing. Believing that someone needs you can take you off the hook in relation to your own needs. Working until you drop is a handy way to anesthetize yourself from inner pain you won't face.

Obviously, there is pride mixed with this temptation. Constant, compulsive overwork says, "I don't need time off like other, weaker people." It says, "See how dedicated I am!" It says, "If I am working all the time, I must be a success."

Overworkers tend to pray in the same manner in which they work. Prayer can become one more thing to do, with a list of people to pray for and a devotional style that is full of words and doing. There is not much room here for the wordless contemplative rest that comes from just being with the One who loves us.

The Quakers have a wonderful insight regarding the tendency to overwork that I have found enormously helpful. Quakers speak of a "bundle" that each person receives from God. Over the course of a life, the contents of your bundle can change, but the only load that you are called to bear is the particular bundle with your name on it. There may be needs crying out all around you, but if meeting those needs is not in your bundle, you are to leave them be. If you pick up another's bundle, you deprive another of the privilege of carrying her own bundle – and you may be crushed by a weight that is too great for you.

This does not mean that you are never called to stretch yourself, and to do things that you "can't" do. Sometimes you are indeed in situations that will exhaust you and demand truly sacrificial giving of your energy and resources. Parents whose young children are sick will know what I mean! Obviously, discernment is vitally necessary here to distinguish what God is really asking of you, from your unhealthy need to keep going – and going and going. Staying alive to the question of what God wants daily, hourly, even minute-by-minute, is a good step toward balance and sanity. As one student in the Gestalt Pastoral Care training group commented, "We are called to die *in* ministry, not *of* it!"

Faith in Your Own Faith

Still another temptation to misuse power is faith in your own faith.[72] You can come to imagine that it is your shining faith that heals, and it is part of your job to keep it in fighting form. This temptation says, "You've gotta be real spiritual, now that you're in healing ministry. You can never, never, miss your time for individual prayer; people's well-being depends on it! You always have to respond to every situation with great faith." Then you begin to worry about how to be a spiritual giant, and you search for some method of prayer that will do the trick.

There is a good motive behind this temptation: indeed it is important to take seriously the disciplines of the spiritual life. God can work more easily through one who is yielded in prayer; indeed it is important to make time for daily prayer and regular corporate worship. The distortion is believing that God must have your highly disciplined superfaith in order to act, and that somehow you can create faith in yourself. Francis MacNutt, in his discussion about the role of faith in healing,[73] points out that God can get around our lack of faith, and that faith is a gift of God in the first place. Our trust needs to be in God, not in the strength of our own faith.

In this regard, I love some of the stories told about St. Therese of Lisieux (1873-1897), a Carmelite nun, who is said to have nodded off more than once during community prayers. She herself writes that she really doesn't know how to pray, or even how to love; she is not big enough. She admits to boredom, distractions, and watching the clock. I can identify with a contemplative like that! But she is clear about trusting Jesus to make up for what she cannot do herself. This "little way," as she called it, opened her to the tremendous flow of grace that has become an inspiration to people around the world.

SPIRITUAL TRAPS: FEAR OF POWER

The above temptations have in common the urge to accumulate power so that one becomes a powerful person. The ones that follow are various ways of running away from the experience of God's power.

---

[72] MacNutt, *Healing*, p. 94.
[73] MacNutt, *Healing*, p. 89-117.

Retreating

Some who encounter God's power to heal get frightened of it. God intervenes in a way that blows apart carefully formed theology, or challenges an old worldview. The result is anxiety, or, at the very least, a period of gulping adjustment. It feels as though one is in far over one's head, and has absolutely no control or understanding of what is happening so powerfully. Some ministers have talked about feeling as if they are falling off a cliff or being swept away and tumbled about in huge waves. I reacted this way when I prayed for the word salad man, whose story is told in the Prologue. I desperately wanted to avoid what was right in front of me – and managed to do so for a while. My temptation was to run the other way as quickly as possible, and to find a less intense way of living out Christian ministry.

A young pastor also had such an experience. One of his parishioners was not expected to live, and the family pleaded with the pastor to pray for healing. He reluctantly went ahead with it, letting his pastoral desire to be there with the family override his own theological confusion about such prayer. The dying man recovered; the very next morning he was sitting up, demanding food!

Soon the family spread the news around the church that the pastor had "healed Dad." The rumor caused some church members to wonder what kind of fool thing the pastor was really into, while others began to gaze at him with awestruck adulation. This was the first time he had ever prayed for healing, and he was not at all sure he was happy about the result. The whole experience seemed just too much: the seemingly miraculous recovery, and the strong, distorted reactions to it, his own shaken theology which did not make much room for modern miracles, and his sense of himself as just an ordinary guy. At the same time there was a voice inside that was saying, "Wow! Wow!" so that he couldn't quite walk away. Nevertheless, his main reaction was "get me out of here!" One Gestalt Pastoral Care student called this reaction, the "Jonah response."

The way through the Jonah response lies in accepting that *of course* God sometimes acts in powerful and surprising ways. It is a matter of allowing one's fear of God's power to change to contemplative awe, and letting one's stunned astonishment change into simple expectation that naturally God wants to heal. Experience helps a lot. After many years of praying for healing I am often surprised at what God is actually doing, but I am no longer stunned that God powerfully acts in ordinary lives.

Limiting God with a System

A strong temptation is to impose a structure on God's activity by adopting an all-purpose technique or system for healing prayer. This temptation springs from a fear that God will act in ways you can't imagine ahead of time, taking you into realms you can't control. Thus, there are some people who greet every kind of brokenness the same way – with insistence on faith imagination, for example, or specifically-worded prayers, or nutrition counseling or deliverance ministry. For those who have succumbed to this temptation, there is little tolerance for nuance, complexity, ambiguity and uniqueness. If God worked in a certain way once, or maybe even several times, they imagine that they have discovered how God works.

Obviously, God won't be put into a box. Nor can God be "figured out." Except in the case of very clear and detailed discernment, you can't predict how God will work in a given instance. Really, the only thing you can say ahead of time is that whatever God does will come from God's overwhelming love and mercy. As a minister of healing you need to live as best you can in a contemplative balance between uncertainty about how God will act, and faith that God will act in some way to bring healing and transformation.

Distancing From Other's Suffering

When you are with suffering people hour after hour, day after day, it wears on you. You hear stories of tragedy, cruelty, terror, failure and pain; it is only natural to try to protect yourself from their impact. The temptation is either to insulate and distance yourself with a "professional" attitude, or to give in to despair, pessimism, and anger. Professionalism reduces human suffering to diagnostic categories and cases; despair weeps and anger rages helplessly, often blaming God for the terrible state of the world. (Therapists who specialize in domestic violence, sexual abuse, and ritual abuse are particularly vulnerable here.) In the process, you lose sight of the resurrection. You lose hope, and you lose your perspective as a Christian visitor in another's world. You are no longer working from a contemplative base.

To do pastoral care contemplatively, you must neither turn away from others' suffering, nor take it on yourself. No one is big enough to carry so much pain. Like the friends who lowered a paralytic through the roof to Jesus, you carry another only long enough to give him to Jesus to care for.

310

When you are with a suffering person, your call is to take a clear look at whatever is presented, no matter how awful. You must not pretty it up, or skip over how really terrible it is. Paradoxically, you must also remember that no matter how terrible, there is still hope. You stay present, knowing that God is very near to those who suffer, bearing in Christ's body both the suffering of the world and the reality of resurrection. Those who are privileged to be with hurting people are witnesses to the crucifixion and the resurrection at the same time. Put another way, the pastor who has learned to listen contemplatively can view even the worst stories of cruelty or tragedy through the lens of the resurrection. Your call is to rest in God's presence while constantly surrendering to the love – and the victory – which surrounds both teller and listener.

Contemplative listening is the best way I know to bear the constant exposure to suffering. The image that often comes to me is God using my ears to listen through me. Then the stories move through my ears and brain and heart, but end up in Jesus' resurrected body. Jesus is the real listener; I just get to overhear what is being said. Other pastors find it helpful to see the cross between them and the sufferer, or to imagine that the stories are swept away by a grace-filled waterfall washing over pastor and sufferer alike, or to imagine that the suffering person is covered with God's light.

Protecting Yourself From Your Own Pain

A temptation similar to the previous one occurs when your own need for healing gets stirred up as you listen to stories with which you personally identify. If you do not deal with your own issues as they arise, then you begin to see every stress, abandonment, rejection, tragedy and sorrow through unhealed eyes. Every encounter becomes weighted with your own pain, especially if someone's work is specifically triggering your own need for healing. When this happens, you can be desperate to turn away from whatever is setting you off, and that is where the temptation to deaden yourself comes in. Most of us have learned how to numb ourselves long before we reach adulthood, and it just comes naturally as a good way to avoid our own issues. We find ways not to feel our own pain by distracting ourselves, perhaps with food or alcohol, or with frantic activity, or by nailing our façade even more firmly in place.

Another way for this temptation to get lived out is to do something to damp down the expression of pain in the person who is coming for help. I have observed therapists making sure that the one who is working is diverted from his depths, because he is getting too close to the therapist's own unhealed issues. Similarly, I have been to healing services in which the slightest hint of tears triggers a bear hug from the entire healing team, effectively stopping the crying before it starts.

This means that every pastor needs to have a way to deal with his own issues, and a commitment to do so. I have an imaginary shelf in my office near a corner of the ceiling. If an issue of mine surfaces during a session, I make a mental note, and place it on the shelf. I know that I must deal with it as best I can before the person returns for the next session. If I'm not able to do it by myself, I have to get the help of another person. If it is an issue of such magnitude that I can't work on it in pretty short order, I am probably not the one to be seeing the person who triggered the issue in me.

BURNOUT

Consistently giving room to even one of these temptations can eventually lead to burnout. Burnout is not a badge of honor pointing to sacrifice and hard work, but a serious, debilitating condition, and is not unusual among clergy. Exhausted by constant demands, wracked with spiritual and emotional pain, beset by unmet needs, and perhaps silently seething at a church that has eaten them alive, some shepherds are so in need of healing themselves that they have nothing left to give. Burnout is an occupational hazard of ministry, both ordained and lay.

Basically a spiritual issue, burnout is a special kind of depression characterized by woundedness and pride. You know you are burned out when everything seems to be colored by ashes, failure, and fatigue. It's hard to get up and face the day. You just can't listen to one more tale of woe; in fact, you don't want to do anything. You can't feel, can't cry, and you can't dig or pray your way out of it. God seems to have abandoned you.

You know you have failed, and the taste is bitter. Your pride is wounded because you were not good enough, not wise enough, just not enough, period. You thought you could do it, but you can't. "But," your misery argues, "I *should* have been able to. Others don't fall apart like this!" You find that your personal need for healing has surfaced with a vengeance, and is intersecting with wounded pride. Your days are full of guilt, shame, pain, and utter fatigue. Your breakdown is spiritual, emotional and physical.

As one approaches burnout, often the response is to work harder. At this stage, some will make a heroic effort to get themselves together. A clergyperson might begin a new program, or initiate Bible study, or campaign for new members. A Gestalt Pastoral Care Minister might toy with starting a new group, or doing more workshops, or enrolling in a training program to gain new skills. These are all wonderful things to do, but will not touch the problem of burnout. Doing more makes burnout worse. Of course, not everyone gets to this point. Some work their way to the brink of burnout, and just plod along there, day after day, hanging on. It is really sad to see these servants of God adjusting to a life of feeling awful. In some ways, full-fledged burnout is better, because burnout brings matters to a crisis.

Healing from burnout takes time. Physical rest is needed, and work pressure needs to be eliminated. A supportive environment in which to work on emotional issues is crucial, as is good spiritual companioning. Time to explore endeavors that have nothing to do with work, such as art, music, or digging in the garden can be helpful too. One who is burned out needs to learn how to take it easy on many fronts at once. The major lesson for the minister to learn is that she is all right even if she is not helping anyone, or getting things done. It is a matter of changing outlook and lifestyle enough so that God has room to work inside.

What We Need

Ministers have needs that should not be ignored! This is especially true of those specializing in healing ministry, for healing ministry can be mightily stressful and, as we have seen, fraught with temptations.

Nutrition and Exercise

We are already aware of the vital importance of good nutrition and regular exercise; I won't dwell on these issues because most of us know perfectly well we need to do better on that score. Our schedules are too full; fast food meals in the car are common; brisk walks or trips to the gym are rare. Churches are notorious for providing sweet treats at coffee hour and carbohydrate orgies at church dinners. Most church activities involve a lot of sitting. Ministers find it all too easy to slide into guilty acquiescence with an unhealthy lifestyle. As we make an effort to eat well and exercise more, it may help to think of doing something good for ourselves rather than somehow "being good."

Sabbath Time

Many ministers fall down when it comes to taking time off. Clergy often think that if they are taking one day off a week, they are doing well. They will allow even that one day to be chipped away by petty details, such as phone calls that can wait or meetings they are not required to attend. Sixty, even seventy hour workweeks are not uncommon, and some work even longer hours. Churches which insist on regular overtime, or who send the message that a good pastor will just naturally put in the extra (unpaid!) time, must bear some responsibility too. However, many ministers cave into this extraordinary pressure by not reminding their churches that they have personal needs that must be respected.

We need regular and generous time off! We need time for rest and a change of scene. We need to piddle and putter and stare at a tree. We need to have fun, to play and laugh, to be goofy with good friends. We need to play with our kids and spend relaxed time with our spouse. We need to encounter beauty in music or art or nature. We need time for contemplation and silence, for prayer retreats and continuing education events *in addition* to our regular time off. If our present schedule does not allow for this, it is our schedule that needs to change, for Sabbath time is sacred.

Participation in Church

Although pastors are naturally in church a lot, the church that employs them may not be the place where they themselves can worship or have their own personal needs met. We ministers need to be in a supportive church community. By this I mean being part of a small group that might be called variously a faith support group, a cell group, a koinonia group, or a ministry to ministers group. These small ad hoc churches share a goal of nurturing each other's spiritual journeys. Committed to telling the truth in love to each other, they can be trusted to tell you if you fall into any of the temptations listed above. The group supports each other's ministries, and members are there for each other in a crisis. They pray for each other's healing and discern together what God might be saying to each person. They worship together, and may share Eucharist. They learn how to enter into communal silence. These groups tend to operate quietly, without much fanfare. I believe that is important for anyone involved in ministry to find one or start one.

Allowing Ourselves to be Healed

Allowing ourselves to be healed means being committed to a healing journey for the rest of our lives. It means being willing to allow God's love to penetrate our defenses and to reach into ancient pain. It means a commitment to facing the worst about ourselves, and welcoming our natural healing process, even if it is scary or painful. It means daring to "step out of the boat" as we are invited to walk on water. No matter how whole we become, there is always more, for we never get beyond our need for growth.

To be on a healing journey, we will need help. For some, this will mean being in therapy. Others may find that a Twelve Step group keeps them on track. Still others will work with a spiritual companion or a healing prayer group.

As we are more and more healed, we will discover something important. After we have experienced terror, anguish, grief, illness, addictions, or rejection, and have allowed God to heal us, we are in a unique position to listen contemplatively to those with similar suffering. When we declare that we are wounded healers, it is not a confession of weakness or a liability. Being a wounded healer is an asset, perhaps even a qualification, for ministry.

Daily Discernment

We need to surrender ownership of our work. Since it is really God's, it is God who needs to direct and empower it. Then our work can flow from constant listening for the answer to the question, "Lord, what do you want me to do now? How do you want to heal this person? What should I do with this day, this hour, this minute?" Our call is to learn to get out of the way more and more, knowing that God will supply what we need to do whatever God asks of us. God will give the energy, the wisdom, the discernment, and the tools to follow God's own direction.

Contemplative Prayer

I have already mentioned contemplative prayer many times. Now I bring it up once more as I close, for contemplative prayer is the natural resting place for those in ministry. Contemplative prayer is not a way to store up power, but a way to surrender to our powerlessness. It is not about recharging our batteries so we can continue to be workhorses for the kingdom, but about letting God love us apart from anything we do.

Contemplative prayer is not about words, nor is it meditation on scripture, discernment, or intercession; these kinds of prayer are important and we do them at other times. Rather, contemplative prayer is deep, wordless resting in God, letting our hearts be inflamed with desire for God. It is being immersed in pure love daily, even hourly, letting our hunger for God's presence take us into deep silence. Here we can get to know God's love first-hand. Here we can release anyone's pain we have carried, as well as our own. Here we can be healed ourselves, sometimes without even knowing that it has happened until later on. It is deeply refreshing. I have found this kind of prayer absolutely crucial for me.

GIFTS FOR THE MINISTER

Finally, I have found that being a Gestalt Pastoral Care Minister has not just been about helping others; it has held enormous gifts for me personally. When I think I am giving to others in ministry, again and again I am on the receiving end. Witnessing another being transformed builds my faith and gives me courage to attend to my own need for transformation, and opens my eyes to the beauty and love that surrounds all of us. As God pours out grace on another, as I watch as a horror is healed and even turned into gift, I am aware of being witness to Resurrection. When someone flings open inner doors and surrenders to God's invitation to grow, I am humbled and moved to pry open my own fearfully guarded boundaries. That other person enables me to be "in church," for we two are gathered in the name of Christ. I've begun to learn to praise God in all circumstances from watching others do it even when their world is collapsing. I'm convinced I have the best job in the whole world, for I get to sit in my office and watch God work all day long.

For me, the bottomest of bottom lines is joy and gratitude. I pray that this will be so for you too.

BIBLIOGRAPHY

All Bible quotes from *The New Jerusalem Bible*. Susan Jones, gen. ed. New York, NY: Doubleday, 1985.

Alken, Martha. *The Healing Power of Forgiving*. New York, NY: Crossroad Publishing Company, 1998.

Bakken, Kenneth L. *The Call to Wholeness: Health as a Spiritual Journey*. New York, NY: Crossroad Publishing Company, 1985.

Barry, William and William Connolly. *The Practice of Spiritual Direction*. New York, NY: The Seabury Press, 1982.

Bender, Sue. *Everyday Sacred: A Woman's Journey Home*. New York, NY: HarperSanFrancisco, 1996.

Brennan, Barbara Ann. *Hands of Light: A Guide to Healing Through the Human Energy Field*. New York, NY: Bantam, 1988.

Brennan, Patrick. *The Way of Forgiveness*. Ann Arbor, MI: Servant Publications, 2000.

Clark, Neil and Tony Fraser. *The Gestalt Approach*. West Sussex, UK: Roffey Management College, 1987. Distributors in North America: Highland, NY: The Gestalt Journal.

Crocker, Sylvia Fleming. *A Well Lived Life: Essays in Gestalt Therapy*. Cambridge, MA: Gestalt Institute of Cleveland Press, 1999.

Cunningham, Lawrence S. *Thomas Merton: Spiritual Master*. Mahwah, NJ: Paulist Press, 1992.

DelBene, Ron. *Alone with God: A Guide for Personal Retreats*. Nashville, TN: Upper Room Books Workbook Edition, 1997.

DelBene, Ron. *The Breath of Life: A Simple Way to Pray*. Nashville, TN: Upper Room Books Workbook Edition, 1996.

Edwards, Tilden. *Living in the Presence: Spiritual Exercises to Open Our Lives to the Awareness of God*. New York, NY: HarperSanFrancisco, 1995.

Edwards, Tilden. *Spiritual Friend: Reclaiming the Gift of Spiritual Direction*. New York, NY: Paulist Press, 1980.

Evans, Abigail Rian. *Healing Liturgies for the Seasons of Life*. Louisville KY: Westminster John Knox Press, 2004.

Fagen, Joen and Irma Lee Shepherd, eds. *Life Techniques in Gestalt Therapy*. New York, NY: Harper and Row, 1970.

Fagen, Joen and Irma Lee Shepherd. *Gestalt Therapy Now: Theory, Techniques, Applications*. New York, NY: Harper and Row, 1970.

Friesen, James. *Uncovering the Mystery of MPD*. San Bernardino, CA: Here's Life Publishers 1991)

Garfield, Patricia. *Creative Dreaming*. New York, NY: Fireside Updated edition 1995.

Gordon, Richard *Your Healing Hands: The Polarity Experience.* Santa Cruz, CA: Unity Press, 1978.

Guenther, Margaret. *Holy Listening: The Art of Spiritual Direction.* Boston, MA: Crowley Publications, 1992.

Heckler, Richard Strozzi. *The Anatomy of Change: East/West Approaches to Body/Mind Therapy.* Boulder, CO: Shambhala, 1984.

Heggen, Carolyn Holderread. *Sexual Abuse in Christian Homes and Churches.* Scottdale, PA: Herald Press, 1993.

Houston, Gaie. *The Now Red Book of Gestalt.* London: Gaie Houston, 1995.

Jones, Paul. *The Art of Spiritual Direction: Giving and Receiving Spiritual Guidance.* Nashville, TN: Upper Room Books, 2002.

Kelsey, Morton T. *Dreams: A Way to Listen to God.* New York, NY: Paulist Press, 1977.

Kepner, James I. *Body Process: Working with the Body in Psychotherapy.* San Francisco, CA: Jossey-Bass, 1993.

Ketterman, Grace and David Hazard. *When You Can't Say "I Forgive You": Breaking the Bonds of Anger and Hurt.* Colorado Springs, CO: Navpress Publishing Group, 2000.

Krieger, Dolores. *Accepting Your Power to Heal: The Personal Practice of Therapeutic Touch.* Santa Fe, NM: Bear & Company, 1993.

Krieger, Dolores. *The Therapeutic Touch: How to Use Your Hands to Help or to Heal.* Englewood Cliffs, NJ: Prentiss-Hall, 1979.

Kurtz, Ron and Prestera, Hector. *The Body Reveals: How to Read Your Own Body.* New York, NY: (HarperSanFrancisco, 1984.

Linn, Dennis and Matthew. *Deliverance Prayer.* Ramsey, NJ: Paulist Press, 1981.

Linn, Dennis and Matthew. *Healing Life's Hurts: Healing Memories through the Five Stages of Forgiveness.* Paramus, NJ: Paulist Press, 1978.

Linn, Dennis and Sheila Fabricant Linn and Matthew Linn. *Good Goats: Healing Our Image Of God.* Mahwah,NJ: Paulist Press 1994.

Linn, Dennis and Matthew. *Healing of Memories.* New York, NY: Paulist Press, 1974.

Linn, Dennis and Matthew Linn and Sheila Fabricant. *Prayer Course for Healing Healing Life's Hurts.* Ramsey, NJ: Paulist Press, 1983.

MacNutt, Francis. *Deliverance from Evil Spirits: A Practical Manual.* Grand Rapids, MI: Chosen Books, 1995.

MacNutt, Francis. *Healing.* Notre Dame, IN: Ave Maria Press Anniversary Edition, 1999.

MacNutt, Francis. *The Power To Heal.* Notre Dame, IN: Ave Maria Press 1977.

McAll, Dr. Kenneth. *Healing the Family Tree. London, UK:* Sheldon Press 1999.

McClain, George Douglas. *Claiming All Things For God: Prayer, Discernment, And Ritual For Social Change. Nashville, TN:* Abingdon Press 1998. (now available only through Penn House Press, 78 Clinton Avenue, Staten Island, NY 10301 718-273-4941)

Norberg, Tilda. "Healing Prayer and Lomi Body Work," *The Journal of Christian Healing,* Fall, 1987.

Norberg, Tilda and Robert D. Webber. *Stretch Out Your Hand* Nashville, TN: Upper Room Press 1998.

Norris, Kathleen. *Dakota.* New York, NY: Haughton-Mifflin, 1993.

Norris, Kathleen. *The Cloister Walk.* New York, NY: Riverhead Hardcover, 1996.

Nouwen, Henri J. M. *The Wounded Healer.* Garden City, NY: Image Books, 1979.

Oksana, Chrystine. *Safe Passage to Healing: A Guide for Survivors of Ritual Abuse.* New York, NY: Harper Perennial, 1994.

Peck, Dr. Scott. *People of the Lie.* New York, NY: Touchstone, Second Touchstone edition, 1998.

Perls, Frederick S. *Ego, Hunger and Aggression: A Revision of Freud's Theory and Method.* Highland, NY: The Gestalt Journal; New edition, 1992.

Perls, Frederick S. *The Gestalt Approach and Eyewitness to Therapy.* New York, NY: Bantam Books, Reissue edition, 1981.

Perls, Frederick S. *Gestalt Therapy Verbatim.* Highland, NY: The Gestalt Journal, Revised Edition, 1992.

Perls, Frederick S. Ralph Hefferkine & Paul Goodman. *Gestalt Therapy: Excitement and Growth in the Human Personality.* The Gestalt Journal, New Edition, 1977.

Polster, Erving and Miriam. *Gestalt Therapy Integrated: Contours of Theory & Practice.* New York, NY: Vintage Books, 1974.

Rohr, Richard. *Everything Belongs: The Gift of Contemplative Prayer.* New York, NY: Crossroad Publishing Company; Revised updated edition 2003.

Rolf, Ida P. and Rosemary Feitis, Editor. *Ida Rolf Talks About Rolfing and Physical Reality.* New York, NY: Harper and Row, 1978.

Rolf, Ida P. *Rolfing: Reestablishing the Natural Alignment and Structural Integration of the Human Body for Vitality and Well-Being.* Rochester, VT: Healing Arts Press; Revised Edition, 1989.

Rose, Emilie P. *Reaching for the Light: A Guide for Ritual Abuse Survivors and Their Therapists. Cleveland, OH:* Pilgrim Press, 1996.

Sanford, Agnes. *The Healing Light.* Ballantine Books; Reissue edition 1983.

Sanford, Agnes. *Sealed Orders.* Plainfield, NJ: Logos International, 1972.

Schoeninger, Douglas and Frances. *Tending Family Roots: Papers on Generational Healing* (The Institute for Christian Counseling and Therapy 1988-

1994) (available from The Institute for Christian Counseling and Therapy, c/o Robin Caccese, 54-1 Holly Drive, Reading, Pa.)

Schroeder, Celeste Snowber. *Embodied Prayer: Harmonizing Body and Soul. Liguori, MO: Triumph Books,* 1995.

Sellner, Edward C. *Mentoring: The Ministry of Spiritual Kinship.* Notre Dame, IN: Ave Maria Press 1990.

Shepard, Martin. *Fritz: An Intimate Portrait of Fritz Perls and Gestalt Therapy.* NY: E.P. Dutton and Co., 1975. Reprinted by ereads.com, 2002

Siegal, Bernie S. *Love, Medicine and Miracles: Lessons Learned about Self-Healing from a Surgeon's Experience with Exceptional Patients.* New York, NY: Harper Paperbacks; Reissue Edition 1990.

Smith, Edward W.L. *Growing Edge of Gestalt Therapy.* Highland, NY: The Gestalt Journal, 1998.

Smith, Margaret. *Ritual Abuse: What It Is, Why It Happens, and How to Help.* New York, NY: HarperSanFrancisco, 1993.

Stevens, John O. *Awareness: Exploring, Experimenting, Experiencing.* New York, NY: Bantam Books, 1973.

Taylor, Barbara Erakko. *Silence: Making the Journey to Inner Quiet.* Philadelphia, PA: Innisfree Press, 1997.

Thompson, Marjorie J. *Soul Feast: An Invitation to the Christian Spiritual Life.* Louisville, KY: Westminster John Knox Press, 2005.

Wagner, James K. *The Spiritual Heart of Your Health: A Devotional Guide on the Healing Stories of Jesus.* Nashville, TN: Upper Room Books, 2002.

Wagner, James K. *Blessed to Be a Blessing: How To Have An Intentional Healing Ministry In Your Church.* Nashville, TN: Upper Room Books, 1980.

Weston, Walter. *Healing Others: A Practical Guide.* Charlottesville, VA: Hampton Roads Publishing Company, 1998.

Weston, Walter. *How Prayer Heals: A Scientific Approach.* Charlottesville, VA: Hampton Roads Publishing Company, 1998.

Wuellner, Flora Slosson. *Prayer and Our Bodies. Nashville, TN:* Upper Room Books, 1987.

Zinker, Joseph. *Creative Process in Gestalt Therapy.* New York, NY: Brunner/Mazel, 1977.

Zinker, Joseph C. *In Search of Good Form: Gestalt Therapy With Couples and Families.* San Francisco, CA: Jossey-Bass, Inc. 1994.

ABOUT THE AUTHOR

Tilda Norberg, the developer of Gestalt Pastoral Care, is a United Methodist minister in the New York Conference. In addition to her private practice, she teaches, writes, and leads retreats. After graduation from Union Theological Seminary in New York City, she was trained at The Gestalt Institute of Canada in Vancouver, and the Gestalt Center of Princeton, NJ. She instituted a two-year training program in Gestalt Pastoral Care 1984, which has now expanded to other locations and includes advanced training. She lives in Staten Island, New York, with her husband, Rev. George McClain. Contact the author at tilda@gestaltpastoralcare.com.

OTHER BOOKS BY TILDA NORBERG

Ashes Transformed: Healing From Trauma. Nashville, TN: Upper Room Books, 2002.

Stretch Out Your Hand: Exploring Healing Prayer. With co-author Robert D. Webber. Nashville, TN: Upper Room Books, revised edition 1998. *Stretch Out Your Hand Leader's Guide* is also available from Upper Room Books.

Threadbear: A Story of Christian Healing for Adult Survivors of Sexual Abuse, illustrated by Joyce Thomas, New York, NY: Penn House Press 1997.

CPSIA information can be obtained at www.ICGtesting.com
Printed in the USA
BVOW08s2012141016

464953BV00004B/157/P